# Witness to Loss

McGill-Queen's Studies in Ethnic History
Series One: Donald Harman Akenson, Editor

1 Irish Migrants in the Canadas
*A New Approach*
Bruce S. Elliott
(Second edition, 2004)

2 Critical Years in Immigration
*Canada and Australia Compared*
Freda Hawkins
(Second edition, 1991)

3 Italians in Toronto
*Development of a National Identity, 1875–1935*
John E. Zucchi

4 Linguistics and Poetics of Latvian Folk Songs
*Essays in Honour of the Sesquicentennial of the Birth of Kr. Barons*
Vaira Vikis-Freibergs

5 Johan Schroder's Travels in Canada, 1863
Orm Overland

6 Class, Ethnicity, and Social Inequality
Christopher McAll

7 The Victorian Interpretation of Racial Conflict
*The Maori, the British, and the New Zealand Wars*
James Belich

8 White Canada Forever
*Popular Attitudes and Public Policy toward Orientals in British Columbia*
W. Peter Ward
(Third edition, 2002)

9 The People of Glengarry
*Highlanders in Transition, 1745–1820*
Marianne McLean

10 Vancouver's Chinatown
*Racial Discourse in Canada, 1875–1980*
Kay J. Anderson

11 Best Left as Indians
*Native-White Relations in the Yukon Territory, 1840–1973*
Ken Coates

12 Such Hardworking People
*Italian Immigrants in Postwar Toronto*
Franca Iacovetta

13 The Little Slaves of the Harp
*Italian Child Street Musicians in Nineteenth-Century Paris, London, and New York*
John E. Zucchi

14 The Light of Nature and the Law of God
*Antislavery in Ontario, 1833–1877*
Allen P. Stouffer

15 Drum Songs
*Glimpses of Dene History*
Kerry Abel

16 Canada's Jews
(Reprint of 1939 original)
Louis Rosenberg
Edited by Morton Weinfeld

17 A New Lease on Life
*Landlords, Tenants, and Immigrants in Ireland and Canada*
Catharine Anne Wilson

18 In Search of Paradise
*The Odyssey of an Italian Family*
Susan Gabori

19 Ethnicity in the Mainstream
*Three Studies of English Canadian Culture in Ontario*
Pauline Greenhill

20 Patriots and Proletarians
*The Politicization of Hungarian Immigrants in Canada, 1923–1939*
Carmela Patrias

21 The Four Quarters of the Night
*The Life-Journey of an Emigrant Sikh*
Tara Singh Bains and Hugh Johnston

22 Cultural Power, Resistance, and Pluralism
*Colonial Guyana, 1838–1900*
Brian L. Moore

23 Search Out the Land
*The Jews and the Growth of Equality in British Colonial America, 1740–1867*
Sheldon J. Godfrey and Judith C. Godfrey

24 The Development of Elites in Acadian New Brunswick, 1861–1881
Sheila M. Andrew

25 Journey to Vaja
*Reconstructing the World of a Hungarian-Jewish Family*
Elaine Kalman Naves

McGill-Queen's Studies in Ethnic History
Series Two: John Zucchi, Editor

1 Inside Ethnic Families
*Three Generations of Portuguese-Canadians*
Edite Noivo

2 A House of Words
*Jewish Writing, Identity, and Memory*
Norman Ravvin

3 Oatmeal and the Catechism
*Scottish Gaelic Settlers in Quebec*
Margaret Bennett

4 With Scarcely a Ripple
*Anglo-Canadian Migration into the United States and Western Canada, 1880–1920*
Randy William Widdis

5 Creating Societies
*Immigrant Lives in Canada*
Dirk Hoerder

6 Social Discredit
*Anti-Semitism, Social Credit, and the Jewish Response*
Janine Stingel

7 Coalescence of Styles
*The Ethnic Heritage of St John River Valley Regional Furniture, 1763–1851*
Jane L. Cook

8 Brigh an Orain / A Story in Every Song
*The Songs and Tales of Lauchie MacLellan*
Translated and edited by John Shaw

9 Demography, State and Society
*Irish Migration to Britain, 1921–1971*
Enda Delaney

10 The West Indians of Costa Rica
*Race, Class, and the Integration of an Ethnic Minority*
Ronald N. Harpelle

11 Canada and the Ukrainian Question, 1939–1945
Bohdan S. Kordan

12 Tortillas and Tomatoes
*Transmigrant Mexican Harvesters in Canada*
Tanya Basok

13 Old and New World Highland Bagpiping
John G. Gibson

14 Nationalism from the Margins
*The Negotiation of Nationalism and Ethnic Identities among Italian Immigrants in Alberta and British Columbia*
Patricia Wood

15 Colonization and Community
*The Vancouver Island Coalfield and the Making of the British Columbia Working Class*
John Douglas Belshaw

16 Enemy Aliens, Prisoners of War
*Internment in Canada during the Great War*
Bohdan S. Kordan

17 Like Our Mountains
*A History of Armenians in Canada*
Isabel Kaprielian-Churchill

18 Exiles and Islanders
*The Irish Settlers of Prince Edward Island*
Brendan O'Grady

19 Ethnic Relations in Canada
*Institutional Dynamics*
Raymond Breton
Edited by Jeffrey G. Reitz

20 A Kingdom of the Mind
*The Scots' Impact on the Development of Canada*
Edited by Peter Rider and Heather McNabb

21 Vikings to U-Boats
*The German Experience in Newfoundland and Labrador*
Gerhard P. Bassler

22 Being Arab
*Ethnic and Religious Identity Building among Second Generation Youth in Montreal*
Paul Eid

23 From Peasants to Labourers
*Ukrainian and Belarusan Immigration from the Russian Empire to Canada*
Vadim Kukushkin

24 Emigrant Worlds and Transatlantic Communities
*Migration to Upper Canada in the First Half of the Nineteenth Century*
Elizabeth Jane Errington

25 Jerusalem on the Amur
*Birobidzhan and the Canadian Jewish Communist Movement, 1924–1951*
Henry Felix Srebrnik

26 Irish Nationalism in Canada
Edited by David A. Wilson

27 Managing the Canadian Mosaic in Wartime
*Shaping Citizenship Policy, 1939–1945*
Ivana Caccia

28 Jewish Roots, Canadian Soil
*Yiddish Culture in Montreal, 1905–1945*
Rebecca Margolis

29 Imposing Their Will
*An Organizational History of Jewish Toronto, 1933–1948*
Jack Lipinsky

30 Ireland, Sweden, and the Great European Migration, 1815–1914
Donald H. Akenson

31 The Punjabis in British Columbia
*Location, Labour, First Nations, and Multiculturalism*
Kamala Elizabeth Nayar

32 Growing Up Canadian
*Muslims, Hindus, Buddhists*
Edited by Peter Beyer and Rubina Ramji

33 Between Raid and Rebellion
*The Irish in Buffalo and Toronto, 1867–1916*
William Jenkins

34 Unpacking the Kists
*The Scots in New Zealand*
Brad Patterson, Tom Brooking, and Jim McAloon

35 Building Nations from Diversity
*Canadian and American Experience Compared*
Garth Stevenson

36 Hurrah Revolutionaries
*The Polish Canadian Communist Movement, 1918–1948*
Patryk Polec

37 Alice in Shandehland
*Scandal and Scorn in the Edelson/Horwitz Murder Case*
Monda Halpern

38 Creating Kashubia
*History, Memory, and Identity in Canada's First Polish Community*
Joshua C. Blank

39 No Free Man
*Canada, the Great War, and the Enemy Alien Experience*
Bohdan S. Kordan

40 Between Dispersion and Belonging
*Global Approaches to Diaspora in Practice*
Edited by Amitava Chowdhury and Donald Harman Akenson

41 Running on Empty
*Canada and the Indochinese Refugees, 1975–1980*
Michael J. Molloy, Peter Duschinsky, Kurt F. Jensen, and Robert J. Shalka

42 Twenty-First-Century Immigration to North America
*Newcomers in Turbulent Times*
Edited by Victoria M. Esses and Donald E. Abelson

43 Gaelic Cape Breton Step-Dancing
*An Historical and Ethnographic Perspective*
John G. Gibson

44 Witness to Loss
*Race, Culpability, and Memory in the Dispossession of Japanese Canadians*
Edited by Jordan Stanger-Ross and Pamela Sugiman

# WITNESS *to* LOSS

*Race, Culpability, and Memory in the Dispossession of Japanese Canadians*

Edited by
Jordan Stanger-Ross *and* Pamela Sugiman

McGill-Queen's University Press
Montreal & Kingston • London • Chicago

This book emerges from the work of the Landscapes of Injustice Research Collective.

ISBN 978-0-7735-5120-6 (cloth)
ISBN 978-0-7735-5121-3 (paper)
ISBN 978-0-7735-5195-4 (ePDF)
ISBN 978-0-7735-5196-1 (ePUB)

Legal deposit fourth quarter 2017
Bibliothèque nationale du Québec

Printed in Canada on acid-free paper that is 100% ancient forest free
(100% post-consumer recycled), processed chlorine free

This book has been published with the help of a grant from the Canadian Federation for the Humanities and Social Sciences, through the Awards to Scholarly Publications Program, using funds provided by the Social Sciences and Humanities Research Council of Canada.

McGill-Queen's University Press acknowledges the support of the Canada Council for the Arts for our publishing program. We also acknowledge the financial support of the Government of Canada through the Canada Book Fund for our publishing activities.

Library and Archives Canada Cataloguing in Publication

Witness to loss : race, culpability, and memory in the dispossession of Japanese Canadians / edited by Jordan Stanger-Ross and Pamela Sugiman.

(McGill-Queen's studies in ethnic history. Series two ; 44)
Includes English translation of Kishizo Kimura's memoir.
Includes bibliographical references and index.
Issued in print and electronic formats.
ISBN 978-0-7735-5120-6 (cloth).–ISBN 978-0-7735-5121-3 (paper).–
ISBN 978-0-7735-5195-4 (ePDF).–ISBN 978-0-7735-5196-1 (ePUB)

1. Kimura, Kishizo. 2. Japanese Canadians–British Columbia–Biography. 3. Japanese Canadians–British Columbia–History–20th century. 4. Racism–British Columbia–History–20th century. 5. Eviction–British Columbia–History–20th century. 6. Japanese Canadians–Evacuation and relocation, 1942–1945. 7. British Columbia–Race relations–History–20th century. I. Sugiman, Pamela H. (Pamela Haruchiyo), 1958–, editor II. Stanger-Ross, Jordan, editor III. Series: McGill-Queen's studies in ethnic history. Series two ; 44

FC106.J3W58 2017　　971.1'004956　　C2017-903559-2
C2017-903560-6

# Contents

# Figures

# Note on Landscapes of Injustice

This book is the result of the collective work and resources of Landscapes of Injustice. Supported by a partnership grant of the Social Sciences and Humanities Research Council of Canada, Landscapes of Injustice is a seven-year project to research and tell the history of the dispossession of the property of Japanese Canadians during the 1940s. Our research collective is united by the conviction that this history still matters. The dispossession is a story about the violation of human and civil rights at a time of perceived insecurity, about measures taken in the name of national defence that made no one safer, about the enduring harms of mass displacement and the loss of home, and about the resilience of people confronting injustice. It is a story for our times.

We comprise dozens of individuals – academics, community leaders, museum professionals, programmers, and students – as well as institutions realizing the benefits of multi-disciplinary and multi-sector collaboration. Participating institutions include the Canadian Museum of Immigration at Pier 21, the Immigration and Ethnic History Society, the Japanese Canadian Cultural Centre, Library and Archives Canada, the National Association of Japanese Canadians, the Nikkei National Museum, the OAH/JAAS Historians' Collaborative Committee, the Royal British Columbia Museum, Ryerson University, the Urban History Association, the University of Alberta, The University of Winnipeg, Simon Fraser University, the Vancouver Japanese Language School and Japanese Hall, and the University of Victoria, our host and headquarters. We are thankful for the support and advice of our Community Council, comprising established and emerging leaders in the Japanese-Canadian community.

Jordan Stanger-Ross
Project Director
Landscapes of Injustice

Figure P.1 Kishizo Kimura on West Hastings Street in Vancouver, circa 1940. Nikkei National Museum (NNM), 2010.4.7.4.3.

# Preface

*Jordan Stanger-Ross and Pamela Sugiman*

This book tells the story of a Japanese Canadian who participated in the dispossession of his own community. Kishizo Kimura's actions call forward the topic of where individuals stand in history, of how their experiences and decisions are connected with their origins. We have felt compelled to ask, and to ask deeply, how Kimura could serve on the government committees that oversaw the forced sale of Japanese Canadian–owned property, because he himself was Japanese Canadian. The participation of Vancouver city alderman Charles Jones and Justice Sidney Smith does not attract similar scrutiny because of where they came from. In important respects, this imbalance is appropriate: none were as affected by this history as Japanese Canadians, and this story cannot be told without careful consideration of their perspectives. It is no coincidence that Kimura – not Jones or Smith – wrote a memoir of his role in these events and urged his children to donate it to a public archive. And yet, this imbalance is also an extension of a history of racism and inequality. Jones and Smith are just as culpable for the dispossession of Japanese Canadians (indeed, more so) as Kimura and should be held to account just as much as he. As the contributors to this volume gather around this history, we are each only partly (but nonetheless powerfully) shaped by where we have come from. Kimura's story and, we hope, our reflections on it invite readers to engage the complex intersection of origins with circumstances and with choice.

As scholars drawn together on this project (and the larger initiative, Landscapes of Injustice, of which it is a part), Jordan Stanger-Ross and Pamela Sugiman come from very different places. Like many in Canada, Jordan grew up with a vague awareness that Japanese Canadians had been interned during the 1940s but without deep personal connection to, or indeed concern about, this history. The informal educational settings of his youth – the blue couch in a family room where his father read aloud a biography of Golda

Meir, the metal shelves of a basement (in a home built two generations earlier by his immigrant great-grandfather) near Bathurst Street, Toronto, where his brother and he picked curiously through neglected family heirlooms, the dreary gymnasium of Beth Jacob synagogue in Waterloo, Ontario, where Israeli-accented teachers exhorted children of the diaspora to understand their roots – the places, in short, where deep connections with the past are forged – pointed him toward different histories. Jordan had his share of encounters with prejudice as a child. He was roughly instructed by older students to use the "Jewish urinal" in his elementary school bathroom. After a rare successful base hit in a Little League baseball game, he was stung by the casual observation of the first baseman that "Hitler should have finished the job." He was startled to learn, in one of the first articles he remembers reading, that the large majority of Canadians would never support a Jew as prime minister. As a result, he cannot remember a time before feeling in his bones an outrage at racism. But it took almost two decades in university classrooms for Jordan to begin to grapple seriously with the importance of the uprooting, internment, and dispossession of Japanese Canadians as events that comprised his own past and the pasts of the students whom he was teaching.

By the time he began a sustained engagement with this history, only one of Jordan's grandparents remained alive. Edith Ross was born in Toronto in 1920 and had her first child (Jordan's father) in 1944, in the midst of the history told here. When Jordan began this project, she was in her early nineties. In response to Landscapes of Injustice, she now reflects on how poorly Japanese Canadians were treated ("it was because they looked different," she often repeats) but recalls little of what she knew or felt at the time, when, for example, thousands of Japanese Canadians (many of them in young families like hers) found their way to Toronto after their exile from British Columbia. On his mother's side, Jordan's immigrant great-grandfather, Sam Strashin, was an entrepreneur: family legend recalls a series of fortunate and clever decisions that led him from owning a small corner store to launching a movie theatre and then eventually to forays into suburban real estate development. Jordan never had the chance to ask him about Japanese Canadians whose similar successes were undone by the Canadian state even as the Strashins built wealth that has been passed down several generations. While Japanese Canadians were being dispossessed, Jordan's family was thriving. Although the traumas of this era for Jews were powerfully felt and communicated in his family (indeed, within its larger tree many were murdered in the global paroxysm of mid-twentieth-century racism), the space between him and Kishizo Kimura is vast. Jordan did not learn on a parent's knee what it meant to be Japanese Canadian in this era; he will never feel Nikkei history in that way, even as he devotes years in efforts to understand it.

Pamela Sugiman has a different relationship to Kimura's memoir and to the larger project of the internment as well as to its scholarly examination. The space between herself and Kishizo Kimura is likewise vast, but the emotions and thoughts that Kimura's memoir generates are close to her heart. For Pam, the narratives of internment merge and depart from family histories – from the personal memories of grandparents, mother, father, and aunts and uncles, as well as from her own memories, formed indirectly and transmitted over time and across generations. The personal impact of the decisions made lay at the core of her family history, but the members of Pam's family lacked the economic resources and education that positioned Kimura as a historical agent.

Not long after Japan's bombing of Pearl Harbor, Pam's mother's family, the Matsuokas, were uprooted from their berry farm in Haney, British Columbia. Along with thousands of other Canadians of Japanese ancestry, they were temporarily placed in Hastings Park, a former livestock building in the Pacific Exhibition fairgrounds in the city of Vancouver. Pam's mother, Ritsuko Sugiman, then a shy young woman, lived for many months, without privacy, in the makeshift quarters that reeked of animal urine and manure. From here, the family was shipped by train to the small, remote town of Rosebery, one of many sites of internment, barren and destitute yet oddly juxtaposed against the natural splendour of the BC Interior. In Rosebery, Haruno and Tsunichi resiliently carved out the shell of a life for themselves and their six children, while their eldest son lived in another BC internment site along with his wife and her family. Not one member of the Matsuoka family again set eyes on their freshly cleared family berry farm and childhood home in the town of Haney.

At the outbreak of the Second World War, Pam's father, Ross Tatsuro Sugiman, was a young man living in "Japan Town," now known as Vancouver's East Side. Ross's parents, Chiyo and Iwazo Sugiman, raised their two sons and one daughter in a modest home in the Powell Street area. Chiyo worked as a homemaker and earned wages as a seasonal cannery worker. Iwazo was employed as a printer for a local Japanese-Canadian newspaper. Like many Japanese-Canadian men of his generation, Ross was for the most part reticent about his experiences during the war years. Though memories were seldom shared in conversation, the one that Pam remembers most vividly is that of her father's years as a prisoner of war in Petawawa in northern Ontario. Ross was detained in a POW camp because in the midst of the chaotic exodus of Japanese Canadians, he refused to leave his hometown. For both Ross and Ritsuko, the years after the internment were filled with struggle and sacrifice, hardship and indignities.

Inspired and fuelled by her father's resistance and her mother's resilience, more than twenty-five years ago Pam initiated a major research study of the internment of Japanese Canadians. For Pam, then, the Kimura memoir is one part of a much larger and long-standing project of memory and reclamation. Long before the birth of the Landscapes of Injustice research collective, Pam had amassed seventy-five oral history interviews with *Nisei* (second-generation Japanese-Canadian) women and men who had resettled after the war in Ontario, Quebec, Manitoba, and British Columbia. The *Nisei* shared memories of ways in which the uprooting, dispossession, relocation, and forced assimilation touched their lives as well as the identities, experiences, and aspirations of their *Issei* parents and *Sansei* children. Among these now elderly *Nisei*, some sadly since deceased, many were "robbed" of fishing boats in addition to sewing machines, china, and dolls. As a researcher, and as a daughter, Pam also heard for the first time narratives that spoke of connections between uprooted Japanese Canadians and Jewish employers and homeowners in the cities of Toronto and Montreal. Not long after she was transported from BC to Ontario, Ritsuko, typical of many *Nisei* women, found a job in a doll factory that was owned by a Jewish man. The Sugimans likewise rented the second floor of a house located on Nassau Street in the Jewish area known as Kensington Market. It was among Jewish communities that many Toronto-based Japanese Canadians began to re-establish their lives and restore their dreams. Jewish business-owners and homemakers, in the memories of many *Nisei*, were among the few groups who would offer them employment as labourers and domestics.

It is not these connections, however, that brought Pam to a research collective that Jordan had initiated. Pam's and Jordan's lives were lived differently, largely because of ways in which race, class, and gender intermingle and shape history. Pam's family did not thrive financially after the war. Her family remained working-class and unashamedly so. The dispossession, forced dispersal and resettlement, and repatriation made a life of poverty and hard work even harsher. But Pam and Jordan, in spite of their many differences – in personal history, political perspective, and relationship to the memoir of Kishizo Kimura – joined in scholarship to produce this volume. And their own complex relationship as scholars speaks to a central tenet of this book. The wartime acts of dispossession, and the ways in which they are memorialized as history, are not black or white, bad or good. They were unjust acts, to be sure. But the ways in which such historical acts are remembered and narrated, and interpreted by scholars, are more slippery questions. Pam and Jordan and the other contributors to this volume, of diverse ethnic origins, seek to find answers.

# Acknowledgments

This book has been generously supported. The enthusiasm and flexibility of Kyla Madden and the team at the MQUP eased the production of a complex manuscript. Funding from the Social Science and Humanities Research Council of Canada, Ryerson University, and the University of Victoria supported publication. The editors thank the translators and the authors for their curiosity about an unknown archival memoir and for taking the time to work so thoughtfully with it. At the Nikkei National Museum and Cultural Centre, Sherri Kajiwara organized and hosted an early meeting of the contributors to this volume and offered generous support for the digital components that accompany this print publication (see http://witnesstoloss.ca). The book would not have been possible without the Landscapes of Injustice (LOI) Research Collective, particularly research assistants Will Archibald, Lauren Chalaturnyk, Kaitlin Findlay, Josie Gray, Adam Kostrich, and Monique Ulysses. Eric Adams and the Legal History Cluster of LOI supported interpretations of legal materials. The support of members of the Community Council of LOI, who saw parts of this work presented in 2015, helped to inspire its further development. Michael Abe's managerial patience and attention kept many moving parts in order. Anne Dodington in Special Collections at the Vancouver Public Library, Cathy Nakagawa at the Nikkei National Museum, and Theressa Takasaki at the Japanese Canadian Cultural Centre offered particular help in locating images from their repositories. Nikkei National Museum archivist Linda Kawamoto Reid deserves singular acknowledgment: her energy for this project started from before we began and helped to carry us to the end. Edmund and Doris Kimura showed courage in donating Ed's father's records to a public archive and in sharing their memories with historians. We hope that they appreciate the results.

Figure I.1 Kishizo Kimura on Bowen Island, BC, 1926. Kimura's personal photographs from this period include many such portraits of lives that would be permanently disrupted by the policies of the 1940s. Nikkei National Museum (NNM), 2010-4-7-1-50.

# Introduction and Reflections[1]

*Jordan Stanger-Ross*

Along with every other Japanese Canadian, Kishizo Kimura saw his life upended by events that began in 1941. His experience of the tumultuous decade that followed – his uprooting and internment, his loss of personal property and livelihood, his effort to forge a new life in a new place after the war – was shared with tens of thousands of others. But his story is also unique: as a member of two controversial committees that oversaw the forced sale of property, Kimura participated in the dispossession of his own community. In January 1942, he assisted officials disposing of Japanese Canadian–owned fishing vessels. Then, in the spring of 1943, he joined officials overseeing the forced sale of Japanese Canadian–owned property in Vancouver. During his service on the two committees, Kimura directly participated in the sale of 950 fishing vessels, 177 parcels of real estate, and an untold volume of personal belongings. Kimura helped to dispossess the fishers among whom he had worked and to destroy the neighbourhood in which he had lived.

Kimura knew that his participation in this process would one day merit attention. For two decades, he carefully preserved the official documents of his committee work, including a ledger detailing the fate of every Japanese Canadian–owned fishing vessel. Kimura treasured these documents. His son recalls that after the war, when Kimura and his wife went on holiday away from their five children, he would entrust key documents to the neighbours so as to protect them from youthful mischief. Then, toward the end of his life, between 1967 and 1974, Kimura reflected on this pivotal period, writing an unpublished memoir, which he instructed his family to donate to a public archive.[2]

The manuscript comprises seventy-seven legal-size pages of dense but elegantly handwritten Japanese. Carefully summarized in a table of contents, the memoir is exclusively devoted to his service on the two government committees, beginning with his participation in the Fishing Vessel Disposal Committee and concluding with his resignation from the committee that oversaw the forced sale of Vancouver-area property. In between, the text oscillates among a variety of strategies, offering a narrow documentary reconstruction of events, an explanation of Kimura's own difficult position, a reiteration of official justifications of the forced sales, a sense of the impact of these policies on Japanese Canadians, and reflections on the history of racism and second-class citizenship in British Columbia.

"I just want young people to understand," writes Kimura. "I would like you to understand," he repeats, "that the first Issei were not an inferior race." Rather, this generation, of which he was a part, persevered in the face of great hardship: "They had to take care of their families in Japan. Even if they studied, sacrificing their families at home, there was no way for them to find good employment. They did not have suffrage, their English was not good enough, and their fields of employment were limited because of exclusionary practices."[3]

To understand him and his controversial choices, Kimura implies, we need to consider his actions within the context of their time and the constraints faced by his generation. This book allows readers to seek this understanding for the first time by engaging directly with Kimura's depiction of his wartime experience. In addition to this introduction and the memoir, it includes four commentaries on Kimura's writings. To supplement this volume, the entire memoir in its original language and an unedited version in translation are available on the website of the Nikkei National Museum, which is the repository of the original memoir and a partner in this publication (see http://witnesstoloss.ca). We hope that readers will join us in grappling with Kimura's rich historical narrative and the difficult past of which he was a part.

## Context

Kishizo Kimura arrived in Victoria, British Columbia, in 1911 at the age of 12. He was one of more than 330,000 immigrants to Canada that year, disembarking at the very peak of mass immigration to the country.[4] Kimura and his parents (he came with his mother, joining his father who had arrived in Canada four years before) took up residence in the East End of Vancouver, in a bustling and diverse immigrant section of the city where Japanese-Canadian businesses, lodging houses, and residences centred on Powell Street. A year before Kishizo's arrival, the Hompa Buddhist Temple had been erected on

Cordova Street, a landmark of the deepening roots of the Japanese-Canadian community in the area.[5]

Japanese newcomers at this time, like other migrants during the first great wave of mass arrivals in Canada, followed in the footsteps of "pioneers" who discovered and built economic opportunity in the decades before. The first known Japanese immigrant to Canada, Manzo Nagano, stayed ashore in New Westminster in 1877 when the ship on which he had arrived departed for Japan.[6] Borrowing a boat with an Italian partner, Nagano was likely the first Japanese fisher in the Fraser River and hence the forerunner of thousands in the half-century that followed.[7] By the mid-1880s, a steady, though still small and difficult to quantify, flow of migrants from Japan arrived annually on Canada's west coast where they found employment in the fishing, mining, lumber, and construction industries in particular. In 1887, Shinkichi Tamura, destined to become one of the great magnates of the Japanese immigrant community, opened a toy shop at the corner of Cordova and Carrall in Vancouver's East End, helping to lay the foundations for a Japanese-Canadian neighbourhood that would be the largest in the country and home to Kishizo Kimura before its erasure during the Second World War (the Tamura family would eventually lose almost a million dollars – in 2017 currency – in the forced sale of their property in the neighbourhood.[8])

In the first decade of the twentieth century, Japanese migrants arrived in British Columbia in unprecedented numbers (many of them via Hawaii). More than 11,000, Tamotsu Kimura (Kishizo's father) among them, came to the province between 1906 and 1908, joining a booming province whose population doubled during the decade.[9] Like other migrants, many among them envisioned only a temporary sojourn in North America. Economic opportunity in British Columbia allowed migrants to return to their home prefectures and towns with sufficient wealth to pursue dreams, often of land ownership, that were otherwise unattainable.[10] A significant share, however, did settle permanently in the province. For the Kimuras, the results of migration were mixed. Kishizo's mother died of the Spanish flu in Vancouver in 1924. His father, after a serious bout of illness, returned to Japan sometime before 1936, when he died in his home village.[11] Kishizo stayed on in British Columbia where he would build a life.

Migrants like the Kimuras weighed many factors in their decisions, but in their case (as Kishizo explained more than a half-century later) pervasive

Figure I.2 The Tamura Building on Powell Street, Vancouver, commissioned by Shinkichi Tamura in 1912, as later depicted by artist Robin Ward. With a hotel above and commerce at street level, the building was an iconic structure in the historic neighbourhood. Courtesy of Robin Ward and the City of Vancouver Archives (CVA).

racism in British Columbia was an unavoidable consideration. Tamotsu's arrival at Vancouver aboard the SS *Kumeric* in 1907 marked a pivotal juncture in this history. "Hundreds of Mikado's Subjects Reached Vancouver," ran a headline in the *Vancouver Province* on the day his ship anchored in Burrard Inlet. "The decks of the steamer," reported the paper, "literally swarmed with the little brown men." Speculating that the passengers (whose actual number included more than 1,100 Japanese migrants) represented "the advance guard of a host soon to locate British Columbia," the paper noted that the ship "attracted no little attention."[12] Indeed, sounding alarm at the impending "invasion" of the province, the Asiatic Exclusion League spent the next month preparing a major Vancouver demonstration to protest the Pacific arrivals. When it occurred, on 7 September 1907, the demonstration spiraled into rioting, with exclusionists ransacking Chinese- and Japanese-Canadian businesses and homes in the East End of the city, causing thousands of dollars of damage and sparking international controversy.[13] Kishizo's father was welcomed to Canada by mob violence.

Scholars have traced the career of white supremacy in British Columbia from the riots that ushered Tamotsu into the country to the internment that changed Kishizo's life forever. Inequality – in housing and labour markets, schooling, political participation, and the application of law – made race a powerful fault line of British Columbian society. And yet race was also a changing, uneven, and unpredictable historical experience. Sometimes, as historian Patricia Roy has surveyed, the "Oriental Question" was a centrepiece of public and political discussion in the province, while at other times race slipped from the spotlight and "British Columbians were preoccupied with other problems."[14] Further, the politics of the "Oriental Question" changed over time, sometimes reflecting class interests (when, for example, employers favoured Asian immigration and organized labour opposed it) and sometimes cutting across ostensible lines of economic self-interest. All the while, Japanese immigrants and their children routinely encountered and built relations with British Columbians of other origins. Canners valued skilled Japanese-Canadian fishers, farming co-operatives benefited from Japanese-Canadian participation, and shoppers of all origins sought out the merchandise (often imported) on offer in Japanese- and Chinese-Canadian stores.[15] As Timothy Stanley's contribution to this volume argues, the province was built on systems of racial and colonial dominance, and yet the structures of racism were endlessly challenged, circumvented, and even ignored. Racism was pervasive at the same time as intermittent.

The Japanese-Canadian community changed significantly in the years between Kishizo's arrival in British Columbia and his uprooting from the coast. Canada, collaborating with Japan, imposed quotas on Japanese immigration starting in 1908, but for two decades these restrictions did not apply to the wives and children of members of the Japanese-Canadian community already residing in the country. Partly as a consequence of this policy, a settlement of male sojourners with strong connections to Japan became, in the course of three decades, a multigenerational Canadian community. By the time of their uprooting from the west coast, 60 per cent of Japanese Canadians were native to the province. In a British Columbia awash with newcomers (only a third of the general population growth came as a result of childbirths), Japanese Canadians stood out as particularly rooted in place.[16] In the face of persis-

Figure I.3 The SS *Kumeric* arrives in British Columbia in 1907, with Kishizo Kimura's father, Tamotsu, aboard. Nativist response to the immigrants crowded on its decks helped to spark riots in Vancouver later the same year. Philip Timms, photographer. Courtesy of the Vancouver Public Library (VPL), Accession 3008.

tent discrimination in the labour market, including the campaign to reduce their access to fishing licences, discussed in Masako Fukawa's contribution to this book, Japanese Canadians diversified their lives and economic activities, transforming Fraser Valley land long regarded as inarable into thriving berry farms, establishing a hub of commercial activity on Vancouver's Powell Street, and finding other niches in the economy and society of British Columbia.[17] By the 1930s, Japanese Canadians farmed the Okanagan, fished the west coast of Vancouver Island and the northern stretches of the mainland coast, and owned (and worked in) lumberyards in the Comox Valley. They laboured in mines, cooked meals, ran groceries, gardened, shaved beards, and ran small businesses in locales throughout coastal British Columbia.[18] In 1935, after an extensive survey of the Japanese-Canadian population, UBC master's student Rigenda Sumida noted the diversity of Japanese-Canadian lives. Their average standard of living was lower than that of the population as a whole, but they had nonetheless achieved considerable economic stability. Countering racist caricatures, Sumida reflected, "They are human beings … as intelligent and progressive as any race on earth, and they are not content to simply exist, but … desire the comforts of fine homes, automobiles, radios, and all the other articles or services which Western civilization provides."[19]

Kimura participated in these larger patterns of Japanese-Canadian lives. Upon his arrival, he took a job as a carrier of *Tairiku Nippo* – the largest circulating Japanese-Canadian daily newspaper, published in Vancouver from 1907 to 1941 – moving into the paper's boarding house, most likely in the East End Powell Street neighbourhood, near the offices of the paper.[20] He would live and work in East End Vancouver until his uprooting in 1942. Kimura studied at both the Alexander Street Japanese School and the Strathcona middle school and as an adult was literate and fluent in both Japanese and English. In his teens, he laboured in local sawmills and lumberyards and, by his early twenties, held a bookkeeping position in the thriving export of salted fish – herring and salmon – from Canada's west coast to Japan. In the mid-1930s, in a context of increasing competition in the industry, Kimura persuaded salted fish exporters to establish two co-operative companies that sought to collectively negotiate contracts and to market Canadian fish in Japan. Kimura became the executive director for both organizations, which continued their operations until the start of the Second World War. During the same period, he established his own household, marrying Haruno Makino on 10 August 1929; the couple settled into a home on McGill Street in Vancouver (to the

Figure I.4 Konko Canada Ucluelet Division, 1934. By the 1930s, Japanese Canadians had established large centres of population in Vancouver and Steveston, and smaller numbers lived as members of communities throughout coastal BC, such as this fishing village on Vancouver Island. Nikkei National Museum (NNM), 2010-31-41.

east of the Japanese-Canadian enclave) where they would have five children. Naturalized a British subject in his early twenties, Kimura was forty-two years of age and well established both professionally and personally when Canada declared war on Japan.[21]

## Debating the Internment Era

In its broad strokes, the internment of Japanese Canadians is well known. After Canada's entry into the Pacific theatre of the Second World War, the federal government used the extraordinary authority granted to it under the War Measures Act to uproot almost 22,000 Japanese Canadians from their homes on the British Columbia coast. The displaced thousands, a large majority of whom were British subjects of Canada (Canadian citizens), were forced to relocate to various sites of internment. Most spent at least some of the years that followed in large camps in the British Columbia interior established to house them. Some, including those who had resisted the breakup of their families, were incarcerated in prison camps in Ontario. Others toiled on farms and in factories in Alberta and Manitoba, while still others moved farther east, establishing themselves in Toronto, Montreal, and even as far as Halifax. In 1946, the federal government exiled almost 4,000 Japanese Canadians to Japan, a country that many among them had never before visited. For the rest, restrictions on their return to the west coast remained in place until 1949, long after the war had ended.[22]

This book draws attention to the forced sale of Japanese Canadian–owned property during the Second World War. Japanese Canadians could take only tokens of their materials lives with them when they were forcibly uprooted from their homes. Of what was left behind, much was quickly lost to theft and vandalism. When the remainder was sold without their consent, Japanese Canadians were given some compensation, but they had no role in setting the (often highly unfavourable) terms of the sales. They were also deprived of the choice not to sell. Those in government camps were forced to use the funds realized in the sale of their property to pay for their own internment. The loss of almost 2,000 homes, businesses, and farms left British Columbians of Japanese ancestry without roots to return to when restrictions were finally lifted. The theft, destruction, and sale of all manner of other property – automobiles, fishing vessels, furniture, musical instruments, dishware, clothing, shrines, cameras – obliterated the accomplishments of generations and ensured, as Mona Oikawa observes, that property belonging to Japanese Canadians became the "antiques" and "inheritance" of others.[23]

Kimura worked with two important government bodies connected with this process. The first, the Japanese Fishing Vessel Disposal Committee, was an ad hoc creation, tasked in the first months of Canada's Pacific War with selling or leasing Japanese Canadian–owned fishing vessels. Established in January 1942, the committee operated until July, when it transferred the remaining vessels in its custody to the Custodian of Enemy Property, the second government body with which Kimura would be associated.[24] The Fishing Vessel Disposal Committee was intended to work quickly, with the aim of maintaining the coastal fisheries where Japanese Canadians, despite discriminatory restrictions, had played a critical role until the Second World War. By contrast, the Custodian of Enemy Property was a bureaucratic body of some longevity that operated under the direction of the secretary of state. Established in 1920 to oversee enemy assets that remained in government custody after the First World War, the office of the Custodian was made responsible in the spring of 1942 for all of the property of uprooted Japanese Canadians.

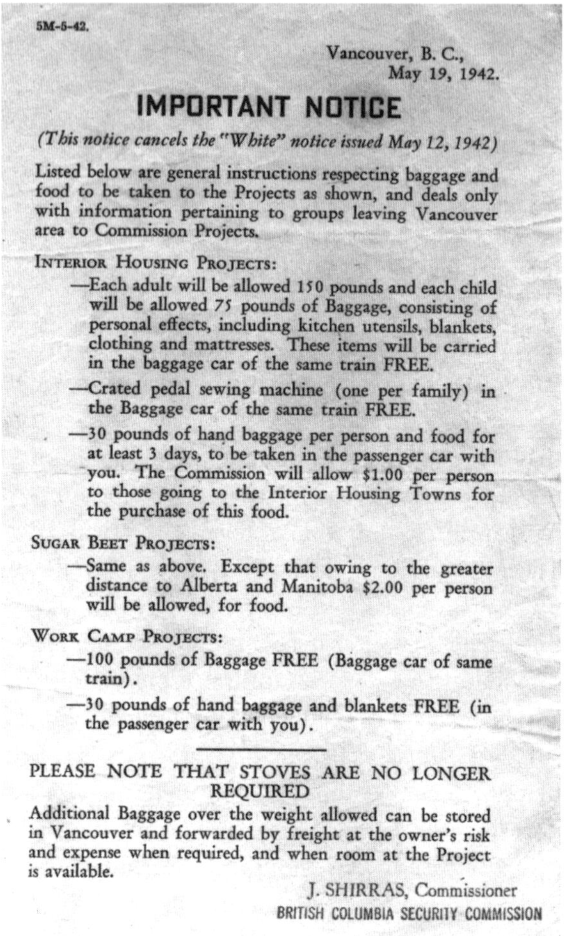

5M-5-42.

Vancouver, B. C.,
May 19, 1942.

**IMPORTANT NOTICE**

*(This notice cancels the "White" notice issued May 12, 1942)*

Listed below are general instructions respecting baggage and food to be taken to the Projects as shown, and deals only with information pertaining to groups leaving Vancouver area to Commission Projects.

INTERIOR HOUSING PROJECTS:

—Each adult will be allowed 150 pounds and each child will be allowed 75 pounds of Baggage, consisting of personal effects, including kitchen utensils, blankets, clothing and mattresses. These items will be carried in the baggage car of the same train FREE.

—Crated pedal sewing machine (one per family) in the Baggage car of the same train FREE.

—30 pounds of hand baggage per person and food for at least 3 days, to be taken in the passenger car with you. The Commission will allow $1.00 per person to those going to the Interior Housing Towns for the purchase of this food.

SUGAR BEET PROJECTS:

—Same as above. Except that owing to the greater distance to Alberta and Manitoba $2.00 per person will be allowed, for food.

WORK CAMP PROJECTS:

—100 pounds of Baggage FREE (Baggage car of same train).

—30 pounds of hand baggage and blankets FREE (in the passenger car with you).

PLEASE NOTE THAT STOVES ARE NO LONGER REQUIRED

Additional Baggage over the weight allowed can be stored in Vancouver and forwarded by freight at the owner's risk and expense when required, and when room at the Project is available.

J. SHIRRAS, Commissioner
BRITISH COLUMBIA SECURITY COMMISSION

Figure I.5
Strict limits on the goods that Japanese Canadians could carry to internment ensured that they would be forced to leave much behind. From the private collection of Masako Fukawa.

Figure I.6 *Opposite*
In the pressure cooker of the uprooting, private companies stepped in to offer services to Japanese Canadians and to take advantage of their hardship. Image courtesy of the Multicultural History Society of Ontario (MHSO) and Simon Fraser University Library.

From an office hastily opened on the fifth floor of the Royal Bank Building in downtown Vancouver, the western branch of the Custodian would continue to handle Japanese Canadian–owned property throughout the 1940s and even into the 1950s. Officials in the employ of the Custodian administered property, helped to steer policy (including the policy of forced sales), communicated directly with Japanese-Canadian property-owners, and responded to claims for compensation after the war.[25]

Federal officials handled the tasks put to them abysmally. Property was lost, stolen, neglected, destroyed, undervalued, and sold without the consent of its owners. The federal records of this process are unambiguous – the of-

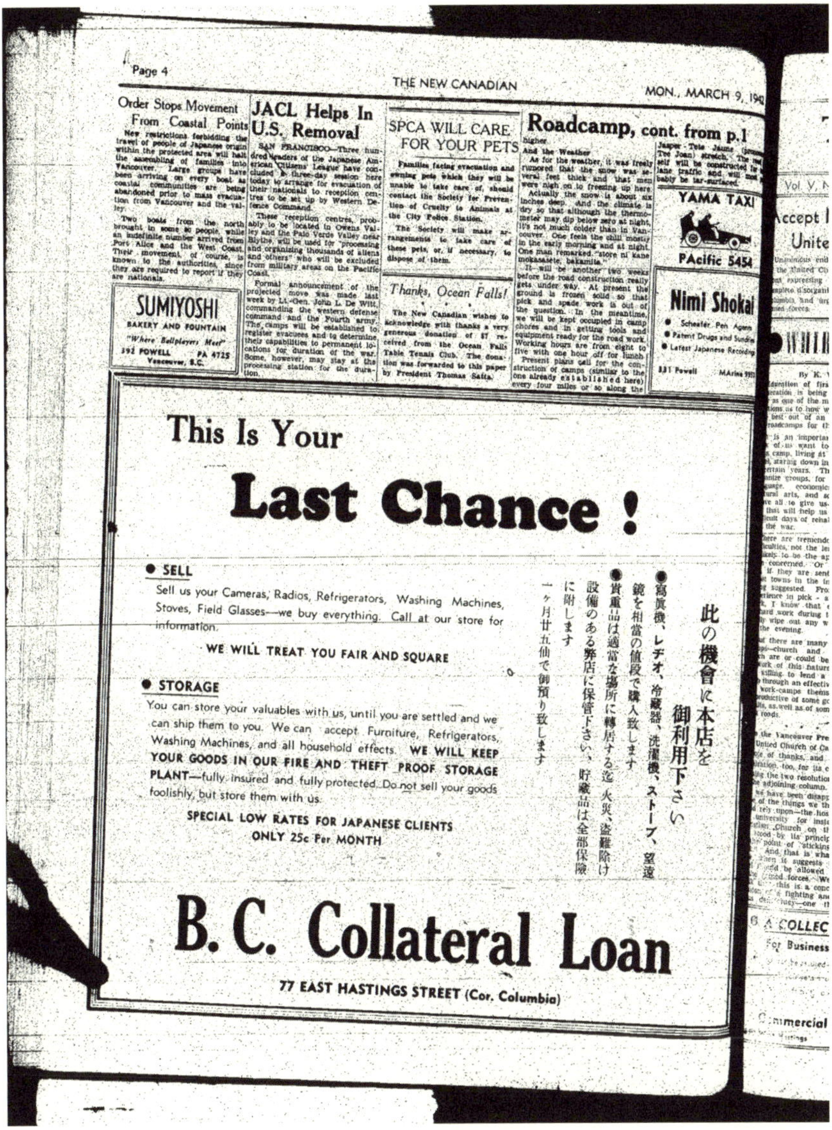

Page 4 THE NEW CANADIAN MON., MARCH 9, 1942

**Order Stops Movement From Coastal Points**

New restrictions forbidding the travel of people of Japanese origin within the protected area will halt the assembling of families into Vancouver. Large groups have been arriving on every boat as coastal communities are being abandoned prior to mass evacuation from Vancouver and the valley.

Two boats from the north brought in some [illegible] people, while an indefinite number arrived from Port Alice and the West Coast. Their movement, of course, is known to the authorities, since they are required to report if they are nationals.

SUMIYOSHI
BAKERY AND FOUNTAIN
"Where Ballplayers Meet"
392 POWELL PA 4725
Vancouver, B.C.

**JACL Helps In U.S. Removal**

SAN FRANCISCO—Three hundred leaders of the Japanese American Citizens' League have concluded a three-day session here today to arrange for evacuation of their nationals to reception centres to be set up by Western Defence Command.

These reception centres, probably to be located in Owens Valley and the Palo Verde Valley near Blythe, will be used for "processing and organizing thousands of aliens and others" who will be excluded from military areas on the Pacific Coast.

Formal announcement of the projected move was made last week by Lt.-Gen. John L. De Witt, commanding the western defense command and the Fourth army. The camps will be established to register evacuees and to determine their capabilities to permanent locations for duration of the war. Some, however, may stay at the processing station for the duration.

**SPCA WILL CARE FOR YOUR PETS**

Families facing evacuation and owning pets which they will be unable to take care of, should contact the Society for Prevention of Cruelty to Animals at the City Police Station.

The Society will make arrangements to take care of these pets, or, if necessary, to dispose of them.

*Thanks, Ocean Falls!*

The New Canadian wishes to acknowledge with thanks a very generous donation of $7 received from the Ocean Falls Table Tennis Club. The donation was forwarded to this paper by President Thomas Saita.

**Roadcamp, cont. from p.1**

higher

And the Weather

As for the weather, it was freely rumored that the snow was several feet thick and that men were nigh on to freezing up here.

Actually the snow is about six inches deep. And the climate is dry so that although the thermometer may dip below zero at night, it's not much colder than in Vancouver. One feels the chill mostly in the early morning and at night. One man remarked "store ni kane mokasasete, bakamita."

It will be another two weeks before the road construction really gets under way. At present the ground is frozen solid so that pick and spade work is out of the question. In the meantime, we will be kept occupied in camp chores and in getting tools and equipment ready for the road work. Working hours are from eight to five with one hour off for lunch.

Present plans call for the construction of camps (similar to the one already established here) every four miles or so along the Jasper-Tete Jaune ([illegible] Tee Joan) stretch. The road itself will be constructed for [illegible] lane traffic and will [illegible] probably be tar-surfaced.

YAMA TAXI
PAcific 5454

Nimi Shokai
● Scheafer Pen Agent
● Patent Drugs and Sundries
● Latest Japanese Recordings
331 Powell MArine [illegible]

This Is Your

**Last Chance !**

● **SELL**

Sell us your Cameras, Radios, Refrigerators, Washing Machines, Stoves, Field Glasses—we buy everything. Call at our store for information.

WE WILL TREAT YOU FAIR AND SQUARE

● **STORAGE**

You can store your valuables with us, until you are settled and we can ship them to you. We can accept Furniture, Refrigerators, Washing Machines, and all household effects. **WE WILL KEEP YOUR GOODS IN OUR FIRE AND THEFT PROOF STORAGE PLANT**—fully insured and fully protected. Do not sell your goods foolishly, but store them with us.

SPECIAL LOW RATES FOR JAPANESE CLIENTS
ONLY 25c Per MONTH

此の機會に本店を
御利用下さい

●寫眞機、レヂオ、冷藏器、洗濯機、ストーブ、望遠鏡を相當の値段で購入致します

●貴重品は適當な場所に轉居する迄 火災、盜難除け設備のある弊店に保管下さい、貯藏品は全部保險に附します

一ヶ月廿五仙で御預り致します

**B. C. Collateral Loan**

77 EAST HASTINGS STREET (Cor. Columbia)

ficials given responsibility for Japanese Canadian–owned property were unprepared for their work. Opportunists took quick advantage. A discussion of "chattels" (personal property other than real estate) in the 1943 annual report of the Vancouver Office of the Custodian offers a glimpse into the sources and scale of losses. Because of vandalism and break-ins at the homes of Japanese Canadians, officials decided to relocate personal goods to centralized

Figure I.7 *Top* Japanese Canadian–owned vehicles were among the first categories of property forced onto the market against the will of their owners. This photograph shows vehicles massed at Hastings Park before being sold to the public in the summer of 1942 while many Japanese Canadians remained in the city. Leonard Frank, photographer. Vancouver Public Library (VPL), 1374.

Figure I.8 *Bottom* Japanese Canadian–owned fishing vessels impounded at New Westminster, BC, 1942. Many vessels would suffer serious damage in this mass mooring. Leonard Frank, photographer. Vancouver Public Library (VPL), 3191.

warehouses. Inadequate security at these facilities, however, only encouraged further thievery: "our central storage places have been broken into several times," reported officials. "The worst feature of this is not so much the amount stolen, but the throwing of the contents of boxes on the floor in the search for valuables makes it difficult or impossible to identify the goods belonging to various owners."[26] The solution to this problem, rather than increased security, was the public auction of all remaining belongings and the denial of responsibility for everything lost.

As Masako Fukawa's contribution to this book describes, Japanese Canadians responded with immediate indignation when they learned of the mishandling of their belongings. Hundreds wrote to the Custodian of Enemy Property in protest. Ryushin Koyanagi expressed the views of many when he wrote the Custodian in August 1944: "I have just received your letter and statement of my account ... To say that I was shocked is putting it mildly. I am sure that my aged parents will be shocked too when they learn that the land which they bought for me with the labour of their sweat and tears have been sold. I know now that my cousins who fought and died in France for Canada during the last war have died in vain." The sense of betrayal implied in his invocation of the sacrifice of his cousins was made explicit in his detailed discussion of the process that led to his family's property losses:

> When we were ordered to register my properties with you ... I was assured that they would be protected and well taken care of until my return to the coast. I had believed you, but now you have betrayed your trust ... The price at which you have sold my land and fishing gear is nothing but highway robbery. Has the price of land and fishing gear depreciated so much during the year that you had to practically give it away? ... You have cunningly taken advantage of this war to deprive illegally the properties which I, a Canadian subject had acquired legally.[27]

Koyanagi's pointed questions went unanswered. For many Japanese Canadians, the sense lingered for decades that the property losses reflected malice that went beyond the exigencies of war. In the late 1940s, Japanese Canadians organized to document the economic impacts of property losses, in part as they prepared presentations for a royal commission that investigated and inadequately addressed these harms.[28] In the 1970s, Ken Adachi described the property sales as a cause of "simmering" anger and "deep rooted … outrage" among Japanese Canadians, and Toyo Takata, writing in the following decade, remembered the property disposals as a "disquieting jolt" that "revealed the government's true intention" to destroy Japanese-Canadian life in British Columbia.[29] Ann Sunahara, whose influential book on the internment era in 1981 devoted a chapter to the forced sale of property, saw it as emblematic of the larger "politics of racism" of the era.[30] In 1986, the National Association of Japanese Canadians commissioned a Price Waterhouse study that provided an estimate of material losses – almost 1 billion in 2017 dollars – that helped to support demands for redress.[31] By participating in the forced sales, Kimura partook of a process that was extremely controversial at the time and has remained so since.

The history of the dispossession opens new historical terrain. Canadians have repeatedly debated whether the internment was a mere expression of racism or a justifiable decision in the context of the war.[32] This question – recently revisited in a *Legion Magazine* forum pitting J.L. Granatstein against Pamela Sugiman in debate – seems to resurface whenever the internment of Japanese Canadians is brought to public attention.[33] The discussions that ensue are often troubling because they tend to expose disturbing elisions of *Japanese Canadians* with the nation and military actions of Japan. And yet, they may also be productive, particularly in the present era as Canadians again confront supposed tensions between national security and civil and human rights.[34] We must continue to discuss the relationship between our values and our fears. The dispossession of the property of Japanese Canadians is part of that discussion, but it also pushes us beyond this well-worn debate and into other stories.

Although property losses began in 1941, the federal decision to forcibly sell everything belonging to west coast Japanese Canadians came in January 1943.[35] Real estate was forced onto the market beginning in the spring that followed and continued to be sold without consent for years. Sales spiked in the summer of 1944, even as the prime minister announced in the House of Commons that the previous two years of battle had "carried the allied war effort across the great divide from uncertainty of victory on the one side to certainty of victory on the other."[36] They continued even once the war was over. Writing from Lemon Creek in February 1946, Takeo Yoshida demanded a permit to return to Vancouver to settle his father's affairs; with hostilities concluded, he could see no grounds for preventing his travel for these purposes. Yoshida argued, "The war was fought to bring peace and justice to all in the world, and to eliminate dictatorial powers, so why practice such dictatorial methods and injustice here in Canada."[37] His plea, like those of hundreds of others, was ignored.

The forced sale of property was neither an act to protect national security nor an expression of panic. Japanese Canadians' former residences – standing empty or (more often) occupied by tenants – and warehouses of their personal belongings clearly posed no security threat. No one ever argued that they did. By the time of most sales, the sense of military threat to the Canadian west had long dissipated.[38] By contrast with the uprooting, the highest levels of Canadian government were largely unconcerned with the situation of Japanese Canadian–owned property after the uprooting: the war cabinet never discussed the forced sales, and Prime Minister William Lyon Mackenzie King never mentioned them in his diary.[39] Nor was there public outcry about the property that Japanese Canadians had left behind. Although they reported on the sale of property, British Columbia newspapers neither mounted nor documented a campaign for the forced sales.[40] Other jurisdictions, notably the United States, did not implement a policy to force the sale of the belongings of incarcerated Japanese Americans. The forced sale of property reminds us that "time of war" is a simplification that obscures as much as it reveals.

This volume introduces new directions of discussion that emerge as we leave behind the long-standing debate over whether racism or the "time of war" necessitated the acts perpetrated against Japanese Canadians. Masako Fukawa's contribution explores the very personal reverberations of property loss within her family. The acts in which Kimura participated undermined long-standing cultural practices, gender roles, and life expectations across multiple generations. Acknowledging that Kimura was in a "difficult position," Fukawa examines his participation in the dispossession of his own community within the context of the norms of the Japanese immigrant generation. Tim Stanley, by contrast, uses the memoir to interrogate Kimura's place, and that of Japanese Canadians more broadly, within the colonial society that surrounded him. Stanley uses the memoir to demonstrate the ways in which dominance was both pervasive and constantly "slipping." Kimura's participation in the process of dispossession reveals, for him, the "complex, competing, and contradictory grammars" of power, the "ill-defined" and unstable categories through which racialized policy operated. Vic Satzewich's approach bridges the previous two, asking explicitly comparative questions about Kimura's apparent collaboration in an injustice against his own community. "Taken in a broader context," he argues, "Kimura's actions are not that unusual." Drawing upon other parallel examples in Canadian history, Satzewich conceives of Kimura's actions as an example of the "collaborative resistance" that often plays a part in making injustice. Maintaining a focus on power and the institutional structures of the state but also returning to the personal implications of these events within the histories of individual families, Laura Madokoro links the dispossession to lifelong performances of citizenship, including her own grandmother's acquisition of a citizenship certificate. Such acts, for Madokoro, illuminate the ways in which "Japanese Canadians sought to move beyond the disappointment of their social experience as citizens to insist upon all the promises that legal citizenship status entailed." In all, the contributions to this volume demonstrate the depth and breadth of this topic, the value of sustained attention to the complex documents of its unfolding, and the connections that can be made between the dispossession of Japanese Canadians and other major historical themes.

## Kimura as a Committee Member and Memorialist

In many ways, Kimura weathered the storm of the 1940s better than most. Because of his work with the federal government, he and his family were offered a special exemption from the order-in-council that uprooted Japanese Canadians from coastal British Columbia.[41] Declining this offer, they instead relocated to Christina Lake, near Grand Forks, British Columbia, joining one of the "self-support camps" where relatively well-to-do displaced people suffered the exclusion associated with the larger internment process but also secured a greater measure of control over their living conditions than did most Japanese Canadians during the uprooting.[42] In Christina Lake, Kimura obtained a pass from the British Columbia Security Commission, allowing him to travel within the restricted area.[43] As late as June 1943, while in Vancouver for his work with the Custodian of Enemy Property, he dined in public at the New Beijing Restaurant with non-Nikkei friends.[44] Such relative privileges, however, came at a cost.

Kimura's first entanglement with wartime federal policy helped to obliterate the long-standing Japanese-Canadian industry in which he had made his livelihood. The seizure of fishing vessels was one of Canada's first acts as a participant in the war in the Pacific. On 8 December 1941, long before the larger course of policy had been set, the Navy demanded that Japanese-Canadian fishers relinquish more than 1,300 vessels, the large majority of which were shortly impounded along the Fraser River near New Westminster. On 13 January 1942, Order-in-Council PC 288 created the Fishing Vessel Disposal Committee, chaired by Justice Sidney Smith, whose mandate was to "make it possible for the present owners of detained vessels to freely negotiate for charters, leases or sales" of their vessels. Smith was joined on the committee by Naval Commander B.L. Johnson and by Kimura, who had agreed to serve as a representative of Japanese-Canadian interests.[45]

The reasons for the selection of Kimura as the committee's Japanese-Canadian member are not entirely apparent. Most likely the choice resulted from his prominence in the industry as well as some impression of his personality and politics. Kimura's agenda of his business activities includes a 6 August 1941 meeting with a "Mr Motherwell," most likely J.A. Motherwell, the chief supervisor of fisheries.[46] It was Motherwell who, just over five months later, called Kimura to invite his participation in the disposal of fishing vessels. In addition, Kimura indicates that other Japanese Canadians supported his involvement with the committee.[47] Whatever the case, in January 1942 Kimura accepted this appointment and began to participate in implementing a policy to encourage, but not (yet) force, Japanese-Canadian owners to sell their boats.

Kimura was not the only Japanese Canadian to participate in this or other aspects of the federal policies targeting his community. As Kimura relates in his memoir, shortly after its formation, the Fishing Vessel Disposal Committee established another body – this one called the Japanese-Canadian Liaison Committee – whose members were charged with encouraging Japanese-Canadian fishers to cooperate in the sale and lease of their vessels.[48] Unosuke Sakamoto, a member of the liaison committee, later recalled that he was "responsible for getting signatures" from boat-owners that allowed their vessels to be marketed and then, once "white men and Indians chose the boats they liked ... I would write [the owners] telling them the prices and asking them what they wanted to do. By that time they had to sell their boats cheap so they sold them, with tears."[49] Yasutaro Yamaga, a prominent community member from Maple Ridge, served briefly on an advisory committee that oversaw the forced sale of rural property. According to Kimura, who consulted with him at the time, Yamaga saw the forced sales as an undoing of his life's work; "this work shall be my own funeral," said Yamaga as he embarked on the destruction of the Japanese-Canadian farming district that he had helped to build.[50] With respect to the uprooting and internment of the Japanese-Canadian population, rather than the property sales per se, Adachi documents a range of organized responses: some Japanese-Canadian groups openly resisted the government's policies, others facilitated compliance, while still others sought to profit. The statements of Kunio Shimizu, general secretary of the Japanese Canadian Citizens' Council, who urged orderly compliance with government orders, are particularly similar to Kimura's own views.[51] The perspectives of such figures have been neglected in our understanding of these events.[52] Kimura himself has been virtually omitted from the historical account altogether. What motivated figures like Kimura and Yamaga to participate in the administration of racist policy? What was the impact of their involvement, both on themselves and on the wider community? Kimura's memoir, perhaps better than any other source, allows us to begin finding answers to these important questions.

Examining Canada's "exclusion era" (when Chinese immigration was taxed and then barred), Lisa Rose Mar finds a political history that was "far more integrated than scholars presume" as Chinese Canadians participated in the implementation of discriminatory law. According to Mar, ongoing collaboration between Chinese and Anglo actors was necessary, even when it came to the "most direct processes of exclusion."[53] The history that Kimura tells in his memoir offers another instance of the complicated processes of racist policy.[54] As with Chinese exclusion, the forced sale of property owned by Japanese Canadians presented officials with significant practical problems, not least of which was a linguistic barrier.[55] As in the case of Chinese Canadians, a small number of Japanese Canadians stepped into this breach, facilitating the operation of power. Close examination of the brokers who were necessary to the operation of Canadian law reveals a history far more complex than stories of heroes and villains, oppressors, victims, and resisters.

Kimura's first step into these murky waters was his decision to join a committee entrusted with arranging the voluntary, not forced, sale of Japanese Canadian–owned fishing vessels. In this context, Kimura, and members of the liaison committee, could well have seen themselves as representing the interests of the owners. They knew the industry and its fishers; they could translate for Japanese Canadians, giving them more choice, rather than less, in the final disposition of vessels that often represented decades of invest-

Figure I.9 Staff at the internment site of Greenwood, BC, in 1945. Kimura was not alone in working in the administration of the internment. In this photograph, Florence Imai (left), Chizu Omae (centre), and Toshimi Ochiai (right) pose with Father Robert O'Farrell and an unidentified man in this portrait of British Columbia Security Commission staff. Nikkei National Museum (NNM), 2011-77-1-4.

ment and hard labour. In these months before the uprooting of the population but after the impounding of fishing vessels, most Japanese Canadians might well have agreed that there was a place for brokerage.

Over time, however, both the context and the policy changed. Japanese-Canadian owners cooperated with officials in allowing their vessels to be impounded, but many resisted the sale of their vessels, hoping to return to gainful employment within the industry. In February and March 1942, the government revealed its intention to uproot the entire Japanese-Canadian population from the coast, and such hopes largely dissolved. Hence, in early March the Fishing Vessel Disposal Committee entered into its "most active" phase, and half of the vessels were sold by the end of May. However, during

Figure I.10 Yasutaro Yamaga (front row, left) served on the committee that oversaw Japanese Canadian–owned property outside of Vancouver until he withdrew in objection to its decision to sell farmlands to the Veterans' Lands Act Administration. Pictured here with other farmers from the Maple Ridge area. From the private collection of Linda Kawamoto Reid, ca. 1939–41.

this period it also "became evident" to the committee "that certain Japanese groups were determined to retain ownership of their vessels," a stance that prompted the committee to adopt what it described as a "'Forced Sales' plan." This plan, to sell vessels at prices that the committee deemed reasonable, irrespective of the views of their owners, was later admitted by federal lawyers to be "something for which they had no legal authority" given the terms of reference in the order-in-council that created the committee.[56] Kimura also notes in his memoir that an organization of Japanese-Canadian fishers immediately questioned the policy.[57] Nonetheless, he remained on the committee and hence, for the first time, became party to the sale of property against the will of Japanese-Canadian owners. Several months later, with only 187 vessels remaining, the committee concluded its business, transferring the rest of the boats to the Custodian of Enemy Property.[58] On 12 December of that year, the committee met for a final time to review its closing report. That afternoon, at 1:15 pm, Kimura boarded a train bound for Grand Forks. He rejoined his family late the next day, having been delayed by heavy snowfall.[59]

This might have been the end of Kimura's involvement in the administration of policy, but the forced sale of the fishing vessels set an attractive precedent for officials. Prior to the uprooting of Japanese Canadians, two orders-in-council, PC 1665 and PC 2483, had assured them that their real estate and chattels would be held in protective custody by the Canadian government.[60] Their assets, they were informed, would be preserved for their benefit for the duration of the war. Almost a year later, however, the government abruptly changed its position. After struggling throughout the summer to perform the task assigned to them, officials in the office of the Custodian encouraged a shift toward forced sales, a position that dovetailed with those of the city government of Vancouver and influential BC MP Ian Mackenzie.[61] In January 1943, this position became law. Order-in-Council PC 469 empowered the Custodian of Enemy Property to "liquidate, sell, or otherwise dispose" of all property, real estate, and chattels belonging to Japanese Canadians.[62] Three months to the day after returning home from his work disposing of fishing vessels, Kimura received a call in the evening, inviting his participation in yet another committee, again chaired by Justice Sidney Smith, which would oversee the forced sale of all property owned by Japanese Canadians in the Vancouver area. As the committee would later put it, because Kimura had already "proved to be a source of willing information and help," it was hoped that he would "be of comparable value" in the sale of the remaining property.[63] Five days later, on 18 March 1943, Kimura attended the inaugural meeting of the Advisory Committee on Japanese Properties in Greater Vancouver. He was to remain on the committee until June, when real estate owned by Japanese Canadians was first advertised for sale. In all, he spent eighteen months, far longer than any other Japanese Canadian, engaged in the dispossession of property.[64]

His account of these events offers a new perspective on the forced sales. Whereas accounts of the dispossession of property have tended to privilege the federal cabinet and the orders-in-council that empowered officials to forcibly sell the property of Canadian citizens, significant discretion devolved to the committees entrusted to implement federal policy. In each case, the committees discussed the advisability of forced sales as against other possible approaches to Japanese Canadian–owned property. Indeed, the committee that oversaw the sale of Japanese Canadian–owned real estate and chattels in the Vancouver area was specifically charged, as its first order of business, with assessing: "is it right to sell properties owned by Nikkei people." Its second responsibility, "if the answer is yes," was to "indicate what is considered to be the best way or conditions or terms of selling these properties."[65] Both matters granted significant discretion to the advisory committee. The committee could have advised against dispossession, especially given that the vast majority, an estimated 90 per cent, of Vancouver-area properties under Custodial supervision, had already been rented to paying tenants.[66] The committee might also have advocated closer adherence to the processes of the earlier sale of the fishing vessels whereby officials had initially sought at least the nominal approval of Japanese Canadians. Instead, the Vancouver property committee recommended forced sales, disregarding the approval of owners. The opportunity to press for a more humane, or indeed merely civil, approach was lost.

The memoir helps us to understand such decisions. Kimura details the process by which narrow, technical discussions served as the ostensible basis for policies that disregarded citizenship and shattered individual lives. The Japanese Fishing Vessel Disposal Committee determined that Japanese Canadian–owned boats should be sold, rather than leased for the duration of the war, as a conclusion of its discussion of the complications of "partial damage" insurance in the fishing industry. In contrast to industry standards for larger, more valuable ships, insurance companies did not allow claims for repairs to small vessels, instead limiting coverage to claims for the replacement of entire boats.[67] A significant majority of Japanese Canadian–owned vessels would have fallen into this category, leaving responsibility for partial damages uncertain.[68] The committee foresaw that "Nikkei fishermen would be anxious about the maintenance standards of Hakujin and Dojin fishermen."[69] Sale, rather than lease, seemed to recommend itself. Thus, the committee's dispossession of Japanese Canadians began in a discussion of the minutiae of insurance policies in the fishing industry. Evil is indeed, at times, banal.

This lesson must be understood in context. The fishing vessels of Japanese Canadians were not disposed of merely because of technicalities of the insurance industry. More deeply, owners lost their vessels because they were caught in the web of a racist wartime policy and popular sentiment, which itself was part of a much longer history of racism in British Columbia. But Kimura teaches us that the discussions that took place in the execution of the policy did not operate at such depths. The committee that made the final decision to sell the fishing vessels was not discussing loyalty and security, racial essences, or land and labour in British Columbia. Its conversations were about other things. This observation helps us to understand how a Japanese Canadian could serve on the committee. It also illuminates the operation of racist policy. In some policy settings at least, the people formulating and executing federal policy found ways of discussing and justifying their actions that avoided deeper motivations and aims. This was not necessarily deliberate obfuscation. Officials could mean what they said, even as they failed to say what their actions meant. As historian Tina Loo suggests in a different but related policy context, taking such perspectives seriously enables us to understand the people involved as "more than abstractions." Listening to what officials said as they enacted policy does not entail a refusal to hold them to account, nor does it absolve us of the responsibility to uncover "masked" and "murkier" agendas. Nonetheless, as we listen to the viewpoints of Kimura and the officials with whom he worked, we can acknowledge "who they thought they were and what they thought they were doing."[70]

An important participant in the dispossession of Japanese Canadian–owned property, Kimura defies reduction to an abstract agent of racism. His presence on the advisory committees forces historians to delve more deeply into the motives of direct participants in the execution of policy. In contrast to government records, which convey his, and Yasutaro Yamaga's, participation as an endorsement of the policy of forced sales, Kimura emphasizes that his involvement was reluctant and ambivalent.

In his memoir, Kimura stresses the difficulty of his decision, particularly when it came to the committee that oversaw the forced sale of real estate. Kimura recognized the new dispossession policy as "a serious matter," and since he "had no experience of property evaluation," he initially declined to participate, recommending others, including Yamaga.[71] Ultimately, Kimura and Yamaga both overcame deep reservations because they saw no better alternative. Thus, in the spring of 1943 each advisory committee indeed had a Japanese-Canadian member, but their presence was no ringing endorsement of the policy. Further, they quickly came under pressure from Japanese-Canadian property-owners to resign. In April, letters from owners interned in Kaslo and Slocan charged that Kimura's participation in the advisory committee ran against the "general public opinion" of Japanese Canadians and advised him to resign "as soon as possible."[72] In response, both Kimura and Yamaga cut ties with the Custodian in May and June when the first properties were advertised for sale.[73]

According to Kimura, his participation on both of the committees reflected his concern about the anti-Japanese sentiment in the province. Prior to accepting a position on the committee, he consulted with Japanese-Canadian "volunteers from Vancouver and the surrounding area" who, in early January 1942, "met regularly … to discuss their wartime safety." According to Kimura, "recalling the anti-Nikkei riots of 1907, which had occurred during peacetime," the group was "afraid of the current mood of the population in this time of war." In this context, Kimura (and, he suggests, many others) deemed it advisable that Japanese Canadians contribute to the smooth execution of federal policy so as to avoid stoking the flames of local "anxiety, fear, and even hatred." Kimura explains his participation in this light: his was an effort to prevent the eruption of violence on the home front in the early days of the war.[74] Once on the committee, Kimura continued to see his role in this fashion, urging the committee to take a position against popular characterizations of all Japanese Canadians as "enemies" and the fishing vessels as "seized" or as "spoils of war." Kimura pushed the committee to establish a public counter-narrative within which it was clear that Canadian citizens of Japanese origins, including veterans of the First World War, had voluntarily and lawfully entrusted their vessels to the government.[75] Kimura, in this reading, was among the first to recognize the importance of the words in which this story would be told.[76]

The memoir also explains the most controversial decision in which Kimura participated – the decision by the Vancouver advisory committee to approve the forced sale of Japanese Canadian–owned property – by reference to rampant racism, the effects of which were already evident in the former neighbourhoods of Japanese Canadians when the committee made its recommendations. Early in their deliberations, the three members of the Vancouver advisory committee (Kimura, Alderman Charles Jones, and Justice Sidney Smith) toured the Powell Street area with a guide from the Office of the Custodian. This practice was, by the spring of 1943, commonplace for federal officials. Tours of the Powell Street area, which highlighted its most dilapidated properties, had been foundational to policy formation over the previous year; such tours encouraged the view, as Ian Mackenzie would put it, that Japanese Canadian–owned properties were "very much in the nature of definite slums," a perspective that, for the Custodian, recommended forced sales.[77]

Kimura was unique among the participants of such tours in having lived in the Powell Street area. Nonetheless, like federal officials, he noted the poor condition of the housing in the district, and at times his explanation of the forced sales seems to echo official justifications. Although many of the dwellings were "already rented out through real estate agents," he explained that "they were generally humble and on the level of temporary dwellings ... It seemed that there were a considerable number of places which required large sums spent on them to comply with city bylaws."[78] However, Kimura differed markedly from federal officials in the context and interpretation that he offered for these observations.

Officials emphasized the long-standing degradation of the neighbourhood as a racialized slum. Summarizing a long discussion of Japanese Canadian–owned properties in the Powell Street neighbourhood, Under-Secretary of State Ephraim Coleman explained that "so long as [the properties] were occupied by Japanese, who apparently had adapted themselves to these conditions ... sanitary inspections appear to have been infrequent." In Coleman's view, inspectors "very properly" intervened when the units were rented to other tenants: "I consider it very doubtful whether, without extensive alterations which might almost amount to rebuilding, the premises can be made fit for habitation by white people."[79] Under such conditions, officials reasoned that Japanese Canadian–owned property would become encumbered by debt and deteriorate in value. On the basis of such (highly specious) analyses, they argued that the forced sales served the interests of Japanese-Canadian owners.[80]

By contrast, Kimura mentioned the quality of housing but emphasized the further deterioration of Japanese Canadian–owned property as the result of "theft and break-ins." Encouraged by "Anti-Nikkei agitators" who "took this opportunity to proclaim, maliciously, that all property belonging to Nikkei people should be disposed of to prevent their return to the west coast" as well as "the general public" that "turned a blind eye to the vandalism of empty houses," criminals grew "increasingly bold."[81] Given an atmosphere of widespread extremism and complicity, "it was easy to see that damages were increasing daily."[82] Six days after witnessing widespread destruction of Japanese Canadian–owned homes and businesses, Kimura joined Smith and Jones in approving property dispossession.[83]

The memoir further contextualizes wartime extremism within the larger history of the "anti-Nikkei campaigns" in British Columbia. Kimura reminds his readers that "all Nikkei immigrants have suffered from the anti-Nikkei movement since they landed in the province of BC." Even naturalized citizens such as the fishers (who were required to be naturalized in order to obtain licences) "suffered from continuous, severe exclusion practices."[84] Long before the outbreak of war, racist movements had sought to restrict Japanese immigration (even encouraging deportation), to limit the economic activity of Japanese Canadians, and to prevent their ownership of land.[85] During the war, "Anti-Nikkei agitators" saw "a great opportunity to lift up nationalistic spirits. They drummed up the fighting spirit of the military, escalated anti-Nikkei propaganda and intensified anti-Nikkei sentiment among the general public."[86] But they did not voice a new sentiment; rather they reflected the "many years of anti-Nikkei propaganda" that set the stage for wartime actions.[87]

In sum, prevalent racism was an essential context for Kimura's retrospective explanation of his decisions. The wider context of racism served as his justification for his participation in the Fishing Vessel Disposal Committee, provided him with a reason for the forced sale of Japanese Canadian–owned real estate and chattels, and formed the crux of his message to younger Japanese Canadians. Kimura's memoir argues that actions such as his, which subsequent generations could take for compliance or even complicity, instead constituted a form of resistance. His generation, he insists, was "by no means ignorant and stupid." Rather, opportunities for resistance varied "depending on the time period, the situation, the environment, and social standing."[88] Resistance, on this view, is historical. It takes form in relation to structures of power.

And it is within this context that Kimura offers his message for the *Nisei* and *Sansei*; he hopes that their assessments of his actions, and those of his generation, will take into account this larger history.[89] "From the current perspective, at a time when protests and demonstrations are the trend," he writes, "there might be some who laugh at the Nikkei who conducted themselves with silence and obedience for decades."[90] Such condescension of posterity, he argues, underestimates the extent of direct resistance – prior to the war Japanese Canadians did press claims for the franchise and unrestricted access to fishing licences – and misreads the historical terrain. "I would like you to investigate, face squarely, and consider the time period, the circumstances, situation, and environment that the *Issei* and some in the *Nisei* were placed in," he writes. "The *Issei* were not an inferior ethnic group"; rather, they achieved remarkable success despite the difficulties of migration and the "vicious anti-Nikkei campaign" that they encountered.[91]

Given this historical setting, Kimura suggests that compliance served to undermine discriminatory norms. The civility of Japanese Canadians, their "diligence, pleasant character, law-abiding spirit, and patience toward past discriminatory treatment" eventually contributed to the undermining of racism.[92] Japanese Canadians "were rewarded for their struggle and finally reached the dawn of a new era after the war" when other Canadians "soon realized that past discrimination was unjust. They gradually came to know the true value of Nikkei people. The accumulated anti-Nikkei sentiment evaporated, and people became open and warm."[93] What a younger generation might mistake for mere docility, he argues, instead laid the ground upon which subsequent and more forceful protest might be staged.

More recently, historians have arrived at similar readings of early civil rights struggles. In a provocative attempt to explain the subtle politics of resistance in the Jim Crow–era South, American historian Robin Kelley uses the work of anthropologist James Scott (also foundational to Vic Satzewich's comparative contribution to this book) to analyze Richard Wright's photographic essay, *Twelve Million Black Voices*. Wright warned readers that African Americans "are not what we seem." Kelley elaborates: "the appearance of silence and accommodation was not only deceiving but frequently intended to deceive."[94] Closer to the history told here, Lisa Rose Mar finds that, in the 1920s, Chinese-Canadian leaders carefully guided social science researchers in British Columbia, suppressing the complexity and transnationalism of Chinese migrants' lives and encouraging scholars to "discover" the potential of the Chinese in Canada to become an "educated, assimilated, deferential, and model minority"; this research finding, it was hoped, would help to "undercut the biological premises of more pessimistic 'sciences'" and encourage a more progressive policy.[95] On this reading, the Chinese-Canadian "model minority" was a deliberate creation, a political claim.

Likewise, Kimura argues that the members of his generation could appear to acquiesce to injustice even as they sought to undermine it. Their civility also disguised deeper maneuvering and subtle argumentation. Kimura counted this strategy a success. Coupled with careful strategic challenges to a racist legal and political order, accommodation begot revolution.

Kimura hoped to extend this logic to his own wartime actions. If civility and apparent compliance could disguise effective resistance, then perhaps his readers would understand his work within structures that were racist and

Figure I.11 Even as Kimura served on the Fishing Vessel Disposal Committee, Gordon Parks took this photograph for the Farm Security Administration in the United States, suggesting the resilience of African-American labourers, who were not always what they seemed. Library of Congress, LC-USF34-013407-C. On comparative contexts, see Commentary 3.

with individuals who were prejudiced. In several pages devoted to the forced sales in his history of the Japanese-Canadian farmers' association in Haney, Yamaga offers a somewhat similar explanation of his role on the advisory committee that oversaw the forced sale of Japanese Canadian–owned farms. Acknowledging that he served despite the objections, and even threats, of other Japanese Canadians, Yamaga insists: "[I] felt it was a duty that was thrust onto me to witness the final liquidation of the Nikkei farms … and to act later as a living witness at some future court of justice."[96] Kimura was not alone in suggesting that resistance could take subtle and unlikely forms.

In contrast to Kimura, Yamaga ultimately spoke truth to power. When Yamaga formally resigned from the rural advisory committee in late May 1943, he sent a telegram explaining that, on the basis of the "atmosphere" of the last meeting he had attended, he concluded that the sale of property would "bring [an] unfair result to the Japanese owners." In this context, he stated, "my service is no longer necessary."[97] Kimura's record in this respect is more ambiguous. In the memoir, he reports having received a telegram from an organization of Nikkei property-owners, urging him to resign, which Kimura would have recognized as part of a much larger movement by Japanese Canadians to resist the forced sale of their property.[98] He raised the issue at a meeting on the twelfth of the month, when he claims to have stated quite forcefully: "first of all, I was not elected to be a committee member by Nikkei people, and it now turns out that they are not supporting my work … I should resign."[99] But he did not do so. While the committee minutes of that day do include a discussion of the protest by Japanese-Canadian property-owners during which "Mr Kimura explained his position," they conclude rather blandly, "it was agreed that nothing need be done by the Committee for the time being."[100] Even after learning of Yamaga's bitter disappointment at the forced sale of rural land, Kimura still failed to resign, instead accepting Sidney Smith's argument that "You have been doing a great job and your resignation will not improve the situation of Nikkei people" and agreeing to remain on the committee until a series of important procedural decisions had been made in June.[101] Thereafter, committee minutes indicate that he went absent, failing to respond to inquiries from the chair, until, on 19 July, he sent a telegram indicating, "Owing to sickness cannot perform my duty as minister of your committee and consequently I hereby tender my resignation."[102] The process for the forced sale of rural property in which Yamaga was involved (a bulk transfer to the Soldier Settlement Board, then the Veterans' Land Act Administration) was in fact different from and more overtly unjust than the process that involved Kimura (transfers to individual buyers on the basis of closed bids). The "atmosphere" of the meetings that each attended may well have been very different as well; these were two separate settings. And yet Kimura tells readers that he saw the forced sales as a consequence of widespread racism, that he understood their implications for Japanese-Canadian owners, and that he knew about the miscarriage of justice with respect to farmlands. In his resignation he might have expressed at least some of this.

Students of this era (like the authors of this volume) will be divided on the credibility of Kimura's characterization of his own actions. Some will argue that he was complicit in racist policy; others will accept the view that cooperation was a strategic response to conditions outside of his control. His participation in the committees surely aided the process of dispossession and bolstered misleading official claims that Japanese Canadians had consented to the sale of their property. However, a refusal to participate might not have changed the policy. Perhaps some benefit was derived from the presence of Japanese Canadians in the process. From a theoretical perspective, such debates may encourage engagement with the very meaning of resistance. Exploring a theme to which he returns in his contribution to this volume, Timothy Stanley has urged historians to understand that "just as there are *racisms*, so too are there *anti-racisms*" and advocated a flexible understanding of both: "Even people actively promoting particular racisms can have their anti-racist moments, and anti-racists have their racist ones … If racisms racialize, anti-racisms trouble racializations. If racisms organize racialized exclusions, anti-racisms promote deracialized inclusions. If racisms have negative consequences, anti-racisms try to mitigate these consequences."[103]

Perhaps Kimura's actions fit somewhere in this description. His presence on the committees put a human face on the victims of the policy in the rooms in which it was implemented; he communicated the policy to Japanese Canadians, and, according to his memoir, undertook small investigations for individual Japanese Canadians concerned about the fate of their belongings. He witnessed and revealed the policy in his memoir at a time when the official government documents remained closed to the public.

Almost three-quarters of a century later, caution is required in any judgment of the character of individuals placed in difficult, and indeed often impossible, situations by the racist policies of mid-twentieth-century states. Recalling his role in the trials of accused Nazi collaborators in postwar Israel, Supreme Court Justice Haim Cohn comments: "I could not rid myself of the feeling that we are altogether unable to judge these people … to put ourselves in their place at all … as one must in order to judge a person."[104] Without suggesting equivalence between the forced sale of property in Canada and mass murder in Europe, I nonetheless gravitate to a similar perspective as I approach figures like Kimura who became entangled in Canada's experiment with mass, race-based incarceration, deportation, and property dispossession. My challenge has been to understand, as well as I can, the wartime era, the enduring damages caused by racist policy, and the ways in which individuals have grappled with and communicated their own experiences of some of Canada's most difficult history.

When Kimura sought to explain his role in the wartime era, his audience was a younger generation of Japanese Canadians in whom he saw little understanding of his experience. Kimura had five children in the generation he was explicitly addressing, but the memoir was not intended exclusively for their eyes. It was written in a language that they could not read, intended for a public archive, and its diction suggests a less intimate audience. Important word choices – for example, in his description of his concern for younger generations (*rōbashin*, which evokes the advice of a more distant, and female, relation) and his final plea for careful consideration of his view (*itadakitai*, which translates to a humble request) – are not suggestive of fatherly authority.[105] Still, upon his death the memoir passed to his children, and today it has found its way back into their hands in translated form. The memoir has thus become a vehicle for the communication of the internment within his family, even as it also aims to communicate on a larger scale. It is thus a complex and unusual instance in the larger effort of interned Japanese Canadians to explain this history to subsequent generations.

Although historians continue to debate the extent of change in the practice of racism in mid-century Canada, for Kimura the matter was clear: his effort to communicate across generations was also a communication across vastly different historical contexts. The younger generation, accustomed as it was to "protests and demonstrations," could scarcely understand submission to second-class citizenship, much less how an individual might find himself in a position of cooperating with authorities to "smooth" the administration of racist policy. Historical change, a transformation in Canadian race relations, opened a gulf within his family and community.

The Kimura memoir and Masako Fukawa's reflections on her own family suggest that Japanese-Canadian men may have felt the difficulty of bridging this gulf with particular acuity. Oikawa has brought important scrutiny to the trope of the "silent survivor," recognizing its racialized and gendered dimensions and its suppression of powerful women's voices. Yet if the "silent survivor" is a misreading of women's experiences, it nonetheless offers a culturally viable female posture. What of men? Oikawa notes that the "usages of silent women" in historical accounts of internment "variously affect the visibility of Japanese Canadian men."[106] Kimura's memoir suggests that we might push such claims further. At least in some instances, the dominant motif of silent submission could impede male communication of the internment. In their efforts to convey their experiences to a generation accustomed to directly confronting inequality, men like Kimura, indeed especially Kimura, faced particular and gendered barriers. Kimura makes repeated mention of a younger generation that he imagines laughing at his silence and obedience.[107] The sense conveyed is one of humiliation, not in relation to the events of the 1940s but, rather, in relation to the mocking jeers of younger Japanese Canadians who fail to comprehend the racism of the pre-war and wartime eras.

Perhaps to push back against such views, the memoir positions Kimura as a protective patriarch within his own family. It was because of this role that Kimura could not accept the exemption of his family from the uprooting order. "I could not," Kimura writes, "have my wife, and especially young children, reside in Vancouver where they could not even go to school."[108] The wider reflections that follow establish that Kimura saw Vancouver – despite his own freedom of movement within it – as a deeply, indeed violently, racist environment. As a father and a husband, he shielded his family to the best of his ability.

Further, Kimura's emphasis on historical context can be read as an effort to create space within which his actions can be understood as manly. Had he lived in a later generation, he too would have expressed himself with greater force; had his young readers lived through his times, they would have tempered their actions. Kimura provides an anecdote to reinforce this point. When Japanese-Canadian property-owners organized a legal challenge to the forced sales, he purports to have suggested strategies for legal argumentation.[109] This recollection demonstrates for his audience that Kimura was able to turn information that he gained, while occupying a position of privilege, against the authorities with whom he had worked. What strong men do, we learn, is navigate fields of opportunity and constraint for the benefit of their families and communities. When this requires the smooth operation of policy, a man steps into a difficult position; when it requires legal battle, he argues; when it demands protest, he takes to the street.

If this was Kimura's core message, it would seem that he harboured doubts about its resonance. The section that forcefully presents his claims about historical context also includes self-defeating gestures. To conclude a paragraph in which he emphasizes the challenges and accomplishments of his generation, Kimura laments: "You might laugh at my slim advice, but I would like to urge you not to foment unconscious ethnic self-hatred without realizing it."[110] In the end, despite whatever justice he saw in his own actions, Kimura continued to feel mocked and even, at least potentially, hated.

Somewhat surprisingly given his tone, there is little evidence to suggest that Kimura suffered publicly as a result of his actions. During the internment, he made no effort to conceal his trips to Vancouver, instead returning to Christina Lake with gifts for the entire community. His son Edmund remembers: "on one occasion he brought back a whole pile of running shoes. From children's size up to adults. So there were a lot of people in the community wearing the same shoes."[111] In the postwar period, the Kimuras remained in Christina Lake where Kishizo worked as a bookkeeper for a mill. After his retirement, however, he returned to Vancouver to spend the final decade of his life within the larger Japanese-Canadian community there.[112] To my knowledge, the lone written comment on Kimura's postwar experience suggests that he remained well placed among Japanese Canadians. Community historian Katsuyoshi Morita, writing in 1988, reflected that it was "nice to see" the accomplishments of Kimura's five children as the two boys succeeded professionally and his "three daughters … all married into prominent Nikkei families."[113] After his death, his children retained his records privately for three decades before donating them to an archive, in part out of concern about the community's potential reaction to the revelation of their father's role in the forced sales. Despite public evidence of this role during the internment, it seems to have been largely forgotten in the years that followed. Rather than documenting any difficulty that Kimura experienced in living among Japanese Canadians after the war, the ambivalence and defensiveness of the memoir seem to emerge specifically in relation to the telling of the past. Kimura struggled as he sought to have his story understood.

Kimura's memoir offers a unique glimpse into an important moment in the history of race in twentieth-century Canada. A memoir of a person in a key position within the dispossession process, it opens a rare window into the operation of Canadian policy. A document of the participation of a Japanese Canadian in actions that victimized his own community, it illuminates the complex political history of racist law. An ambivalent and uneasy document, it conveys the difficulty of communicating political violence, especially across historical change.

The internment of Japanese Canadians has been told, by and large, in black and white. And rightly so. It is a story of profound harms in which there are unmistakable perpetrators and definite victims. Kimura's memoir, far from absolving guilt, instead intersects with other sources in conveying the profound and enduring human impacts of such historical eras. The internment forced itself on Kimura, as it did upon other Japanese Canadians. But when his life was interrupted by Canadian officials, he received a troubling proposition. Kimura accepted. His memoir challenges us to understand such choices, to grapple with their implications, and to join in their difficult telling.

NOTES

1 Portions of this chapter appeared in an earlier form as an article. See Stanger-Ross, "Telling a Difficult Past." Note that this article used an earlier translation of the memoir. Thank you to Eric Adams, Jason Colby, Audrey Kobayashi, Graeme Wynn, and the contributors to this volume for their comments on earlier versions.

2 Edmund Kimura and Doris Kimura, interview by Jordan Stanger-Ross, 4 March 2015, Vancouver.

3 Kimura Memoir, 57. All references to Kimura's memoir will reference the page numbers of the manuscript as it appears in this book. In addition, the entire unedited volume is available online via the Nikkei National Museum at http://witnesstoloss.ca.

4 Immigration figures were higher still in the two years that followed. As a proportion of the resident population, the annual figures of this period have never again been approached.

5 Adachi, *Enemy That Never Was*, 112. A Methodist church had served the spiritual needs of Japanese-Canadian Christians in the neighbourhood since 1906. Ibid., 111.

6 Ibid., 9–13; On Japanese migration to Canada in this era, see Takai, "Navigating Transpacific Passages; Geiger, *Subverting Exclusion*.

7 Sumida, "The Japanese in British Columbia," 23.

8 Adachi, *Enemy That Never Was*, 51. The Tamura family lost an equivalent of more than $800,000 (2017 dollars) in the forced sale of a single property that they owned in the Powell Street neighbourhood. This figure is based on the author's calculations made in consultation with the Landscapes of Injustice real estate database.

9 Sumida, "The Japanese in British Columbia," 28; Belshaw, *Becoming British Columbia*, 32. Although the overall population (and economy) was booming in this period, it also marked a period of demographic catastrophe for First Nations people. Ibid., 72–90.

10 Kobayashi, "Emigration from Kaideima, Japan"; Adachi, *Enemy That Never Was*, 17; see also Morawska, "From Myth to Reality."

11 The family's household register in Japan shows that Tamotsu died in his home village in 1936. Access to register courtesy of Edmund Kimura and Doris Kimura.

12 "Dominion Policy in Favor of Influx," 1.

13 Adachi, "The Riot of 1907," in *Enemy That Never Was*, 63–87; Roy, "The Vancouver Riot and Its Consequences," in *White Man's Province*; Gilmour, *Trouble on Main Street*; Atkinson, "Out of One Borderland, Many."

14 Roy, *Oriental Question*, 5; Roy, *White Man's Province.*

15 Dunae et al., "Making the Inscrutable, Scrutable"; Mawani, *Colonial Proximities*; Stanley, *Contesting White Supremacy*; Roy, *Triumph of Citizenship*; Anderson, *Vancouver's Chinatown*; Roy, *White Man's Province*; Lai, *Chinatowns Towns*; Sunahara, *Politics of Racism*; W. Peter Ward, *White Canada Forever*; Adachi, *Enemy That Never Was.*

16 Belshaw, *Becoming British Columbia*, 57.

17 Adachi, *Enemy That Never Was*, 142–53.

18 Sumida, "The Japanese in British Columbia," 102–3, 419; Switzer, *Gateway to Promise*; Fukawa and Fukawa, *Spirit of the Nikkei Fleet*; Ayukawa, *Hiroshima Immigrants*; Takata, *Nikkei Legacy*; Adachi, *Enemy That Never Was.*

19 Sumida, "The Japanese in British Columbia," 218–19.

20 Adachi, *Enemy That Never Was*, 123.

21 "Biography," Kishizo Kimura fonds, NNMCC, http://nikkeimuseum.org/www/collections_detail.php?col_id=F461 (accessed 22 February 2013). This brief biography was developed by the Kimura family. Morita, *Powell Street Monogatari*, 54; "British Columbia Security Commission Permit No. 00076 March 26, 1943," Kishizo Kimura fonds, NNMCC, File 1, MS42.

22 For the details of these policies, see Adachi, *Enemy That Never Was*; Sunahara, *Politics of Racism*; and Roy, *Triumph of Citizenship.*

23 Oikawa, *Cartographies of Violence*, 231.

24 For the records of the Japanese Fishing Vessel Disposal Committee, see file "General Correspondence – Disposal of Japanese Fishing Vessels," and file "Japanese Fishing Vessel Disposal Committee," LAC, RG23, Vol. 2292, Pacific Region Federal Records Centre, Vancouver.

25 The records of the Custodian of Enemy Property constitute RG 117 at Library and Archives Canada (LAC), Ottawa. Many key records of the Vancouver Office are available online at heritage.canadiana.ca. On the origins and records of the Custodian of Enemy Property, see Roberts-Moore, "Office of the Custodian of Enemy Property." On the role of staff in the office of the Custodian in administering and steering policy, see Stanger-Ross and the Landscapes of Injustice Research Collective, "Suspect Properties."

26 F.G. Shears to Norman McLarty, Report, 28 January 1944, Canadiana Heritage, Office of the Custodian of Enemy Property: Vancouver Office, RG117, microfilm reel C-9469, image 228, http://heritage.canadiana.ca/view/oocihm.lac_reel_c9469/228?r=0&s=1.

27 Ryushin Koyanagi, letter, 5 August 1944, *Canadiana Heritage*, Office of the Custodian of Enemy Property: Vancouver Office, microfilm reel C-9476 RG117, image 1460, http://heritage.canadiana.ca/view/oocihm.lac_reel_c9476/1460?r=0&s=1.

28 Nakashima, "Economic Aspects of Japanese Evacuation"; Sunahara, "Seeking Civil Rights and Compensation, in *Politics of Racism*, 147–60; Bird, "Royal Commission."

29 Adachi, *Enemy That Never Was*, 261; Takata, *Nikkei Legacy*, 141; Miki, *Redress*, 87–8.

30 Sunahara, "Dispossession," in *Politics of Racism*.

31 National Association of Japanese Canadians and Price Waterhouse, *Economic Losses of Japanese Canadians*. Increases in the value of real property since 1986 in Vancouver and elsewhere in British Columbia mean that this figure is very conservative.

32 Adachi, *Enemy That Never Was*; Ward, "British Columbia and the Japanese Evacuation"; Sunahara, *Politics of Racism*; Roy, *Triumph of Citizenship*; Robinson, *Tragedy of Democracy*; Oikawa, *Cartographies of Violence*; Roy et al., *Mutual Hostages*; Granatstein and Johnson, "Evacuation of the Japanese Canadians."

33 *Legion Magazine*, "J.L. Granatstein vs. Pamela Sugiman"; Stanger-Ross, interview by Pamela McCall.

34 Stanger-Ross, Adams, and Madokoro, "Lessons from the Japanese Canadian Internments."

35 "Report to the Under Secretary of State regarding the Japanese Evacuation Section of the Office of the Custodian at Vancouver, B.C.," 26 June 1942, LAC, RG117, Vol. 2. Property loss began almost immediately after the order to uproot Japanese Canadians as a result of privation, theft, vandalism, and the handling of fishing vessels, automobiles, and other kinds of property that were deemed "perishable." On dispossession prior to Order-in-Council 469, see Oikawa, *Cartographies of Violence*, 106–7.

36 "House of Commons Debates, 1944."

37 Takeo Yoshida to Mr P. Douet, 12 February 1946, Canadiana Heritage, Office of the Custodian of Enemy Property: Vancouver Office, microfilm reel C-9476, images 1596–7, http://heritage.canadiana.ca/view/oocihm.lac_reel_c9476/1596?r=0&s=1.

38 Weinberg, "Halting the Japanese Advance"; Granatstein, *Canada's War*, 211–12, 249–50. The contrast between the political contexts of the uprooting and the dispossession of property is apparent in William Lyon Mackenzie King's diaries. See William Lyon Mackenzie King, "Diaries," February 1942, December 1942, and January 1943, LAC, http://www.bac-lac.gc.ca/eng/discover/politics-government/prime-ministers/william-lyon-mackenzie-king.

39 The journals of the Provincial Legislature in British Columbia similarly contain no direct discussion of the dispossession of Japanese Canadians in the period leading to Order-in-Council 469. In contrast, the war cabinet, King's diary, and the records of the provincial government all touch upon uprooting and internment. The federal House of Commons engaged in heated discussion of the uprooting of Japanese Canadians, particularly in the summer of 1942. When Parliament resumed in January 1943, the forced sales had already been ordered. See "House of Commons Debates,

19th Parliament, 3rd Session" and "House of Commons Debates, 19th Parliament, 4th Session."

40 This claim is based on a reading of the *Vancouver Daily Province* and the *Vancouver Sun* in the summer and fall of 1942. The papers regularly published stories related to Japanese Canadians, including news of property sales, but they followed, rather than led, the Custodian in this respect.

41 Kimura Memoir, 33.

42 See Oikawa, *Cartographies of Violence*, 168–72.

43 "British Columbia Security Commission Permit No. 00076."

44 "Agenda, June 8, 1943," *Kishizo Kimura fonds*, NNMCC MS42.

45 "Report of the Fishing Vessels Disposal Committee, December 1942," NNMCC, Kishizo Kimura fonds, MS43, File 10. On the disposal of the fishing vessels, see Fukawa and Fukawa, "Loss of Licences, Vessels and Livelihood," in *Spirit of the Nikkei Fleet*; Sunahara, "The Decision to Uproot Japanese Canadians," in *Politics of Racism*; Adachi, *Enemy That Never Was*, 228–9.

46 "Agenda, August 6, 1941," *Kishizo Kimura fonds*, NNMCC MS42.

47 Kimura Memoir, 5–7.

48 Kimura indicates that requests were sent to seven individuals: Unosuke Sakamoto, Mitsujiro Noguchi, Kuninosuke Miwa, Kohei Nakai, Matsunosuke Shinde, and Mr Hideo Fukuyama. Fukawa and Fukawa name four members: Sakamoto, Miwa, Nakai, and Shinde. Fukawa and Fukawa, *Spirit of the Nikkei Fleet*, 127.

49 Quoted in Marlatt, *Steveston Recollected*, 58.

50 Kimura Memoir, 63.

51 Adachi, *Enemy That Never Was*, 242.

52 Ibid., 235–46; Sunahara, *Politics of Racism*, 16–7; Miki, *Redress*, 44–5.

53 Mar, *Brokering Belonging*, 131. In this way, as Mar suggests, the administration of policy was similar to the production of knowledge about "Orientals" in North America, which also required the participation of Japanese and Chinese Americans (and Canadians); see Yu, *Thinking Orientals*; Mar, "Fixing Knowledge," in *Brokering Belonging*. For additional discussion of the role of Chinese migrants as "managerial elites" in the processes of exclusion, see Chang, "Brokering Empire."

54 There is little evidence that Kimura was a long-time broker between Japanese Canadians and the state. Although his business activities brought him into contact with Canadian officials before the war (including J.A. Motherwell, who, as chief supervisor of fisheries, would play a role in the seizure and liquidation of Japanese Canadian–owned fishing vessels), there is no archival record to suggest that he played a role in pre-war policy.

55 One of the many administrative challenges facing the Custodian of Enemy Property was the difficulty of finding "interpreters" to work in the Vancouver office. See "Report to the Under Secretary of State."

56 "Japanese Fishing Vessels," submitted to the Japanese Property Claims Commission,

13 February 1948, Canadiana Heritage, Office of the Custodian of Enemy Property: Vancouver Office, microfilm reel C-9434 RG117, image 458-477, http://heritage.canadiana.ca/view/oocihm.lac_reel_c9434/458?r=0&s=4.

57 Kimura Memoir, 24.

58 "Report of the Fishing Vessels Disposal Committee."

59 "Agenda, December 13, 1942," *Kishizo Kimura fonds*, NNMCC MS42.

60 Order-in-Council PC 1942-1665, LAC, RG2-A-1-a, Vol. 1750, File 2516G; Order-in-Council PC 1942-2483, LAC, RG2-A-1-a, Vol. 1752, File 2531G.

61 "Report to the Under Secretary of State"; Sunahara, "Dispossession," in *Politics of Racism*; Stanger-Ross and Landscapes of Injustice Research Collective, "Suspect Properties."

62 Order-in-Council 1943-469, LAC, RG2-A-1-a, Vol. 1789, File 2710G.

63 "Report of the Advisory Committee on Japanese Properties in Greater Vancouver," City of Vancouver Archives, AM199, Box 513-E-2, File 7.

64 "Report of the Fishing Vessels Disposal Committee"; "Report of the Advisory Committee on Japanese Properties in Greater Vancouver."

65 Kimura Memoir, 66. These instructions are also available in the official records of the committee. See "Report of the Advisory Committee on Japanese Properties in Greater Vancouver."

66 A.A. Hamilton to C. Norman Senior, 7 January 1943, LAC, MG27-IIIB5, Vol. 24, File Vancouver Centre Japanese in BC, 1942–1944; "Memorandum, General Policies," 29 March 1943, City of Vancouver Archives, AM199, Box 513-E-2, File 6.

67 Kimura Memoir, 8–9. There is no evidence in the memoir that the committee sought to lease larger vessels for which partial loss insurance might have been obtained.

68 The committee's records provide a summary of the kind and value of vessels under their authority. Of the vessels sold by the committee, 67 per cent were gill-netters, which sold for an average of $629 per vessel. An additional 6 per cent of vessels (classified as "cod-fishing boats, trawlers, and other boats") sold for an average of $810. Hence, almost 75 per cent of vessels were likely subject to this concern about "partial damage" insurance. By contrast, larger seiners, packers, and trollers sold for averages of $6,795, $3,256, and $1,588, respectively.

69 Kimura Memoir, 8.

70 Loo, "Africville and the Dynamics of State Power," 43.

71 Kimura Memoir, 61.

72 Ibid., 103.

73 Minutes of the Advisory Committee on Japanese Properties in Greater Vancouver, 7 July and 21 July 1943, City of Vancouver Archives, am199, Box 513-E-2, File 3.

74 Kimura Memoir, 6–7. This justification of the wartime policies (i.e., that they were put in place for the protection of Japanese Canadians) has more recently been a controversial dimension of the scholarship on this era. Kimura, of course, was writing before that scholarship emerged.

75 Kimura Memoir, 9–10.

76 On the importance of terminology in the telling of this history, see National JACL Power of Words II Committee, "Power of Words Handbook"; Oikawa, "The Forgetting Subjects and the Subjects Forgotten," in *Cartographies of Violence*; Daniels, "Words Do Matter"; Miki, "In Defense of Rights," in *Redress*.

77 Ian Mackenzie to Norman McLarty, 23 December 1942, LAC, MG27-IIIB5, Vol. 25, File 70-25c: Liquidating Lands in the Fraser Valley That Are Jap Owned.

78 Kimura Memoir, 69.

79 Memorandum by Ephraim Coleman, "Real Estate Owned by Persons of the Japanese Race Evacuated from the Defence Area of British Columbia," December 1942, Ian Mackenzie fonds, LAC, Vol. 25, File 70-25c.

80 Stanger-Ross and Landscapes of Injustice Research Collective, "Suspect Properties." In reality, evidence that was readily available to officials demonstrates that the vast majority of properties were not accumulating debt. Only a small proportion of them were in the East End neighbourhood on which official justifications rested. Even in that area, the cash ledgers of the Custodian showed healthy earnings on Japanese-Canadian–owned properties, with rental incomes far exceeding costs. The Pemberton Company, whose manager offered dismal tours of the neighbourhood for government officials, earned commissions for its supervision of more than a dozen properties on Powell Street alone. When it came time to sell, Pemberton and its competitors clamoured for the opportunity to represent the properties on the market. Although the reimagining of real estate as perishable proved powerful, it was a fiction.

81 Kimura Memoir, 98, 67.

82 Ibid., 67.

83 Ibid., 70.

84 Ibid., 87, 53.

85 Ibid., 87–92.

86 Ibid., 97.

87 Ibid.

88 Ibid., 57.

89 *Nisei* refers to second-generation Japanese Canadians; *Sansei* refers to third-generation Japanese Canadians.

90 Kimura Memoir, 57.

91 Ibid., 57.

92 Ibid., 54.

93 Ibid., 58, 100.

94 Kelley, "'We Are Not What We Seem,'" 76; Wright, *Twelve Million Black Voices*. On Wright, I am also indebted to Allred, "From Eye to We."

95 Mar, *Brokering Belonging*, 11, 108; Yu, *Thinking Orientals*.

96 Yamaga, *History of Haney Nokai*, 67. In 1958, Yamaga also wrote a Japanese-language manuscript devoted to the "Forced Disposition of Japanese Property Due to Wartime

Decree." (Yasutaro Yamaga fonds, UBC Special Collections.) The translation of that manuscript is not within the scope of this chapter but will be part of the larger project of which this is a part. Yamaga, like Kimura, should be incorporated into a fuller history of this period and policy.

97 "Fifth Meeting of the Advisory Committee on Rural Properties," Minutes, 1 June 1943, *Canadiana Heritage*, Office of the Custodian of Enemy Property: Vancouver Office, microfilm reel C-9469 RG 117, image 1900, http://heritage.canadiana.ca/view/oocihm.lac_reel_c9469/1900?r=0&s=1.

98 See Stanger-Ross and Blomley, "My Land Is Worth a Million Dollars"; Adams and Stanger-Ross, "Promises of Law."

99 Kimura Memoir, 77.

100 "Minutes," a meeting of the Advisory Committee on Japanese Properties in Greater Vancouver, 12 May 1943, *Canadiana Heritage*, Office of the Custodian of Enemy Property: Vancouver Office, microfilm reel C-9475 RG117, image 52, http://heritage.canadiana.ca/view/oocihm.lac_reel_c9475/52?r=0&s=1.

101 Kimura Memoir, 81.

102 "Minutes," a meeting of the Advisory Committee on Japanese Properties in Greater Vancouver, 21 July 1943, Canadiana Heritage, Office of the Custodian of Enemy Property: Vancouver Office, microfilm reel C-9475, image 72, http://heritage.canadiana.ca/view/oocihm.lac_reel_c9475/72?r=0&s=1.

103 Stanley, *Contesting White Supremacy*, 14, 30–1 (emphasis in original).

104 Ronen, Agmon, and Danziger, "Collaborator or Would-Be Rescuer?," 147. Examining the "last great trial" of this kind, Ronen et al. herald the emergence of a historical perspective that "is neither accusatory nor apologetic and, instead, is mindful of the paradoxical complexity that envelopes these institutions and individuals." Ibid., 167; see Nicosia, *Zionism and Anti-Semitism*; Kaplan, *Between Dignity and Despair*.

105 Kimura Memoir, 57–8. My thanks to Daniel Lachapelle Lemire for this analysis of diction in the memoir and to Midge Ayukawa for helping to refine my understanding of these terms.

106 Oikawa, *Cartographies of Violence*, 57.

107 Kimura Memoir, 57.

108 Ibid., 33.

109 Ibid., 50–2.

110 Ibid., 57.

111 Kimura and Kimura, interview.

112 *Kishizo Kimura fonds*.

113 Morita, *Powell Street Monogatari*, 56.

# Translator's Note

*Matsuki Masutani*

I came to Vancouver in early 1976, several months before Kishizo Kimura passed away at the age of seventy-seven. A friend who came to Vancouver a few years before me remembers him walking around Powell Street looking like a scholar. One day he was even invited to Mr Kimura's house and had a look at his historical manuscript. (The date on the handwritten manuscript is '70/7/15, but it seems he revised it until the end of his life.)

Kishizo Kimura was born in 1899, only three years earlier than my father, who was also a scholar. He came to Canada at the age of eleven and finished his junior high school education in Canada. He studied Japanese reading and writing whenever he had spare time. Curiously, his Japanese vocabulary has no trace of the English language he was surrounded by. He must have used English all the time in his daily dealings with businessmen and officials. On the other hand, my father hardly left Japan, but his writings were clearly influenced by the English language, this being the new orthodoxy in post-war Japan.

When I looked at Mr Kimura's handwritten manuscript for the first time, I thought I was dealing with pre-war writing. It was full of Kanji (Chinese characters) and expressions derived from the classics. It looked as if he was determined to prove that traditional Japanese could sufficiently express new ideas in English culture without borrowing any vocabulary from it. Meanwhile, in my father's writing, English vocabulary appeared often, expressed in the phonetic Japanese alphabet, Katakana. He also uses fewer Kanji than Mr Kimura does, which makes his writing look smooth and modern. In spite of these stylistic differences, some personal qualities shone through that were very similar. Both of them believed in justice, fairness, and the concept of doing one's duty in service to something greater than oneself.

The translation was done by me, a Japanese native, and my partner, Jane Masutani, an English native. I translated the text into English, and Jane made the English read more fluidly. I then compared this English text to the original and fixed it wherever I found deviation from the original intent. Jane went over this text one more time for proofreading. I tried my best to be faithful to the original, and Jane endeavoured to make it read smoothly.

There was an issue of how to translate an idiomatic Japanese expression such as "I do this work as if it is my own funeral," which has no equal in English. This was the remark Yasutaro Yamaga, Mr Kimura's colleague who assisted (for a short time) in the disposition of rural property, used to describe his participation in that work. There is also an echo, with this phrase, of the death of the Japanese community that was taking place at the time. Jane insisted that talk of a funeral was too awkward and had to be translated as "This shall be my legacy" or "This work shall be my own funeral" because the phrase was not idiomatic in English.

With suggestions from Jordan Stanger-Ross and Eiji Okawa, we decided to adopt the transliteration term *Nikkei* instead of *Japanese Canadian* for the translation of *Nikkei* 日系. *Nikkei* means simply Japanese lineage and does not explicitly mean Canadian, possibly a closer rendering of the original term. When we translated *Nikkei* as *Japanese Canadian* following convention, the term *Canadian* appeared far too often compared to the original, distorting the overall impression. This tendency was further magnified by the difference in grammatical convention between English and Japanese. In Japanese, subjects, in the grammatical sense, can be implied, rather than explicitly included in sentences. Therefore, when we translate the Japanese text into English, we have to resurrect these implied subjects. In this text, they were very often *Japanese Canadians*, further increasing the frequency of *Canadian*.

Mr Kimura constantly used the word *Nikkei*, except in the chapter "Recollections," but the irony was that the official names of committees he served in were the "*Japanese* Fishing Vessels Disposal Committee" and the "Advisory Committee on *Japanese* Properties." Also, the department created for the removal of all Nikkei people was named the "Department of *Japanese* Placement," not *Nikkei*. Mr Kimura, probably to keep consistency in the writing, uses *Nikkei* instead of *Japanese*, discreetly obscuring the official names. Other Nikkei people, who demanded that he resign from the "Committee on *Japanese* Properties," used the term *Japanese*, not *Nikkei*, in their letter and resolution.

Canadian newspaper articles and other publications quoted in the writing constantly called *Nikkei* people *Japanese*, but in his memoir, Kimura translated these statements as *Nikkei*. In these cases, we have preserved the terminology used in Kimura's memoir (e.g., Nikkei) rather than those of the original sources that he was translating. This results in some awkward renderings of historical materials; resolutions of Vancouver City Council and a speech by Prime Minister William Lyon Mackenzie King, for example, here appear to use *Nikkei* rather than "Japanese." This awkwardness is a result of our effort to faithfully convey the memoir rather than the sources upon which Kimura drew. His persistent use of *Nikkei* throughout the memoir is one of the noticeable undertones.

Another point for us was how to translate the term 白人 *Hakujin*. We first translated it literally as *white people* and then considered using *Caucasian*. In the end, we decided to use *Hakujin*, another transliteration, in the same spirit of choosing the term *Nikkei* over *Japanese Canadian*. We did the same thing with the terms *Toyojin* and *Dojin*, which are usually translated as *Oriental* and *Native*, respectively. Rather than imposing our own racializing terms or guessing at how Kimura might have named these origins in English, we transliterated the words he used, leaving further interpretation of racial terminology in the memoir to our readers.

*Nikkei-Jin* 日系人 literally means Japanese lineage people. They are *Japanese Canadian* in Canada but *Japanese American* in the US, *Japanese Brazilian* in Brazil, and so on. Whenever I encountered the word *Nikkei-jin*, I interpreted it as an abbreviation of *Nikkei-Kanada-jin* 日系カナダ人. When *Nikkei-Kanada-jin* appeared in its full form, I translated it to *Nikkei Canadian* and *Nikkei-jin* into *Nikkei people*.

The term *Nikkei Canadian* appeared once in the beginning, and Mr Kimura never used it again until toward the end when he was evaluating the historical struggle Nikkei people went through: "meaningful points because these could *make the Canadian general public recognize that Nikkei Canadians carried out their responsibilities as Canadian citizens* in spite of extremely difficult circumstances."

It was an honour to translate Mr Kimura's life's work.

20 November 2015

# Editor's Note

*Jordan Stanger-Ross*

Kishizo Kimura's memoir is presented below in edited form. Where indicated with ellipses, material has been removed (some 3,500 words in total) from the full translated text to improve narrative flow and accessibility. The full memoir, in Japanese and in translation, is available on a website hosted by the Nikkei National Museum (http://witnesstoloss.ca) as a companion to this book.

To the numbered "Parts" below, we have inserted a summary introduction, images with captions, and footnotes as editorial interventions to facilitate comprehension and analysis. These insertions are not included in the digital versions on the Nikkei National Museum website. All other subtitles and in-text notes are original to the manuscript. Where appropriate, the year has been added to the running heads to clarify the timing of events chronicled by Kimura.

The appendix lists key individuals and legal enactments mentioned in the memoir and is available online.

# *Memoir*

Kishizo Kimura

*Translated by Matsuki Masutani and Jane Masutani*

Figure M.1 Kimura (aged fifty-one) outside his home at the south end of Christina Lake where the family settled along with a small number of other Japanese Canadians after the war. From the private collection of Edmund T. Kimura, 1950.

# Part One

# The Fishing Vessels Disposal Committee

As one of its first acts after Canada entered into the Pacific Theatre of the Second World War in December of 1941, the Canadian Navy impounded Japanese Canadian–owned fishing vessels in coastal British Columbia. In early January, the federal cabinet promulgated Order-in-Council PC 288, creating the Fishing Vessels Disposal Committee, chaired by Justice Sidney Smith. As he recounts in the pages that follow, Kishizo Kimura agreed to serve on this committee along with Naval Commander B.L. Johnson. The two would take the most active roles on the committee, overseeing the disposition of 1,337 vessels. In this part of the memoir, Kimura explains his role on that committee and details its work.

Figure M.2 Impounded Japanese Canadian–owned fishing vessels at Annieville Dyke, BC, 1942. Nikkei National Museum (NNM), 2010-4-2-1-001.

Figure M.3 Nikkei-owned vessels varied in size, kind, and value, complicating the work of the Fishing Vessel Disposal Committee. Nikkei National Museum (NNM), 2010-31-58.

# A Memorandum on the Events Surrounding the Liquidation of Fishing Boats Owned by Nikkei People

This document includes matters prohibited for release at the time by the Wartime Secrecy Act. The main section concerns matters reported exclusively to the minister of fisheries, Hon. J.E. Michaud, the officer responsible by an order-in-council. I shall record the events chronologically based on the memos of those days.

## Establishment of the Committee for the Liquidation of Fishing Boats

*8 January 1942:*

One month after the outbreak of the Pacific War, Major J.A. Motherwell, chief supervisor of fisheries, contacted me. He urgently wanted to have a private consultation with me at the Ministry of Fisheries. He told me that the provincial government wanted to increase the food supply. They planned to promptly release impounded Nikkei fishing boats into the hands of Hakujin and Dojin fishermen so that they could go out fishing. An order-in-council was being drafted for this purpose. To facilitate the sale or rental of these boats, they were creating a special committee. A judge would be appointed as chairman, with a representative from the Ministry of Defence as another member. Mr Motherwell was to recommend myself as a representative from the Nikkei community and urged me to accept.

The recommended sale prices for seiners and packers were clearly stated in the yearly survey report for the purpose of disaster and fire insurance. Their rental price could be easily ascertained by checking past charter contracts. However, regarding the smaller boats such as gill-netters, trollers, trawlers, and cod-fishing boats, no one placed insurance on them because insurance was limited to the total loss. Therefore, there was no price recommended in the survey report and hardly any examples of their chartering fees, making it

Figure M.4 Kimura (front, second from right) pictured with community leaders, including Asahi star Frank Nakamura (front, centre) and Japanese Language School Principal Tsutae Sato (front, fourth from right). Japanese Canadian Cultural Centre (JCCC), 2001-4-029, 1930s.

very difficult to determine a price. So it was difficult for me to carry out my duties as a committee member.

I stated that there was a Nikkei fishermen's organization, that Mr Ritsu Ide had been its director for many years, and that he would be the right person for the job. The following day, on the ninth, I called Mr Ide, and he said he had already spoken to Mr Motherwell that morning and that he had recommended me to him. He encouraged me to accept the position, and I made it a condition that the Nikkei fishermen's organization would support me. I promised that I would make up my mind after one day of deliberation.

I reported back to Mr Motherwell, and he told me that the draft of the order-in-council had already been completed because of the urgency of the situation, and it would take effect on the twelfth. The committee chairman and member from the Ministry of Defence had already been chosen.

Before this happened, Nikkei volunteers from Vancouver and the surrounding area had met regularly in Vancouver to discuss their wartime safety. Recalling the anti-Nikkei riots of 1907, which had occurred during peacetime, they were afraid of the current mood of the population in this time of war.

There was anxiety, fear, and even hatred being directed toward them. If an incident occurred, it would be very difficult to protect women, children, and the elderly. The group had been discussing their temporary evacuation to a safe place before the threat became urgent. On the eleventh of January, I visited their meeting place and summarized, to the people in the fishing industry, the conversation I had had with Mr Motherwell. They promised to back me up whenever necessary.

Early on the morning of the twelfth, there was a call from Mr Motherwell. He persuaded me to accept the committee position, saying that both the chairman and the member from the Ministry of Defence were familiar to me.

## The Appointment of Liquidation Committee Members

*13 January:*

Order-in-Council PC 288 was announced, stating that the chairman of the committee would be Hon. Justice Sidney S. Smith, a justice at the BC Supreme Court and a full-time judge at the Marine Affairs Court. The representative from the Ministry of Defence was Commander Barney L. Johnson of the reserved forces. He volunteered to active duty and was an associate partner of Johnson Walton Steamship Ltd. Mr Kishizo Kimura was also appointed to represent Nikkei people.*

*15 January:*

There was a phone call from Justice Smith asking me to visit him in his private room at the courthouse. The content of our conversation was as follows:

1. Once the management of the committee was on track, he wanted Mr Johnson and me to run the committee. Should any disagreement occur, he would join the discussion.

2. He also said that we needed to hire someone to handle the business end of things, and he wanted me to recommend someone.

I accepted the first proposal, but regarding the second I responded that the recommendation should come from Justice Smith and then Mr Johnson will probably accept it.

* Here, and elsewhere in the manuscript, Kishizo Kimura refers to himself in the third person. He often does this when copying committee minutes into his memoir, which he had preserved among his personal papers.

*18 January:*

Mr Johnson returned to Vancouver from Halifax, and on the nineteenth, the three of us gathered at the private courthouse room of Justice Smith for an unofficial meeting. We discussed the hiring of a deputy director. The judge recommended Mr A.E. McMaster, the former manager of the Powell River Pulp & Paper Company, as a very able and competent person with a great personality. He also held Mr Ginjiro Fujiwara, at Oji Paper Manufacturing Company, in high esteem. Mr Johnson and I agreed and asked him to proceed with the hiring. We decided to have an official meeting the next day including Mr McMaster and then discussed other necessary matters.

## The Start-up of the Committee

*24 January:*

In Justice Smith's private courthouse quarters, the three of us, plus Mr McMaster, held the first official committee meeting.

1. We decided to name the committee "The Japanese Fishing Vessels Disposal Committee."

2. We approved the appointment of Mr McMaster as deputy director and left it to him to open the office, hire office workers, and do other necessary things, as well as writing a draft of the proposal.

3. We established the offices in rooms 1528, 1529, and 1530 of the Marine Building.

4. Large fishing vessels (registered in the British Shipping Registry) could be easily chartered, but chartering the simply licensed small vessels would be another matter. Protecting the owners, the vessels had to be insured for total loss. (The insurance company did not issue partial insurance.) Also, to prepare for the event of partial damage, a deposit equivalent to the repair work would be required. (In order to make absolutely sure, an amount equal to the value of the vessel had to be deposited.) Also, Nikkei fishermen would be anxious about the maintenance standards of Hakujin and Dojin fishermen, and cases of dispute about the extent of deterioration of vessels would be confusing to settle. Considering these points, the committee decided in the end that small fishing vessels should be sold at market value.

(Note: If we adopt an instalment payment method, in the case of a total loss, the mortgage and insurance will kick in, and the insurance company will cover the remaining portion for the former owner. In the case of a partial loss, the insurance company will not cover it. The new owner must pay for the cost of rescue and repair. If these costs are too high, the new owner, who is unable to pay, will abandon the boat, and the former owner will possibly end up with an abandoned and damaged boat.)

5. To raise office operating costs, although the amount needed was unknown, we decided to charge 1 per cent of the sale price or charter fee and pay the rest to the owner immediately.

(Note: This was enacted into law by Order-in-Council PC 987, issued on 14 February. The BC Security Commission* felt uneasy handing over such a huge amount of money to the fishermen, proposing instead to put the money temporarily into the hands of the Custodian, with gradual payouts to fishermen. However, it was decided eventually to pay the fishermen as the order-in-council indicated.)

6. To prepare for eventual damage to the fishing boats, we would create a damage investigation organization. This to be comprised of insurance surveyors, Navy surveyors, and licensed civilians, who would be charged with making an appraisal report. They would examine the time of damage, its extent, and make a repair estimate.

7. We decided to create a detailed catalogue of all the fishing boats.

8. We created a Nikkei Liaison Committee to mediate between the owners and people wishing to purchase the boats. (Note: The work of this committee and the disposal committee was all on a volunteer basis.)

9. We entrusted Mr Kimura and Nikkei liaison officers with the job of making a catalogue of fishing boats (mentioned in item 7).

10. To avoid mistakes and misunderstandings with media outlets, the announcement would be exclusively communicated through the deputy director.

11. The committee would submit a weekly report to the minister of fisheries and an overall report when it completed its work.

After all these decisions had been made, Mr Kimura requested the following points, with all members accepting them.

Because newspaper reports (*Sun*, *Province*, *News Herald*, etc.) on this matter were so brief and unclear, people had the impression that enemy Japanese

* The British Columbia Security Commission was established by Order-in-Council PC 1665 on 4 March 1942. Its main function was to administer the forced uprooting and internment of thousands of Canadians of Japanese descent from coastal British Columbia. Order-in-Council PC 1942-1665, LAC, RG2-A-1-a, Vol. 1750, File 2516G.

fishing boats had been seized and liquidated as the spoils of war. Therefore, it was necessary to clarify the following points through the deputy director to the people hired by the committee.

1. Boat owners are Nikkei Canadians or Canadian companies established, approved, and registered according to the Canadian Company Act. Also, some of the boats belong to Nikkei veterans who had volunteered in the Canadian armed forces at the time of the First World War.

2. Presently, the fishing boats are impounded in an enclosed area under the control of the Ministry of the Navy. However, each owner voluntarily and lawfully entrusted their boats to the government, which ordered the impoundment of the boats by an order-in-council. Almost all the boats impounded near New Westminster were navigated there by the boat-owners from various remote places such as Skeena River, both the east and west coasts of Vancouver Island, the Fraser River, and the Port of Vancouver, following the order or request of the Ministry of the Navy.

3. This has nothing to do with this committee directly, but the boats under the control of Mr W.G. McPherson, authorized deputy of the secretary of state and/or Custodian, have not necessarily all been seized.* With the exception of boats belonging to owners who violated the law and were interned,† the remainder of the boats belonged, as I mentioned in item 1, to Nikkei companies whose stakeholders or owners happened to be in Japan when war broke out and were unable to return to Canada.

## Requesting the Appointment of Nikkei Liaison Committee Members

*26 January:*

The committee decided the following items:

1. To request the following persons to be Nikkei Liaison Committee members.‡

* Here, Kimura reverses McPherson's first two initials (Glenn Willoughby). This is a mistake repeated in the memoir.

† Here, Kimura uses the word *yokuryu*, which could be translated as "arrested" or "incarcerated," but he has added in brackets the English word "interned," which was the official term at the time to refer to Japanese Canadians who were incarcerated in prisoner-of-war camps under the Defence of Canada Regulations. This group comprised a small fraction of the total population that was uprooted and forced to relocate to sites of internment.

‡ Starting in the early 1920s, Japanese Canadians formed local *Kyogikai*, or fishers' associations, to represent their interests within geographic districts. Shortly thereafter, the local associations

- Representing the first area of Fraser River: Mr Unosuke Sakamoto and Mr Mitsujiro Noguchi
- Representing the second region, the Northern Fishing Area: Mr Kunisaburo Miwa
- Representing the third area, the west coast of Vancouver Island Fishing Area: Mr Kọhei Nakai and Mr Hideo Fukuyama
- Representing the Cod Fishing Union: Mr Matsunosuke Shinde and as a deputy representative Mr Hideo Fukuyama

2. When Liaison Committee members handle sales on behalf of the owners, a letter of attorney from the owner is required.
3. The letter of attorney mentioned in item 2 shall be created by Mr Roy Ginn, KC, and the cost shall be covered by the committee.
4. In the impoundment area (Annieville Dyke Slough), a guide and a Navy barge has to be employed for the inspection of the boats. To avoid congestion, there is a need to limit the issue of inspection permits to those who have already reached some agreement with liaison personnel. However, for the inspection of canneries, a special arrangement shall be considered.
5. Chief clerk, Mr Alexander J. Martin, shall exclusively issue permits for boat inspections. Those without a permit are not allowed to go into the impoundment area.
6. Vancouver Harbour officials are campaigning to convert two large fishing boats into supplemental fire boats. However, because this is not in line with the purpose of the order-in-council, it is not possible to agree to this.

## Inspection of the Impoundment Area

Hearing a rumour that many fishing boats were damaged and sunk in the impounded area, three committee members went to investigate. We got onto the Navy barge from New Westminster harbour and entered the impounded area. As we embarked on the inspection, the accompanying Navy officer told

formed the BC-*Shu Nikkei Gyosha Kyogikai*, which was generally referred to as the "Liaison Council." The council advised on matters of general and specific concern to Japanese-Canadian fishers and provided market analysis to fishers to assist in negotiations with canners. After the seizure of Japanese Canadian–owned fishing vessels, some prominent members of the council, such as Unosuke Sakamoto, took up a new role of brokering interactions between the federal government and dispossessed fishers. Fukawa and Fukawa, *Spirit of the Nikkei Fleet*, 95–7.

***

## Jap Fishermen Out—Perhaps For Good

**Many Problems to Be Solved; Mortgages; Unpaid Engines; Three-Man Committee**

By DON MASON

News from Ottawa Tuesday and today spells finish for Jap fishermen on this British Columbia coast for the duration . . . and perhaps for all time.

Yesterday Ottawa said that no fishing licenses could be issued to Japanese. Today's news said that the Jap fishing fleet, now tied up, will be operated by whites and Indians.

But, until Tuesday, the Japanese were still hopeful. They refused to talk about selling, chartering or leasing their boats to white fishermen. They still thought that Ottawa might relent, might re-issue fishing licenses to Japanese who could prove their citizenship and loyalty.

More than one white fisherman has tried to negotiate with a Jap for a boat, but the Japanese would have none of it.

Now that Ottawa has made up its mind, the Jap boats will be taken over by whites, but there are many problems to be ironed out first.

Some of the Jap fishboats . . . a good percentage of them, in fact . . . . are wholly or partly owned by cannery companies. Some are mortgaged to banks, some have new engines that are not paid for.

All these claims must be settled before the boats can be sold, or even chartered.

Commander B. L. "Barney" Johnson, named a member of the three-man committee to supervise the distribution of the Jap fishboats, will arrive in Vancouver from the east on Monday.

In Ottawa, in his capacity as a naval intelligence officer, he sat in with the Standing Committee on Orientals during their conferences with government officials.

Vancouver fishermen are pleased but cautious about Ottawa's decisions regarding the Japanese fishermen and their boats. But they want to know:

1. Will individual fishermen be given priority over fishing companies when the boats are placed on sale?

2. Is the Ottawa order compulsory, or can a Japanese decide that his fishing boat shall remain idle for the duration?

The inference drawn here is that the Japs must sell their boats if a buyer is available.

K. Kimura, Japanese member of the Ottawa-appointed committee, is well known in British Columbia. Since 1920, he has been general manager of the Canadian Salt Herring Exporters.

Mr. Kimura has not been officially informed of his appointment.

His only hope is that Ottawa will give the committee a definate plan of procedure.

* * *

Figure M.5 *Left* Kimura worried that newspaper depictions of the seizure of fishing vessels failed to convey Nikkei cooperation with authorities. This article linked Kimura to the seizures, and the journalist appears to have interviewed him. *Vancouver Sun*, 14 January 1942.

Figure M.6 *Above* Japanese Canadian–owned vessels were badly mishandled in custodial care. Vancouver Public Library (VPL), 1352.

us that they were not sure about the number of damaged boats because they were still investigating. They speculated that the Fraser River had frozen and pieces of drifting ice had damaged the boats and, in time, sunk them. We went around the impounded area on a barge but could not see very well because the water was very murky. Even when we tried to see the sunken boats from directly above them, all we could see was a dim exterior shape, and we could not identify the boats. Damage was not confined to the boats impounded outside; the boats in the centre were also damaged. Some of the masts were barely above water. This impoundment area was shallow, with mud shoals, and there was a rumour that the boats leaned on their sides and ran aground at low tide and were swamped at high tide. The committee requested the Navy to investigate promptly and take appropriate action.

*28 January:*

A committee office was set up.

*3 February:*

1. "About 900 of the impounded boats are small fishing vessels. After an initial rush of sales, the committee will be stocked with hundreds of unsold boats, which they will be unable to dispose of."
2. "Nikkei fishermen are purposely pricing their boats too high," stated by a Hakujin fisherman.
3. "Nikkei fishermen are removing all the important equipment from their boats and storing it in warehouses. Fishing boats without nets are useless." Such talk shows a complete lack of knowledge of fishing.
4. "Among Nikkei fishermen, some believe that if they hold on to their boats, eventually they can get a fishing licence and go fishing again." A newspaper article gave rise to this rumour.

It seems that these three rumours had their start either with those who attempted to lower boat prices or those who believed the lies and propaganda of anti-Nikkei fanatics.

The fourth rumour was due to a newspaper article reporting on Mr Reid, the representative from New Westminster. He declared in the Legislature that right after the Nikkei boats were impounded by the order-in-council, some fishery companies started a campaign to re-release boats to Nikkei fishermen. He was then forced to name these companies. He explicitly named a Canadian fishing company and BC Packers. Both companies refuted Mr Reid's claims in the newspaper.

The committee keenly recognized the need to wipe out these misunderstandings whenever and however possible.

## Making a Catalogue of Fishing Boats

*4 February:*

The Liaison Committee, Fisherman's Association, Fisherman's Union, and the boat-owners together collected information to make a catalogue of the 1,037 Nikkei fishing boats. Then, office clerks at the Canadian Salt-Cod Export Company typed up forms with the necessary memos attached. The catalogue was completed much faster than expected and submitted to the committee.
[ … ]
(Note: Among the 1,037 boats, those belonging to interned* owners or absent owners stuck in Japan were not included. The committee has nothing to do with those boats.)
[ … ]

The Ministry of the Navy had also created a simple catalogue of fishing boats, so we compared it with our committee's catalogue. It seemed to be randomly put together by an assortment of people. There were many mistakes, especially relating to boats from Prince Rupert. There were mistakes with boat names and columns left blank, such as the registry number or the naval control number. Also, the forms were not unified, and typists were obviously not experienced. In some cases, the numbers weren't in order, and the owners' names were misspelled.

The majority of the fishing boats impounded in New Westminster were originally tied up randomly as the Nikkei owners brought them in. Under such circumstances it was difficult to find a desired boat. Mr McMaster pointed this out to the Navy. The Navy promised to rearrange the rows of boats according to their usage when they refloated the sunken boats.

*5 February:*

The Navy had started to lift the sunken boats and arrange them according to their use. They said they planned to complete the job in a week. Later, we had

* Kimura has transliterated the English word "interned" into Japanese characters.

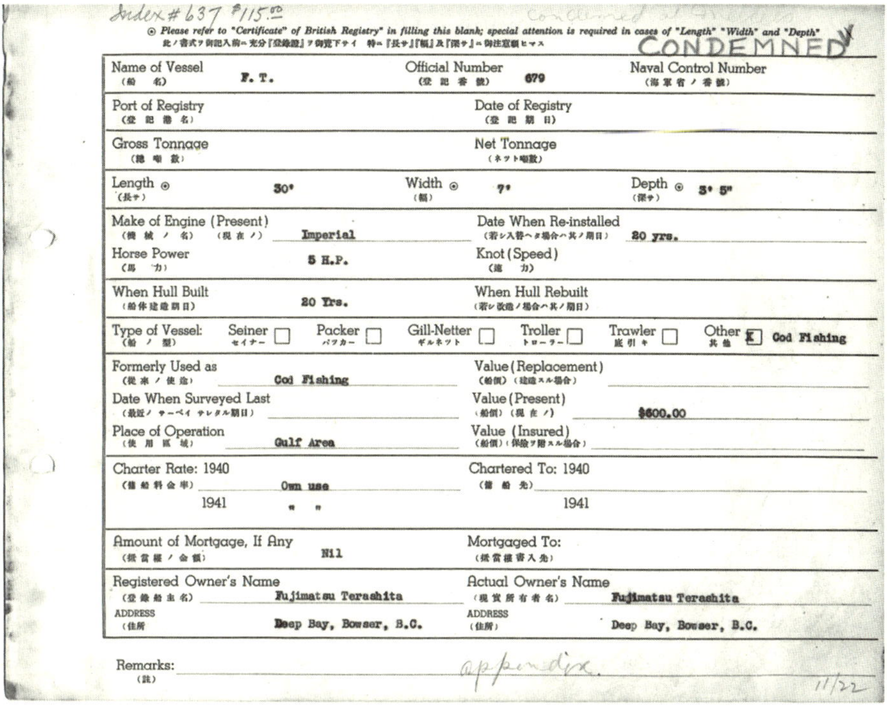
Index #637 $115.00 CONDEMNED

⊙ Please refer to "Certificate" of British Registry" in filling this blank; special attention is required in cases of "Length" "Width" and "Depth"

Name of Vessel: F. T.
Official Number: 679
Naval Control Number:
Port of Registry:
Date of Registry:
Gross Tonnage:
Net Tonnage:
Length ⊙: 30'
Width ⊙: 7'
Depth ⊙: 3' 5"
Make of Engine (Present): Imperial
Date When Re-installed: 20 yrs.
Horse Power: 5 H.P.
Knot (Speed):
When Hull Built: 20 Yrs.
When Hull Rebuilt:
Type of Vessel: Seiner ☐ Packer ☐ Gill-Netter ☐ Troller ☐ Trawler ☐ Other ☒ Cod Fishing
Formerly Used as: Cod Fishing
Value (Replacement):
Date When Surveyed Last:
Value (Present): $600.00
Place of Operation: Gulf Area
Value (Insured):
Charter Rate: 1940 Own use; 1941 " "
Chartered To: 1940; 1941
Amount of Mortgage, If Any: Nil
Mortgaged To:
Registered Owner's Name: Fujimatsu Terashita
ADDRESS: Deep Bay, Bowser, B.C.
Actual Owner's Name: Fujimatsu Terashita
ADDRESS: Deep Bay, Bowser, B.C.
Remarks: appendix 11/22

Figure M.7 For decades after the war, Kimura preserved a ledger recording the Fishing Vessel Disposal Committee's decisions. Nikkei National Museum (NNM), 2010-4-4-1-4.

a report that six sunken boats were rescued from the water and sent to the Celtic Shipyard.

[ … ]

*11 February:*

There was the following report from the Navy:

The total number of sunken boats in the impounded area was 162. Some of them had already been sent to a shipyard, and the rest of them would be sent gradually to the following shipyards: Celtic; Vancouver; Stanley Park; Wright's; Mercer's; Chapel Bros; and others. The cost of repairs would be covered by the government.

(Note: By Order-in-Council PC 3737, issued on 5 May, and Order-in-Council PC 6787, issued on 31 July, $80,000 was estimated for this expense, and it was decided that it would be covered by war expenditure.)

## The Appointment of Surveyors

*12 February:*

Articles began appearing in newspapers stating that some fishermen considered the prices suggested by fishing boat–owners to be too high. There were inquiries from the Fisheries Institute of BC about which course of action to take when a price could not be agreed upon. At the same time, there was the need to supervise the repair of the damaged boats, to estimate fair repair prices, and to estimate boat values. In order to mediate between boat-owners and purchase applicants, the committee decided to hire two official boat appraisers and requested one civilian with knowledge of fishing boats.

[ … ]

*16 February:*

The deputy minister of fisheries, Dr D.B. Finn, came to Vancouver and met with Mr Johnson and Mr Kimura, the committee members. We explained the decisions we had made and clarified the reasons behind them. Also, we pointed out that once rearrangement of the impoundment area was completed, the sale of fishing boats would be more active.

On the same day, in the conference room of the Canadian Manufacturing Association, we met with several representatives from the Fisheries Institute of BC, the deputy minister of fisheries, Dr Finn, Mr Motherwell, and all the committee members, including the deputy director, and explained matters similar to how we had explained them to Dr Finn. There were fishing boats belonging to canneries, but they had been impounded because they were operated by Nikkei fishermen. The canneries wanted to ready these boats for fishing as soon as possible and asked the committee for help. We promised to negotiate on their behalf with the Navy and to take measures to release them from impoundment once the companies came up with legal papers to prove ownership. Everyone was satisfied, and the meeting was dismissed.

[ … ]

*21 February:*

The Custodian of Enemy Property placed an advertisement of tender in the newspaper to open bids on fishing boats, with bidding to close on 9 March. We have asked the Custodian to cooperate with us on the liquidation of fish-

ing boats, even though they are enemy property. They attached a condition on tender, limiting it to bona-fide fishermen or fishing companies.
(Note: Among the forty boats advertised, those belonging to the Nanaimo boat manufacturer Matsuyama Shokai were the largest in number. Besides the boats owned by absent owners, such as Mr Masataro Mukai, Mr Kototaro Oota, Mr Numasaburo Yoshiaki, Mr Kazuichi Shirai, and Mr Genichi Kodama, there were six boats that seemed to belong to interned people.*)
[ … ]

## The Announcement of the Removal of All Nikkei People

The BC Security Commission announced that by Order-in-Council PC 1665 promulgated yesterday, on the fourth of the month, all people holding Japanese nationality would be removed as soon as possible from coastal areas designated as defence regions.
[ … ]

It happened that not only naturalized Nikkei people but *Nisei* who were born in Canada also were forced to move as soon as preparations were completed. Through the RCMP, I made an arrangement to postpone the removal of Liaison Committee members until the liquidation of fishing boats was almost complete.

For the four days between 2 March (Monday) and today, the committee issued 122 survey permits, and 258 people have been surveyed.

### *10 March:*

The Custodian published a notification for Nikkei people, as a protective measure, to report all property to them except that which they could carry with them when they were relocated (except fishing boats, savings, stocks, bonds, and security certificates). Because of this, I assumed that the time for removal of all Nikkei people would be imminent, so:

1. I requested Liaison Committee members to obtain letters of attorney from as many boat-owners as possible so they could act on their behalf.
2. Young men tended to be moved first, leaving family members behind. There was a case where a negotiation had concluded after the owner's removal. I

* Kimura uses both Japanese and English terms. He transliterates "internee" to Japanese characters and writes *yokuryusha*, which could also be translated as "incarcerated person."

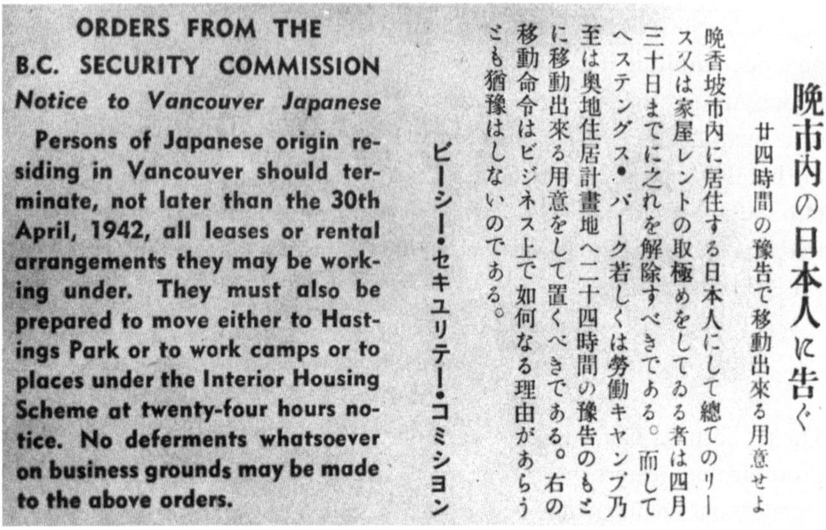

**ORDERS FROM THE B.C. SECURITY COMMISSION**

***Notice to Vancouver Japanese***

**Persons of Japanese origin residing in Vancouver should terminate, not later than the 30th April, 1942, all leases or rental arrangements they may be working under. They must also be prepared to move either to Hastings Park or to work camps or to places under the Interior Housing Scheme at twenty-four hours notice. No deferments whatsoever on business grounds may be made to the above orders.**

**晩市内の日本人に告ぐ**

廿四時間の豫告で移動出來る用意せよ

晩香坡市內に居住する日本人にして總てのリース又は家屋レントの取極めをしてゐる者は四月三十日までに之れを解除すべきである。而してヘステングス•パーク若しくは勞働キャンプ乃至は奥地住居計畫地へ二十四時間の豫告のもとに移動出來る用意をして置くべきである。右の移動命令はビジネス上で如何なる理由があらうとも猶豫はしないのである。

ビーシー•セキユリテー•コミシヨン

Figure M.8 The hardship of the uprooting process was intensified by its unpredictability. Japanese Canadians were ordered to prepare to leave in less than twenty-four hours from unspecified dates of notice. Japanese Canadian Cultural Centre (JCCC), 2001-3-60.

requested Liaison Committee members from now on to advise owners to appoint someone to whom payment would be made, for example, a wife, father, or mother. Also, owners should submit request letters for payment, following a certain format.

## Committee Decision regarding Difficult Contracts

A Canadian fishing company was negotiating with a Nikkei salt-cod company about the sale of five seiners, but they were unable to reach an agreement. They eventually requested the committee to make a settlement. For the committee, this was their first settlement proposal, and the deal was finally concluded as a result of going through the process stated below. (Note: The price is the total price of the five vessels.)

The catalogue price put forward by the owner of the vessels was $45,550.
The corrected owner's price was $38,600.
The final price suggested by the applicant for purchase was $34,500.
Evaluation by the surveyor, Mr Clarke, $33,450.
Evaluation by the surveyor, Mr Pilkey, $35,126.
The price settled on was $35,065.

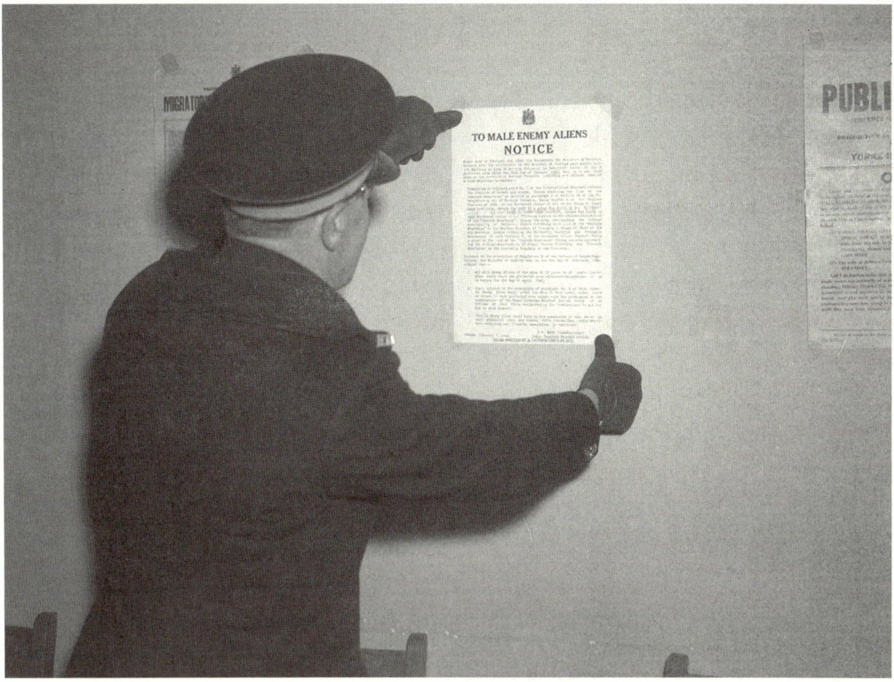


Figure M.9 The expulsion of Japanese Canadians from coastal British Columbia unfolded in waves. In this photograph, an officer posts an order regarding male Japanese nationals. Eventually, the entire population, including all Canadians, would be expelled. Vancouver Public Library (VPL), 1342.

(Note: Looking back on the negotiation process, it could be summed up that it was caused by the opposing positions of seller and buyer, with a classic high price followed by a low offer. The fact was, the owners were considering the operation value of the boats and generally came up with numbers based on insured value, which was replacement value, a half of the building cost plus the actual value. On the other side, the purchasers naturally considered the actual value to be the building cost minus depreciation, which was subtracted by some percentage every year. If we apply a compounded depreciation rate of 7.5 per cent [in the case of an income tax return, the official depreciation rate allowed for wooden boats was within 15 per cent], at the end of the first year the price of the boat would be 92.5 per cent of the building cost. If we take another 7.5 per cent from this number, at the end of the second year the price of the boat would be 85.6 per cent. If we follow this formula every year, by the end of nine years it would be about 50 per cent of value, and by the end of eighteen years the price would be 25 per cent and about 12 per cent at the end of twenty-seven years. [If the owner repairs the boat, the cost would be added to the total cost, and the depreciation would be subtracted from there.] The life of a fishing boat varies depending on the way it is being operated or maintained, but let us suppose it is twenty-seven years for the sake of debate, and then let's recap the above. In the first nine years, the owner recovers half of the building costs, but in the next nine years, only 25 per cent will be recovered, and in the next nine years, a mere 12.5 per cent will be recouped. Furthermore, for these later years, the owner has to anticipate a substantial amount for repairs.)

The owner of the boat and the purchaser had to compromise in each case to make a deal, but it seems that in general the newer boats fetched higher prices, while the older boats brought lower than the surveyed price.

*14 March:*

The Navy had already requisitioned and utilized several large fishing boats belonging to Hakujin and Nikkei fisherman. This time, the Air Force and an office of the Army requested the requisition of eight small packers or trolling boats. They had special requirements about the structure of the boats, the speed and make of the engines. We requested that Mr Pilkey carefully select and survey ten boats to begin with.

Furthermore, the British Admiralty Technical Mission (BATM)* in Ottawa proposed to requisition about twenty middle-sized diesel engine packers with lower cabins and low draft and less than ten feet width. We also asked Mr Pilkey to select and survey these.

[ … ]

*19 March:*

A newspaper article stated that Mr Reid, the elected representative from New Westminster, was going to question the minister of fisheries about the discrepancy between the catalogue price and the actual agreed upon prices of impounded Nikkei fishing boats. So we included the following chart in our weekly report to the minister.

* The British Admiralty Technical Mission (BATM) was established in July 1940 as part of a larger technical mission in which British scientists and engineers shared the United Kingdom's technical and scientific military secrets with their Canadian and American counterparts. The BATM's specific role was to provide technical assistance and supervision to North American firms undertaking contracts for the Admiralty. Its actions to this end included an active hand in researching, developing, and manufacturing radio, radar, and munitions capabilities for the Canadian and American navies. Zimmerman, *Top Secret Exchange*, 102; Smith, "History of the British Admiralty Technical Mission in Canada," typescript (Ottawa: British Admiralty Technical Mission, 1946), LAC, RG28, Box 29.

1. The boats we have sold up until today were as follows:

| | | |
|---|---|---|
| Seiners | 26 boats | $196,061 |
| Trollers | 10 boats | $20,775 |
| Gill-netters | 76 boats | $53,322 |
| Packers | 31 boats | $81,689 |
| Others | 5 boats | $9,235 |
| Total | 148 boats | $362,082 |

2. The actual sale price of the small fishing boats was 25.8 per cent lower than the listed catalogue price.

[ … ]

*30 March:*

We placed a newspaper advertisement on 10 February concerning the liquidation of fishing boats, but at the time, the Navy had a complex method of showing the boats. They looked for specific boats and towed them, one by one, to the New Westminster docks to be surveyed. If the buyer wanted to see other boats, he had to check the committee's catalogue again, talk to the Liaison Committee, obtain a permit again, and come back to New Westminster to survey the actual boat. It was not only time-consuming but also expensive for the buyer. We heard rumours criticizing the committee and the Navy for the complex and repetitious bureaucratic process preventing sales. It was true that the process was complex, but in the beginning the Navy took an especially responsible and careful attitude, worrying about theft or damage to the boats. Now that the impoundment area had been rearranged and organized more efficiently, we placed another advertisement. In the ad, we made it clear that we could arrange a reasonable way of reaching a settlement in case the buyer could not reach an agreement with the owner.

[ … ]

## The Peak of the Fishing-Boat Sale

*30 April:*

The number of boats disposed of, up until and including today, is as follows:

| | |
|---|---|
| 1. Sold | 540 boats |
| 2. Requisitioned | 59 boats |
| 3. Released to registered owners | 144 boats |
| 4. Total | 743 boats |

By use:

| | |
|---|---|
| Seiners | 49 boats |
| Trollers | 39 boats |
| Gill-netters | 497 boats |
| Packers | 107 boats |
| Cod fishing & others | 51 boats |
| Total | 743 boats |

*1 May:*

The Navy informed us that they want to remove the guard duty on the marine impoundment area at month's end. The sale of the small boats is inactive, and there is some criticism concerning the committee's sale methods. They say that the committee's full cash payment method is inconsiderate toward small, individual fishermen with limited funds. Many canneries are providing an interest-free instalment plan.

For canneries, fishing is a vital resource, and they were providing generous deals only to experienced and proven fishermen based on many years' records. Our committee cannot do the same. Also, because of the above discussed reasons, there was little scope to make deals by changing the method of payment. However, to counter the criticism, and thinking there might be a limited number of deals possible, we came up with the following method and advertised it.

1. One third of the sale price shall be paid in cash.
2. The remaining two-thirds will be mortgaged at an annual interest rate of 7 per cent.
3. Insurance must be obtained to secure the total loss to the former owner.
4. The Montreal Trust Company shall represent the person who sets the mortgage (a former owner) and, at 5 per cent commission, demand payment. The commission fee shall be covered by the former owner.

We also advertised a minimum "suggested negotiation price," which was displayed on all the remaining fishing boats in the catalogue. We made it known that our committee was capable of making deals on purchase offers if they were above these prices.

(Note: There was not a single case of a deal through the instalment method. After all, this was just to counter criticism. However, through the suggested price method, about 153 boats were quickly sold without the owner's consent. From among them, 136 boat-owners consented after the deal was done and received payment. The other 16 cases, including the issue of payment, were entrusted to the Custodian's department.

The sale total was $72,031, and the estimated price total was $60,000. That is to say, we sold the boats for 20 per cent more than the surveyor's estimate.)

*14 May:*

Regarding the BATM requisition order of twenty boats, three were already outfitted and on their way to Halifax by train, and another four were ready for shipping. The committee is pressuring the rest of them for early completion. All these boats are heading to England by ship to engage in minesweeping activities at sea.

*15 May:*

Within a week, we sold seventy-five fishing boats, which saturated the demand from the fishing industry. Therefore, the committee sent a telegram to the minister of fisheries asking whether we should stay on course by concentrating on the fishing industry or if we should begin to open up the boats to more general demand.

*16 May:*

The minister of fisheries responded by telegram saying that he wished us to come up with the best way to dispose of the remaining fishing boats as soon as possible. He wanted to decide the liquidation strategy after careful deliberation based on a more detailed report and advice from the committee.

## Releasing the Boats to General Demand

*18 May:*

We explained to the minister that by opening up the remaining boats to general demand, we can possibly stimulate business in the fishing industry where the demand seemed to be slowing down. The minister approved our strategy.

*25 May:*

We advertised the fishing boats to be released for general use.

(Note: Because gasoline rationing was in effect, this strategy did not accomplish much, and only a few boats were sold for logging tenders, but it somewhat stimulated demand in the fishing industry.)

[ … ]

*29 May:*

By the order of the Navy, suddenly Mr Johnson has to go east tomorrow for his new assignment. It was arranged that he still keep his position in the committee and shall be consulted about important matters.
(Note: I considered a send-off party for him but changed my mind and instead organized a thank-you party in Yoshino restaurant for all the committee members, the deputy director, Nikkei Liaison Committee members, and office staff. We had been tense with logistical discussions in the office for days, but we were all relaxed there and had pleasant chats.)
[ … ]

*18 June:*

A letter, dated on the fifteenth, from Mr Finn, the deputy minister, told us to come up with alternative guarding plans for the remaining fishing boats or, if impossible, to dispose of them all before 30 June when the Navy removes its guard.

*19 June:*

We shipped five boats on a requisition order from the BATM.

*25 June:*

The inquiry dated the fifteenth came from Mr Mitsujiro Noguchi, the director of the Fishermen's Association in the first district, regarding "Fishing boats sold without owner's consent" (the so-called forced sales).

I asked the deputy director to explain at length and to their satisfaction the background and circumstances, as well as the results of the sales, etc.

*26 June:*

[ … ]
We must decide quickly how to safely store the remaining fishing boats after the Navy removes their guards.
1. Ask a minimum number of marines to stay
2. Place under the Custodian's supervision
3. RCMP's supervision

(1) To make such arrangements as will make it possible for the present owners of detained vessels to freely negotiate for charters, leases, or sales of such vessels as they own to persons other than those of Japanese origin, provided that the committee approve of such charters, leases, or sales,which approval shall be a prerequisite for the use of such vesael under fishing license.

(2) Where necessary, to arbitrate disagreements on price between owners and intending purchasers with a view to preventing advantage being taken of duress.

(3) To report on claims which may be made on the government for damage to, or deterioration of, the vessels and equipment while under detention.

(4) To report on claims which may be made on the government for the returning of the detained vessels from their present storage place to places where they were picked up.

(5) By consultation with the Department of Fisheries, to determine which of the detained vessels shall first come under the arrangements to be put back into production.

(6) To report on steps that should be taken to dispose of vessels which the present owners are unable to sell, charter, lease or otherwise transfer.

Figure M.10 The duties of the Japanese Fishing Vessel Disposal Committee, as articulated in Order-in-Council PC 288 of 1942. The committee lacked the legal authority to force the sale of vessels without the consent of Nikkei owners, and the illegality of its actions in this respect was later acknowledged by federal lawyers. Reproduced with the permission of Library and Archives Canada (2016). LAC, RG 2, Vol. 1744, File 2484G, PC 1942-288.

4. Ministry of Fisheries' supervision
5. Place under private company's control

To investigate these possibilities, we started meeting with Mr Motherwell, the chief supervisor of fisheries, Col. C.H. Hill, the divisional commander of the RCMP, and Mr McPherson.

*2 July:*

Colonel Hill issued a command from Ottawa to transfer guard duty of the marine impoundment area into the hands of the RCMP. All other duties, including maintenance, shall be under the control of the Ministry of Fisheries. We felt that divided responsibility tends to give rise to inconvenience and conflict and requested a wait until our committee could come up with an alternative plan.

After several meetings with Mr Motherwell, Col. Hill, and Mr McPherson, the committee pointed out to the minister of fisheries that apart from protecting the fishing boats from water damage, fire damage, burglary and maintaining the boats, there were other manual and administrative tasks required. These were: surveying; checking boat equipment; removing claims against the Navy; making sale-related documents at sale completion; and the actual handing over of boats. Since the Custodian is an established office within the Department of the Secretary of State and already holds several fishing boats under its control, as well as all the property owned by Nikkei people, it is proper to move the remaining fishing boats under its control. Also, we recommended the temporary transfer of our committee staff, experienced as they are with matters pertaining to fishing boats, to the Custodian's office for the sake of administrative continuity. This would also save the trouble of hiring new staff. We recommended this proposition in a detailed report at a meeting with Mr McPherson.

We also made it clear that we will collaborate as much as possible with the RCMP and the Ministry of Fisheries as long as the command of Col. Hill stands.

An Army section applied to requisition eight small fishing boats on 14 March, and we have been preparing them. Today, 2 July, they officially requisitioned ten boats.

*8 July:*

We proposed to transfer the task of the protection and management of the remaining 217 fishing boats in the New Westminster marine impoundment area to various governmental departments, but they all had a mountain of work in front of them, and none of them could take over the task. Our committee looked into the possibility of continuing to handle them ourselves.

We estimated that we needed about $3,000 a month for the salaries of guards who would replace the present Navy guards and for various expenses in the impoundment area. However, if present sale trends continue for two weeks, the number of boats will decrease to the point where we can store them on land. Then we might be able to proceed with a budget of just $1,000 a month. We communicated this idea to the deputy minister of fisheries.

We also decided, withdrawing our past allocation plan, to ask the three largest canneries to reconsider and take any number of fishing boats on either an entrusting or a storage basis. In case this plan does not work, we are also looking for a company with storage facility on land and will check the possibility of just storing the boats there.

The removal of Nikkei people gathered momentum, and contact with boat-owners became more difficult and slow. On the other hand, we faced increasing pressure from the Navy, who wanted to remove their guards from the impoundment area. Under these circumstances, the number of boats sold without owner consent amounted to 154 boats … To normalize these sales, we decided to send letters to the owners explaining the situation and asking them to sign the sale contracts as soon as possible. We also promised the immediate settlement of the account upon completion of the sale.

[ … ]

*9 July:*

The Custodian moved twenty boats under their control from New Westminster to the North Arm of Bedwell Bay in Burrard Inlet.

*16 July:*

Negotiations with the canneries concerning the entrusting or storing of fishing boats is going well. Therefore, while the companies are selecting boats, to avoid confusion we temporarily stopped issuing survey permits as well as conducting boat sales.

*18 July:*

The acting deputy minister of fisheries, Mr A.J. Whitmore, sent a telegram informing us that they have decided to transfer the remaining boats, as well as the remaining committee duties, to the Custodian at the end of the month. Therefore, when a negotiation with canneries about entrusting or storing the boats reaches an agreement, the effective date of the contract shall be after 1 August. This is to give the Custodian responsibility for the official contract, with consideration for possible future boat sales.

[ … ]

## The Transfer of Remaining Boats

*25 July:*

The deputy minister of fisheries wrote to us that by the Order-in-Council PC 6247, issued on 20 July, all the remaining boats will be transferred to the protection and control of the Custodian. The deputy minister heard that the Custodian was aware of negotiations the committee was now engaged in with the canneries. He also asks the committee to complete its remaining work as soon as possible to save costs. However, he expected the committee to come up with a comprehensive report listing various procedures, actions taken, and their results. At the same time, the minister of fisheries sent us a thank-you letter.

*31 July:*

The transfer of the control of Nikkei fishing boats to the Office of the Custodian progressed smoothly. The surveyors from the Navy and the Custodian were assessing the condition of the remaining boats together. The Custodian will use the same impoundment area until they find another location. The remaining five boats requisitioned to the BATM were shipped. This makes twenty vessels in total that have been sent to them.

## The Expense of Moving the Fishing Boats

Immediately after the Naval Order to Impound Nikkei Fishing Boats was announced, many owners delivered their boats to Steveston from various places in BC and made their way home. We were aware of the issue of compensation for costs incurred delivering the boats, but Order-in-Council PC 288 did not authorize the committee to handle this issue. However, we considered that if we submitted the issue to the Navy, unofficially, though an immediate solution may be unlikely, there might be a way to solve the issue from a different perspective once the Custodian took over the committee's remaining tasks. So we estimated the minimum cost of boat delivery and a trip home and prepared the following chart.

1. From Skeena River to Prince Rupert $5 each – 48 cases
2. From Prince Rupert to Steveston $50.25 each – 48 cases

| | |
|---|---|
| 3. From Ucluelet or Bamfield to Steveston | $12.15 each – 64 cases |
| 4. From Tofino or Clayoquot to Steveston | $21.75 each – 28 cases |
| 5. From Victoria to Steveston | $9.70 each – 6 cases |
| 6. From the Deep Bay area to Steveston | $14.45 each – 8 cases |
| 7. From the Nanaimo area and Galiano Island to Steveston | $10.35 each – 35 cases |
| 8. From Chemainus to Steveston | $10.35 each – 5 cases |
| 9. From Kosiaski Cove to Steveston | fee unclear – 8 cases |

(Note: Due to the removal of the Nikkei owners, we did not have a chance to talk with many of them. However, we put together this request, thinking that even a small number of claims will prove that the owners accepted the order or request from the Navy.)

Regarding entrusting or storage of the boats, collaboration with the canneries was disappointing, and only Nelson Brothers Fishery Company agreed to keep fifty-two boats. Therefore, there were ninety-seven boats remaining in New Westminster.

*3 August:*

The committee reported on 1 August to the Ministry of Fisheries concerning travel expense compensation for Nikkei boat-owners. Today we requested Commodore W.J.R. Beech, the Pacific Coast commanding officer in Esquimalt, to advise the related parties on compensation.

*5 August:*

Protection and management of the remaining fishing boats in New Westminster and Prince Rupert (Tuck's Inlet) was finally transferred from the Navy to the Custodian.

*10 August:*

There was a communication from the deputy minister of fisheries, Mr Whitmore: "Regarding compensation for expenses incurred by Nikkei owners navigating their boats, stated in your letter of August 1st, because this matter is totally different from compensation for the damage of fishing boats during impoundment, it is considered to be outside the business of the Committee (namely, an excess of authority). I have not received a report from the Commodore of the Pacific Coast Naval Office, so I cannot give a decisive opinion, but apparently, it seems that it is part of expenses caused by the enforcement of the Vessel Impoundment Law. Accordingly, in case this view is correct, I would pass on the Committee's intention to the Navy."

From Commodore Beech, there was a response issued on the eighth, whose contents are stated below:

> When the fishing boats owned by Nikkei people were locked in the marine impoundment area, there was of course, no Order for the Removal of Nikkei people, so the owners of boats went home. Thus the reasonable expenses stated in your proposal are naturally meant to be paid to the boat owners. According to the Order issued on 10 December 1941 (attached), from the commanding office regarding this matter, I think it is reasonable to consider that the RCMP is responsible for the compensation of the incurred expenses.

Attached: An overview of the order:
0038 z/10 the matter of protection of fishing vessels owned by Nikkei people:
1. As soon as all vessels are gathered at the designated gathering point, the engine of each small fishing vessel should be locked, and the captains should board the few large fishing vessels able to tow 5–10 of these vessels, and tow them to Steveston under the protection of the F/R ship.
2. Have all Nikkei people disembarked at Steveston, and have them stay at Nikkei homes there. If necessary, build temporary housing. This area is already under the protection of a unit dispatched near the area. All fishing vessels must be impounded in appropriate flat, shallow water about 10 miles upstream, and be protected by guards sent from headquarters.
3. The most appropriate twenty boats from among these vessels will be requisitioned and chartered. Charter fee at market price should eventually be paid to the owners. If these twenty vessels are utilized, it will be enough for patrolling.
4. In the case of these vessels being owned by Japanese nationals, the boats would be the spoils of war.
5. *The Navy's responsibility toward Nikkei crews will be finished upon their landing in Steveston*, and they will be under the control of the RCMP, according to an arrangement. The crews cannot land until preparation by the RCMP is complete.

(Note: An article similar to the overview above was printed in newspapers at the time. One newspaper praised the well-planned government preparations for the mass landing of Nikkei people. Another newspaper report emphasized the protection of Nikkei people. Even reports that "*Japanese* crews will be locked in, at temporary housing," appeared in some papers. These reports had the effect of calming down citizens' minds, preventing misplaced war hysteria. Also, considering the result, careful efforts by the government could be inferred.)

(Note: Following a similar method, stated in the first section of the Navy order, boats were towed from Prince Rupert. This was limited to boats fit for navigating the Skeena River during winter. Moreover, when these boats reached the Queen Charlotte Islands (situated north of Vancouver Island), the waves were very high, and it was difficult to tow. The boats would be damaged if they were towed, so the majority of boats navigated southward independently, from various places, to Steveston.

With a copy of communication from the Navy, as well as the above order, the committee requested Commodore Hill of the RCMP to consider this matter. He responded that he felt the order merely indicated who was responsible for the protection of the Nikkei crews. We concluded that there seemed to be no other way than transferring this matter to the Office of the Custodian and having them make a proper arrangement.

[ … ]

*24 August:*

During negotiations over the purchase of boats requisitioned by the Navy, a Nikkei owner of three requisitioned boats demanded a charter fee be paid for a period beyond the setting of the sale price. The Navy insisted that it was not going to pay a charter fee at all because it was going to purchase boats based on the price evaluated by Lloyd's of London. The Navy said that the owner had agreed to this at the meeting of inquiry held by the Advisory Committee at the time of requisition. By the way, the matter of requisitioned boats involves not just Nikkei owners but Hakujin boat-owners as well, so the Navy gives uniform terms on purchases, and if an owner refuses to accept these terms, the Navy will continue to argue until a judgment by the Court of the Exchequer in England. Therefore, considering the cost and time involved with a lawsuit, the Nikkei owner decided to take the amount offered.

*30 August:*

A month has already passed since the impoundment area was transferred to the Office of the Custodian.

Because the majority of Nikkei boat-owners have been relocated to various places, all negotiations for the purchase of requisitioned boats have had to be done by mail. Things are very slow and do not progress smoothly.

The Custodian wants to take over after the committee is near completion of its administrative tasks, so we are trying to arrange the purchase of the requisitioned boats mentioned above, but even if business negotiations are agreed upon, they are different from private sales, and we must:

1. Complete the procedure for transferring vessel registry
2. Send the new vessel registry and the bill to the government
3. Receive payment and settle the account with the owner
4. Receive a receipt from the owner and submit the receipt to the government

Thus, the task requires many complicated procedures and time-consuming negotiations. Accordingly, the matters the committee has to communicate to government and the owners increase. So, the committee is very busy with various complicated office procedures.

[ … ]

*6 October:*

The Custodian reported to the committee that due to the late-comer salmon gathered in mass in the Fraser River, they have sold forty-three boats from 1 August up until today. The Custodian sent six additional boats for safekeeping, under special conditions, to the Nelson Brothers Fishery Company.

[ … ]

*15 October:*

The committee had one administrative clerk handling procedures for damaged fishing vessels transferred to the office of the Custodian. Negotiations regarding the Army, Navy, and Air Force moved forward, and the committee received approval from about 80 per cent of boat-owners.

## Transferring the Committee's Remaining Tasks to the Custodian

*31 October:*

Inspection of the account began on the twenty-second, and it was decided that all committee tasks would be transferred to the Custodian after its completion.

The sale of requisitioned boats is progressing smoothly, with completion in sight. Among 152 small boats sold without the owner's permission, the so-called forced, sixteen of those cases remain unsettled. The committee will transfer several procedures to the Custodian: boat registry, claims against the Navy if necessary, and money from sales, amounting to $8,000. On reflection, things were thought to be much simplified if the committee were to complete the transferral of boat registries, then transfer sale amounts to the Custodian. The Custodian preferred this option, and with its authority signed the document transferring boat registries on behalf of the owners.

The removal of all Nikkei people from the coast is nearing completion, and it was decided that after today, any Nikkei people remaining in the Coastal Defence Region without permission from the RCMP will be detained.

Although there was an offer from the RCMP to issue a permit for me to stay, I declined their offer. I could not have my wife, and especially my young children, reside in a Vancouver where they could not even go to school. It would also be very sad for the family to leave Vancouver by themselves, so for the time being, we have all moved to Christina Lake (PO Box Cascade), joining those who have come before us.

I visited Vancouver on 17 November and helped to organize the remaining tasks. Negotiations on boats with ties to the military were settled, and a comprehensive report to the minister of fisheries was completed.

Various records were organized, and necessary records on individual boats were reorganized after the inspection of accounts, and all of them were made ready for transferral to the Custodian.

On 23 December, I finally said my good-byes and returned home to Christina Lake.

[ … ]

Figure M.11 Japanese Canadian–owned fishing vessels in Steveston, BC, 1927. Japanese Canadians had invested generations of labour and care in crafting and working fishing vessels. Nikkei National Museum (NNM), 2010-31-2.

Part Two

# Unusual and Exceptional Cases

In this section of the memoir, Kimura describes the cases of individual Japanese Canadians that, years later, he continued to see as exceptional or troubling. Some individuals, such Mr I in the first anecdote recounted, seemed to Kimura to make decisions that resulted in unnecessary losses of compensation. Others, such as the case of Mr E (the second anecdote), are memorable for the light they shed on the extremism occasioned by the war when, in Kimura's view, "ignorant fanatics" saw an opportunity "to take … actions to express their enmity" toward Japanese Canadians. On the whole, the cases convey the difficulties faced by the committee: Kimura seems in part to have been troubled by how much of the process lay outside of his control despite his role on the committee.

# Unusual and Exceptional Cases

## 1. The Case of Mr I

Not long after we established the committee office, an old man we will call Mr I came to call. He said, "A very kind man is willing to buy my boat, and I want the committee to approve this deal." I checked the catalogue but could not find anything to match the boat, so I questioned him further. Mr I replied, "In order to receive my pension [or allowance?], I registered my boat with the government as my sole property and didn't report it to the committee. When I receive the $400 boat payment, I would like to give that money to the Compensation Board." It happened that Mr Pilkey came along, so I asked him what he thought about the price of the boat. He replied that it was hard to estimate the price of any boat without actually seeing it, but Mr I was an old man and would not operate the boat in a reckless manner; consequently he thought it would be worth about $600. I told Mr I of Mr Pilkey's estimate and told him not to rush into a sale. Mr I insisted that since the boat had supported him, so to speak, he wanted to hand it over to someone kind and able to take proper care of it without fussing over the price. So I created the necessary documents and phoned the clerk in charge at the Compensation Board. The clerk said that it was all right to hand over the whole amount of the sale to the owner. But the old man said, "It is worrisome to move with such a lot of money; if I lose it, I will be destitute. If I pay the Compensation Board now, I will continue to get my pension. That is much better and safer." So I processed it in the end as he wished.

## 2. The Case of Mr E

Mr E had a plan to replace his boat engine during winter and put his boat in the shipyard with a new engine right beside it. As soon as the announcement of the Vessel Impoundment Law, a group of people looking like marines, with military caps on, came in and ordered him to "Tow the boat to the gathering spot as soon as possible." While he was installing towlines and blocks, part of the engine was destroyed by someone. Because it cost money to repair and return the engine to the store, he wanted us to negotiate with the Navy to cover that cost. Of course, an engine was not a fishing boat, and it was outside our jurisdiction. But if his story was the fact, it was a terrible thing, so I pushed the Navy to do something about it. But the individual who had done it was unidentified, and there was no way of investigating.

We heard a rumour that the engine of a Nikkei fishing boat tied at the Gore Street dock had been destroyed, but the facts were unclear to us. It was right after the outbreak of war, and ignorant fanatics might have taken the announcement of boat seizures as a chance to take such actions to express their enmity. But there was no obvious evidence, so there was no way to take action.

## 3. The Case of the Skeena Fishing Group's Boat

From Navy headquarters in the Skeena area, there was a report that the boat *Mioria* was damaged, foundering, and drifting on the Skeena River, so the committee immediately reported this to Mr Kunisaburo Miwa. "The boat was not usually used during winter and was kept in dry dock, the same as in other years. I think someone forcibly towed the boat into the water," and then he said, with his usual frankness, "Because it is wartime, such things tend to happen. It can't be helped," he continued.

Around this time, because of the removal order, all Nikkei people in the Skeena area had already been moved into temporary lodgings in Hastings Park. They were in a situation where there was no way to find out the facts; thus, he realized it was useless to say anything while the guilty person was unknown. The committee appreciated the Navy for its report and requested the boat be towed to a convenient river ford, if possible.

## 4. The Case of Mr A

Mr A was a carpenter who lived in a small village about 200 miles north of Vancouver. In September of 1941, he purchased a fishing boat from a Hakujin, and on land he leisurely started repairing it, but the transfer of the boat registry was incomplete. (Thus, officially it was a boat registered under the name of the Hakujin.) After the announcement of the order to impound vessels, marines came and said the boat was to be transferred to the marine impoundment area near New Westminster. Mr A worried about possible damages and attempted to make excuses why it couldn't be moved, but eventually it was moved to the impoundment area, and Mr A registered himself with the committee as the real owner of the boat and the Hakujin as the registered owner.

There was no applicant wanting to purchase the boat by the end of the boat liquidation period. When boat custody was transferred from the Navy to the Custodian, with the presence of the surveyors from both sides, it was decided that the boat had become a total loss since its impoundment. Because the committee had heard about the situation from Mr A, the committee claimed that the boat had been further damaged by forcibly being towed to the area of impoundment. This happened despite it being already incapable of navigation at the announcement of the vessel impoundment order. The committee requested $300 as compensation for damages, but Navy surveyors showed a piece of the ship's planking which was riddled by teredo worm damage, and this bolstered their opinion that the boat was a total loss. Other surveyors agreed with this, so there seemed to be no hope for compensation. The committee left the record of the claim for compensation, complying with Mr A's request.

## 5. The Departure Bay Case

This concerns a seiner that belonged to the Nanaimo Shipyard. Because the stockholder of the shipyard was in Japan at the outbreak of war, it was under the control of the Custodian. The boat was very well equipped, with a very strong searchlight, so at the beginning, the Navy requisitioned it and used it as a guard boat within the marine impoundment area. The Navy flag flew on the mast, and two guards with bayonets were always on the boat. However, one day the boat suddenly caught fire. It was quickly extinguished, but the boat suffered considerable damage and was sent to the shipyard for repair. It is unknown how much repairs cost, but as with other requisitioned boats, this boat was purchased by the Canadian Navy according to the surveyor's price evaluation after going through the committee's review process.

## 6. The Case of Mr N

Soon after the establishment of the committee, Mr N and a company manager making a purchase brought us a sales contract that was already notarized and requested transfer approval. However, this contract included, besides several fishing boats: fishing nets; boat parts; a camping scow; and various tools to go with it. The committee approved this comprehensive contract, charging 1 per cent of the sales amount as a commission. The committee suggested that Mr N make a separate contract just for the fishing boats. However, because the contract needed to be completed immediately, Mr N was okay with paying the extra commission. They insisted the committee approve the contract, and the committee accepted the request.

## 7. The Case of Mr T

Mr T entered into a sales contract with a cannery in order to sell all five of his fishing boats. He submitted the contract to the committee and requested their approval. In the contract, besides an instalment plan, there was a section stating that the repair costs and remodelling that the buyer wanted would be subtracted from the payment. Of course, because all Nikkei-owned fishing boats were impounded after the fishing season, there might be some boats that required repairs, but if the buyer were to use the conditions stated above as a legal statement, the former owner would be in a very disadvantaged position. The committee pointed this out and advised Mr T to cancel his conditions, even give a discount, or set a maximum amount for repairs. He was advised to reach an amount which deducted repair costs, making an arrangement to get the remaining sum, if there was one, after repairs. However, Mr T entreated the committee for approval, repeating that there was no need for such concern because this was a contract with a company he had been dealing with for a long time. The committee eventually accepted the agreement. According to what was later discovered, because the packer, *The B*, was remodelled as a seiner at large expense, the remodelling cost exceeded the price of the vessel. Due to it being a package deal, this exceeded amount had to be deducted from the price of the other boats. (In other words, Mr T could have gotten more money if he had given away *The B* for free.)

In the early spring of 1944 when I visited the city for business, Mr T took the trouble to attend a tea gathering, and we had an opportunity to talk there.

Recalling the past, he said, "Regarding that matter of the fishing boats, you helped me a lot. I learned the hard way how much the war had changed people's minds and their sense of honour."

## 8. The Case of Mr M

Mr M sold his boats to Mr K when he went back to Japan in 1941. There were proposals to decrease the number of fishing licences given to Nikkei fishermen, and there was counter-litigation from Nikkei people, which achieved some result in 1929. After that, the government kept a policy of maintaining the number of the fishing licences given to Nikkei people. Therefore, it was understood implicitly among Nikkei people that the trading of fishing licences accompanied the sale of fishing boats. (In other words, it was useless to purchase a fishing boat if a buyer could not get a fishing licence with it.) Because of such a situation, just like paying a price for a certain brand, the value of fishing licences was naturally included in the price of boats. I am not sure if this was exactly the case with Mr M, but buyers tended to postpone registering their boat until getting a licence. Usually, licences were applied for after January 2nd at the earliest each year. When war broke out, Mr M's fishing boat was put under the control of the Custodian (the Department for the Liquidation of Enemy Property), since the boat belonged to an absent owner. If Mr M returns to Canada after the war, he will get the sale amount, but I do not know if Mr M is still alive or not.

## 9. The Case of Mr U

Mr U's boat was very old, built in 1921, but because the engine had been replaced in 1931, it had been evaluated by the surveyor at $316. In late April, he sold this boat to a cannery for $75 (thus, 13.07 per cent of the estimated value). The committee did not have a chance to meet Mr U, so we did not know the details of the transaction, but probably it was not only due to the anxiety of having to relocate. Mr U had bought the boat about a year before the outbreak of war and had given a mortgage to the cannery; thus, it seems that Mr U stated the amount deducted from the mortgage as the sale price. Among cases similar to this one, there were ten other cases where the sales contracts were agreed to at below 50 per cent of the estimated value.

## 10. The Case of Mr C

Mr C owned a boat built in 1920, and he maintained it in immaculate condition. The surveyor evaluated his boat at $661 because it did not look like a twenty-year-old boat. However, because of the old registry date, no one seems to have actually surveyed the boat, and the boat wasn't sold for a long time. Around mid-July, it was eventually liquidated based on the method of forced sales, with a price evaluated by a surveyor. I felt sorry because the date of registration disadvantaged this boat.

## 11. The Case of Mr G

It was in the beginning of March that I happened to meet Mr G. He said, "I'd like you to sell these boats as soon as possible because we have to relocate, and if we don't have any money we'll be in trouble." I was surprised at Mr G because, when I was collecting documents to make a fishing boat catalogue, I heard a rumour that Mr G was saying, "Report the price of your boat as high as possible, and never sell it, even though it decays." Because it was wartime, I expected there to be false rumours among Hakujin. I realized that even among Nikkei people there are those who spread false rumours and slander.

However, in mid-April, I heard from someone else that Mr G was telling people, "I've sold off all three of my boats. If I'd hesitated, they would've soon been worthless." I felt strange and checked the accounts book. It turned out that the agreed price of his sales contract had been one-third of the catalogue price. When this was happening, surveyors had not yet systemically evaluated the boats, so it is unclear whether Mr G's sale price was one-third of the market price or the reported price of the boats was an inflated 300 per cent of the market price. To this day, I am still mystified with Mr G's motives for saying and doing these things.

## 12. The Case of Mr Y

Mr Y was a fisherman on the Skeena River. Following the order of impoundment, he navigated his boat to Prince Rupert and, at the request of the Navy, further navigated as far as Steveston. The boat was impounded in the New Westminster marine impoundment area, but later, at the request of a cannery that turned out to be the registered owner, the boat was released and passed on to that company. Mr Y did not have to navigate a boat that wasn't his, so it was assumed that he hadn't registered the boat yet because there was a balance remaining with the company. Similar to the case of Mr Y, there were six other boats navigated from Prince Rupert that were later released to their registered owners.

## 13. The Case of Mr T and Mr Y

A boat owned by Mr T and Mr Y sank in the impoundment area and was towed to a shipyard for repairs. The cost of repair exceeded the value of the boat, so the Navy declared the boat a total loss. With the mediation of the Liaison Committee, the boat-owners submitted a $400 compensation claim, but when the committee tasks were transferred to the Custodian, this case remained unsettled. In May of 1943, there was a request from Mr T and Mr Y to speed up the settlement. I visited the Custodian to find out that the payment of $393.50 from the government had just arrived, so I asked the Custodian to make an arrangement to send the payment. (However, because the Custodian could only send a maximum of $100 a month based on an agreement with the BC Security Commission, it took four months to complete.) There were twelve other boats in total that the Navy determined to be total losses.

## 14. The Case of Mr S

Mr S was a gill-net fisherman on the Fraser River, but he also used his boat to ferry children to school. When the impoundment order was announced, he requested special permission from the Navy and continued to ferry the children until 24 April. After that, he navigated his boat to the impoundment area. This was the only case where a boat belonging to a Nikkei person continued to operate for four months after the outbreak of war.

## 15. The Case of Nikkei Veterans

This is an opposite case to the ones above. It concerns the Nikkei people who volunteered to the Canadian military at the time of the First World War and fought courageously on the European front. After coming home from the war, they acquired Canadian citizenship and the right to vote. However, they were not exempt from the impoundment order, and their boats were liquidated. They, as well, had to follow the order for removal of all Nikkei people from the coast.

## 16. The Case of Mr T, a Logging Operator

Mr T owned two log-tender boats for his logging operation. Since he had to close his business and move somewhere soon, he contracted a sale with a Hakujin for his two boats. He demanded permission for the sale from the committee. I explained to Mr T that they were not fishing boats; therefore, there was no need to get our permission. However, Mr T insisted, to satisfy his buyer even paying 1 per cent commission, so I decided to give him the committee's permission.

Apart from this case, I handled three other cases of tender boats for Nikkei logging operators in the same way.

## 17. The Case of Small Pleasure Fishing Boats Owned by Nikkei People

Mr K at Ocean Falls requested us to approve the sale of a few small pleasure fishing boats. Of course, these were not professional fishing boats and were free to be sold, but the buyer insisted on obtaining the committee's approval. We decided to give it to him.

By the way, we collected money from the boats we handled, but because of the relocation of all Nikkei people, some of the owners' addresses got lost, and we could not send their money to them. In those cases, we sent it to the Custodian and asked them to keep it for the owners.

## 18. The Case of Mr F

Mr F did have a boat, but this story concerns something else.

On a day when many Nikkei people had already been moved, two RCMP officers came to see me regarding a request from Mr F.

When Mr F was relocated, he was anxious about carrying a large sum of cash with him, so he buried it in his garden. Now he wanted RCMP officers to dig it up, following the instructions on his map, and send the money to him.

The two officers wanted me to come along with them. I thought of going with them, but a past incident came to mind.

It had happened when I was in back-and-forth discussions with the Navy about missing parts and tools from the boats of Nikkei fishermen. A newspaper had reported, "Many boat parts and tools are being found under the empty houses of Nikkei fishermen." When the impoundment order was announced, many fishing boats were navigated from faraway places to Steveston. The Navy allowed Nikkei fishermen to take their personal belongings with them when they disembarked from the boats. However, some removed boat parts or tools from the boats. There were people in the Navy who believed this report. (Nikkei people place a high value on tools and equipment, and they would not bury them. If they had something of value, they would report it to the Custodian before moving.)

I was worried about being the subject of a newspaper report and told this to the officers. "I haven't met Mr F in person," I said, "but I hear he is a very honest man. There is no need of my being a witness. I firmly believe you will find exactly the amount of money written here. Please follow up on his wishes." I was very much relieved later on when I received a report from the RCMP that they had found exactly the amount of money mentioned by Mr F and they had forwarded it to him. Newspaper reports and gossips kept this a much repeated story.

# Part Three

# Concluding the Forced Sale of Fishing Vessels

Having recounted the activity of the Fishing Vessel Disposal Committee as well as the individual cases that concerned or troubled him, Kimura now turns to broad reflections on these events. He makes the case that Japanese Canadians were poorly compensated for the sale of their fishing vessels, a matter that, in his view, might be integrated into a larger claim for material compensation for the forced sale of property. At the same time, he argues that the Fishing Vessel Disposal Committee, and Japanese Canadians themselves, did as well as possible under the circumstances that they confronted.

# Afterward

A few weeks after the remaining committee tasks were transferred to the Custodian, the chairman of the committee, Justice Smith, was again appointed by the federal government to be chairman of the Advisory Committee for the Liquidation of Nikkei Property … After that, he continued to work as the chief justice at the BC Supreme Court and as a full-time justice at the Marine Court. He passed away in 1959.

Mr Johnson, a committee member and representative from the Ministry of Defence, went to the Port of Halifax on 29 May 1942 where he was in active service. After the war, he was promoted to Navy captain and transferred to the reserves. Returning to Vancouver, he lived a tranquil life. In 1968, he passed away in Shaughnessy Hospital.

Mr McMaster worked as a deputy director on the Advisory Committee on Japanese Properties, directed by Justice Smith. He was then appointed by the Hon. C.D. Howe, the minister of munitions and supplies, to work in his ministry. After the war, he worked as a port manager at Vancouver Harbour, retiring in 1958. He died from an illness in 1960.

The following members of the Nikkei contingent who served with devotion have all, regrettably, passed away:

Mr Kunisaburo Miwa in New Denver; Mr. Hideo Fukuyama at Christina Lake; Mr Kohei Nakai in Toronto; Mr Matsunosuke Shinde in Greenwood.

The following members are still alive: Mr Unosuke Hashimoto in Richmond; Mr Mitsujiro Noguchi in Guelph, Ontario; Mr Ritsu Ide in Toronto, although he was not a member but the former director of the Nikkei Liaison Association.

## My Impressions

Although there is no document that records exactly the total worth of the fishing boats owned by Nikkei people, I have the impression that it was approximately $2,000,000 in total, taking into account what I heard before the war.

1. The actual sales amount was $1,423,182.
2. There were 187 vessels transferred to the Custodian with an estimate of $400 per vessel, equaling $74,800, although the exact price is unknown.
3. There were twenty remaining vessels under the control of the Custodian of Enemy Property estimated at $350 per vessel, making $7,000.
4. There were seventy vessels semi-owned by Nikkei people estimated at $400 per vessel, equaling $28,000.
5. Nine vessels for which compensation for total loss was requested. (However, one of them was denied. See "The case of Mr A" and "The case of Mr T and Mr Y.") $3,918.
6. Three vessels where the procedure of request for compensation of total loss was not completed, estimated at $400 per vessel, coming to $1,200.
7. Cases where the sale price was written down as the sale amount minus the rest of the mortgage, $5,116.

Total = $1,543,216

This figure is the assumptive total amount. If we suppose $2,000,000 as the correct amount, the total amount above equals 77.2 per cent of $2,000,000, and we can tentatively say that the boats were sold at a 22.8 per cent discount.

Except in the cases of the 152 boats the committee had to forcibly dispose of due to the urgency of the situation (among them, 136 cases later approved by the owners) the committee left all of the sales contracts as free negotiations between buyers and sellers.

Despite that, if the owners suffered a loss, it was because they were heavily pressed by the emergency situation of wartime and the order to remove all Nikkei people. They were concerned with various points:

1. Anxiety about the expense of keeping a boat during a war that no one knew how long would last.
2. There was no guarantee that the boats would not be damaged if the owners kept them.

3. Owners could not expect any income even if they made charter contracts.
4. Anxiety about the cost of living at their place of relocation.

Therefore, the owners were not in a position to negotiate a fair price.

At one time, volunteers from various places examined the possibility of compensating the loss of Nikkei property. Three Greenwood committee members visited me and requested I submit documents relating to the sale of Nikkei fishing boats. They said they would amalgamate the accounts from Nikkei fishermen with other property under the care of the Custodian. They would submit them, through Mr McMaster, a lawyer, the associate partner at Norris and McLennan.

Even though we arrived at the loss figures mentioned above, there was no documentation on individual fishing boat estimates authorized by surveyors to prove the total amount was $2,000,000, the basis on which the result was reached. Also, the committee left the sales negotiations to the discretion of the boat-owners, so I think it unfair to complain there were problems in the process.

However, if we generalize the matter of compensation to include everything that was sold, even voluntarily, to consist of: real estate; fishing vessels; fishing tools; forests; furniture; shops; rooming houses; business brands; and so on, you can argue that Nikkei people had to sell at bargain prices because of anxiety about their forced removal. The Order of Removal was definitely a biased order, which was applied only to Nikkei people, from among all other enemy foreigners. We could make a convincing claim that property sold under pressure should be compensated for. Testimonies could be collected from various fields. Even if somehow the claim proved unsuccessful, it would at least contribute to making the general Canadian public recognize the sacrifice Nikkei people had to make.

"Why don't you suggest this claim to Mr McMaster, the lawyer?"

"I would respond to a summons and certainly testify," I replied.

This attempt at a claim did not materialize for some reason, maybe because they did not acquire enough support from the Nikkei community, or they failed to obtain an agreement with Mr McMaster, or for some other unknown reason.

In eastern Canada, this issue of general compensation was debated, but it was called off there as well. I heard there was some difficulty raising expenses, but it remains unclear.

Now, some might argue that these fishing boats, which used to be owned by Nikkei people, could have been a resource when Nikkei people returned to the west coast if they hadn't been sold, but at the time, no one could predict the future. Moreover, the boats were necessary "to ensure food supply," a government policy, and in the end Nikkei people gave up their boats.

After the war, there was progress in the quality of fishing boats and equipment, and I think Nikkei people would eventually face the necessity of having to renew their boats. Be that as it may, if Nikkei people suffered the estimated losses mentioned above, I would like to investigate whether they came out with something positive.

It has not been investigated, but I think it is a small matter that the owners saved costs for boat maintenance and damage repairs, which they had to cover, in case their boats did not sell.

Even though these are invisible achievements, they are very significant:

1. All Nikkei fishermen not only followed the law to impound vessels, navigating their boats to the impoundment area but also:
2. Accepted the request by the Navy and took further trouble navigating the vessels to the impoundment area at New Westminster.
3. All Nikkei fishermen understood the necessity to ensure the food supply, giving up their boats and cooperating promptly to release the boats to go out fishing.

I think these are meaningful points because they could *make the Canadian general public recognize that Nikkei Canadians carried out their responsibility as Canadian citizens* in spite of extremely difficult circumstances.

At the end of January, soon after the committee started the liquidation of fishing boats, one newspaper that usually reported anti-Nikkei stories reported that "Nikkei boat owners are insisting on absurd prices." This was according to a Hakujin fisherman. Another rumour was that "Nikkei owners removed boat parts and equipment and stored them in warehouses with fishing nets," related in the typical manner of some abusive Hakujin fisherman. Moreover, the newspaper reported that it was predicted that "the Committee would suffer from hundreds of old, unsold vessels." In late April, the newspaper reported "We give praise to the Committee which is successfully managing difficult problems even Solomon might fail to manage. The Committee has already released more than half the vessels to people who need them." Also, in late May the newspaper reported, from a speech made by Mr Mc-

Master, that "Mr McMaster gives praise to the Nikkei owners of vessels who were willing to cooperate." I felt that this might be evidence that the profile of Nikkei people with the general public had improved and the newspaper could not ignore it.

Two years after Nikkei people were allowed to return to the west coast (beginning in 1949), I was asked by an acquaintance to accompany him to Vancouver. We had a meeting with Mr C, section chief of the N fishery company. I had known him for a long time since Mr R and his brother were fresh-fish traders. Mr C suddenly hugged me and said, "Thank you for coming! My flagship packer, the *Dara-Dog*, was alone and lonely, but fortunately I could purchase the *Kitaka* and the *Nakamoto* from the Custodian. Now I have the same number of packers as long ago, and I am going to keep them for a long time, for sentimental reasons. I was pleased to meet with R. Also, I saw S at the office a while ago. He has been working here for two years. He would be happy to see you!"

Mr C got so excited to see me that my acquaintance was surprised. Both of us could understand the conversation, but for those who didn't know the circumstances, it was of course odd. I finished the business with my acquaintance, and when I was talking with other old acquaintances, Mr S arrived.

Soon after Nikkei people were allowed to return to the coast, Mr S went to Vancouver. He pioneered the revival of fishing by Nikkei people. He was expecting threats from Hakujin fishermen. The cannery he had worked for before hesitated to work with Nikkei fishermen, so he switched to the N fishery company.

"Remembering the old days, I was tense and nervous, but, contrary to my apprehensions and as if the world had completely changed, people kindly assisted me with all sorts of matters. It was dream-like, I don't know how many times I pinched myself," he recalled.

All Nikkei immigrants have suffered from the anti-Nikkei movement since they landed in the province of BC, but especially Nikkei fishermen. Although they were all naturalized citizens, they suffered from continuous, severe exclusion practices. The number of fishing licences was limited, and moreover, the licences themselves were limited by discriminatory conditions. So throughout the fishing season, they operated only within the small fishing areas accorded them by licence. However, after the war the limitation on the number of licences was abolished (note: the current law for limitation is merely to protect certain kinds of fish and to increase the revenue of fishermen and is not anti-Nikkei), and all types of licences are granted to Nikkei fishermen. They can fish any areas, the same as other fishermen.

Common sense among the general public no longer condones anti-Nikkei practices, and I believe there is no room for anti-Nikkei propaganda. It was definitely the behaviour of the Nikkei fishermen who created such an atmosphere, by following the law, making sacrifices, and cooperating with government policy during the war.

There might be some people who insist that this is "because Nikkei people received suffrage," but it is too simple to conclude that it is a matter of course that naturalized citizens and Canadian-born citizens have suffrage. In reality, Nikkei people in general raised their profile with the Canadian general public by demonstrating their diligence, pleasant character, law-abiding spirit, and patience toward past discriminatory treatment, and these formed the basis whereby Nikkei people were granted suffrage.

Part Four

# A Message to Younger Japanese Canadians

In this short but important section of the memoir, Kimura addresses himself directly to generations of Japanese Canadians coming of age when "protests and demonstrations are the trend." Emphasizing the interwoven effects of economic struggle and racist exclusion, Kimura defends his own generation, asking young people "to investigate, face squarely, and consider the time period, the circumstances, situation, and environment" before judging the actions of their forbearers. He further claims that "Nikkei people were rewarded for their struggle and finally reached the dawn of a new era after the war."

# To the Second and Third Generations

From the current perspective, at a time when protests and demonstrations are the trend, there might be some who laugh at the Nikkei who conducted themselves with silence and obedience for decades. In fact, there were lawsuits claiming suffrage in the old days by *Nisei* representatives. Regarding the limitation of fishing licences, Nikkei people fought in the Supreme Court of Canada and the Privy Council in England, winning both cases. But Parliament gave the minister of fisheries the authority to discriminate when they issued fishing licences. We swallowed our tears. Recently, the *Nisei* conducted a protest against the draft of the removal of all Nikkei people, but this also ended with disappointing results.

Depending on the time period, situation, environment, and social standing, the outcomes are different. There might also be different opinions among us; however, I just want young people to understand that the *Issei* were by no means ignorant or stupid.

At the risk of sounding too insistent, I would like you to understand that the *Issei* were not an inferior ethnic group. They had to take care of their families in Japan. Even if they studied, sacrificing their families at home, there was no way for them to find good employment. They did not have suffrage, their English was not good enough, and their fields of employment were limited because of exclusionary practices. They had to take care of their family in Canada, and they somehow built up a base in the face of a vicious anti-Nikkei campaign. You might laugh at my slim advice, but I would like to urge you not to foment unconscious ethnic self-hatred.

Last year when the atomic bomb exhibition was held at a department store in Tokyo, a magazine reported that many young people who saw the photos of the terrible scenes of both Hiroshima and Nagasaki said, "There was notice of bombing from the United States, why didn't people evacuate? They must have been really dumb." These young people laughed without knowing that the atomic bomb was kept strictly a secret and people of the era did not know its power. I do not want similar thoughts repeated among Canada's Nikkei community.

When you criticize, I would like you to investigate, face squarely, and consider the time period, the circumstances, situation, and environment that the *Issei* and some in the *Nisei* were placed in. I would like you to recognize that Nikkei people were rewarded for their struggle and finally reached the dawn of a new era after the war. With this understanding, I would like you to leap forward into various fields with self-awareness and self-respect.

[ … ]

## Part Five

# The Forced Sale of Vancouver Property

In January of 1943, a new order-in-council (469) reversed the federal government's previous commitment to protect and preserve the property of Japanese Canadians. As the first three parts of the memoir make clear, significant losses had already occurred. Nonetheless, the new order-in-council authorized the wholesale disposal of everything that Japanese Canadians had been forced to leave behind when they were uprooted from coastal British Columbia, including their real estate, which had been previously managed by the Custodian of Enemy Property, under the authority of the secretary of state. Shortly after this shift in official policy, Kimura was once again contacted to serve in an administrative capacity, this time of the forced sale of the property of Japanese Canadians in the Vancouver area. This part of the memoir recounts Kimura's difficult decision to join this committee and then its conduct in the forced sale of Vancouver area property.

# The Advisory Committee on Nikkei Properties in Greater Vancouver

## The Course of Events Leading up to the Establishment of the Committee

*13 March 1943:*

In the evening, a telegram came from Colonel C.H. Hill, divisional commander of the RCMP, stating: "Regarding property owned by Nikkei people, the Custodian, as well as Mr. George Collins of the BC Security Commission (where he is a Commissioner of Japanese Placement), wishes to consult with you. Please come to Vancouver as soon as possible."

I thought I would travel to Vancouver in a few days' time. The next day (Sunday), Corporal William Durnin of the Grand Forks RCMP detachment came to visit and prompted me to go to the head office in Vancouver, handing me a travel permit to do so. That same night, I left Cascade for Vancouver.

*15 March:*

I met Col. Hill, who told me that he would report to Mr Collins about me. He prompted me to see Mr W.G. McPherson, executive assistant to the Hon. Mr McLarty, secretary of state. Mr McPherson said he was creating an advisory committee to deal with the liquidation of Nikkei properties and wanted me to represent the Nikkei community.

It was a serious matter, and I had no experience of property evaluation. So I declined the offer and recommended several other people. I should have consulted with those people before recommending them, but I had no time to do so. I recommended four people, all of them Nikkei businessmen, to deal with Vancouver properties and Mr Yasutaro Yamaga to handle rural properties. If he needed more people, I suggested he ask those who had been recommended to put forward other names for consideration. Mr McPherson asked me to stay in Vancouver a few more days while he spoke to Ottawa and investigated candidates before reaching a decision.

Figure M.12 Glenn W. McPherson (right) and his supervisor, Under-Secretary of State Ephraim H. Coleman (centre), were both integral to the operation of the Vancouver Office of the Custodian of Enemy Property (figure on the left: Frank Delaute). Photo courtesy of Rare Books and Special Collections, University of British Columbia Library (Glenn McPherson fonds, Box 4, File-4-03).

Two days later, Mr McPherson told me they had accepted Mr Yamaga to be in charge of rural properties and that he would soon be coming to Vancouver. The government did not accept any other candidates for Vancouver properties, and he wanted me to accept the position. They were going to reappoint Justice Smith as the committee chairman and suggested I consult with him. I wanted to know why none of the candidates I believed to be appropriate were accepted by the government, but I refrained from asking in case that put them in an awkward position.

*18 March:*

Mr Yamaga came to Vancouver from his place of evacuation and expressed his resolve to do the job, stating: "I thought I would devote my life to farming in the Fraser Delta, but it turns out that this will be my final life's work. Fortunately, my friend Mr. Harold Menzies,* a real estate agent who knows the Haney district well, will also be a member. This work shall be my own funeral. You as well, must again, give your best."

I had already shut down the salted salmon business I had devoted myself to since 1920 when I accepted the job of liquidating the Nikkei fishing boats. (On another occasion, I'll disclose why the Nikkei salted salmon business could not be rehabilitated while the salmon fishery could.) When I was burying the Nikkei fishing industry, I was well supported by a few like-minded members of the Liaison Committee. This time around, I didn't feel as comfortable or confident. I knew nothing about property liquidation and had no support staff. I said this to Mr Yamaga and then decided to consult with Justice Smith.

## Advisory Committee on Nikkei Properties, Rural Division

*20 March:*

At ten-thirty in the morning, in the Custodian's office, the first meeting of the Advisory Committee (Rural Division) was held. Mr McPherson recommended I attend the meeting as an observer. The committee consisted of the following people:

Chairman: His Honour, Justice Whiteside of New Westminster
Member: Mr Yasutaro Yamaga, Tashme, BC
Member: Mr D. MacKenzie, New Westminster
Member: Mr J.J. McLellan, Fort Langley
Member: Mr Hal. Menzies, Haney

Besides these, from the Custodian's Office there were Mr McPherson and his deputy Mr Shears, as well as their lawyer, Mr Wright. Mr McPherson made introductions, explained the duties and rights of the committee, and then explained that Mr Shears would consult with the committee from time to time.

* Menzies's first name is Halbert, but Kimura wrote Harold (transliterated) in Japanese.

After that, the chairman said that the meeting would usually be held in the New Westminster courthouse and if not, a notice of assembly would make clear where the meeting place would be. Then the meeting was dissolved.

*19 March:*

I visited Justice Smith, who informed me that he had sent a letter to me in Cascade. In the letter, he said that when he was asked by the secretary of state to form the Advisory Committee under the Custodian, he told them that he would appoint Alderman Charles Jones and me. I said that the Custodian is supposed to protect and manage the property of Nikkei people after they have been relocated. People who wanted to sell or lease their property could request the Custodian to assist them. Also, there should be a few bilingual people in the office. They could certainly deal with these demands and facilitate them more efficiently than Nikkei committee members like myself who had no experience dealing with property.

He persuaded me that this Advisory Committee was different from the Fishing Boat Disposal Committee. This committee would simply give advice after consultations with the Department of Japanese Placement within the Office of the Custodian. We had Mr Jones, who was well versed in finance and city zoning. Furthermore, Justice Smith had informally appointed Mr McMaster … as deputy director. Justice Smith spoke at length on a proposal, from the BC Security Commission and the Custodian that had taken place during cabinet discussions, about Nikkei properties. He persuaded me to accept the appointment, and I said I would try my best.

On returning to the hotel, I found the letter that Mr Smith had sent from Cascade. The authorities checked the mail, and often letters took a long time to arrive. Reading this letter, it became clear why the government had not accepted the people I had recommended to handle Vancouver properties. They had already selected the Nikkei committee member.

*22 March:*

At ten o'clock in the morning, after receiving word, I went to Justice Smith's room at the courthouse. Besides the chairman, committee member Kimura, and deputy director McMaster, Mr McPherson and his deputy, Mr Shears, acting director of the Custodian, were present. Alderman Jones could not attend because of a conflict with city council scheduling. We decided to postpone the meeting until the next day, and we listened to Mr McPherson's explanation, as follows:

### Clarification of Orders-in-Council and an Explanation of the Function of the Custodian

By Order-in-Council PC 1665 of 4 March 1942 and Order-in-Council PC 2483 of 27 March 1942, both issued based on the War Measures Act (chapter 206 of the Revised Statutes of Canada, 1927), property (except fishing boats, bank accounts, bonds, securities, and stock, etc.) owned by all removed Nikkei people was put under the protection of the Custodian. People on the street called this the "Enemy Property Disposition Act," but it is the "Consolidated Regulations Respecting Trading with the Enemy Act" of 1939. This originally applied to enemy products. This regulation would be applied to the protection of property of removed Nikkei people, with necessary modifications.

According to these regulations, the property of Japanese nationals who lived and were not interned* in this country was not necessarily considered to be enemy property. On the other hand, the property of Canadians or naturalized citizens who resided in enemy countries would sometimes be treated as enemy property. The Custodian has already disposed of a few properties, based on a request from removed Nikkei people and, with the cooperation of the BC Security Commission, are sending a hundred dollars a month until the account is exhausted. This policy will be ongoing, with an increase beyond the hundred-dollar limit if necessary.

Later on, to clarify and to make partial changes to the two orders-in-council mentioned above (PC 1665 and 2483), another order-in-council was passed (PC 469 of 19 January 1943). According to this order, the right of entrustment and responsibility of the Custodian consisted of the control and effective governance of property owned by Nikkei people. Therefore, it became clear that the Custodian functions to liquidate, sell, or dispose of by other methods all Nikkei property when the Custodian finds it necessary to fulfill their responsibility.

* Again, Kimura uses the term *yokuryu* (or, more precisely, its negation) to describe these owners. In keeping with his uses earlier in the manuscript, we translate this as "interned." What Kimura means is that they were not incarcerated in prisoner-of-war camps. In this use of "interned" he follows the official convention of the time.

The Custodian had been making an effort to fulfill their mission of protecting the property of Nikkei people left in the area of coastal defence. They observed that under the circumstances, properties could not escape theft or damage and thus concluded to sell them in due course. Please understand that this was not a confiscation of property because we applied the Enemy Property Disposition Act only after adding the necessary modification to it, as mentioned previously.

Points the Custodian wanted to put to the Advisory Committee were as follows:

1. Considering the present circumstances, is it right to sell properties owned by Nikkei people as its primary function?
2. If the answer is yes, please indicate what is considered to be the best way or conditions or terms of selling these properties.
3. What is the best way to evaluate them?
4. Is it in the public interest to dispose of, as soon as possible, property owned by religious groups?
5. Under the circumstances, it was difficult to protect movable assets, and theft and damage of these assets was rampant. The BC Security Commission considered sending assets to removed owners not only inconvenient but unnecessary. Whether this was just or not, these assets were disposed of. (Because the Custodian has no intention to dispose of religious objects or things of sentimental value, the committee doesn't need to advise on this issue.)

## First Meeting of the Committee

*23 March:*

From eleven o'clock in the morning, all of us, including Mr Jones, gathered in Justice Smith's room and had the first meeting of the committee.

Mr McPherson repeated the points he discussed yesterday in the unofficial meeting and informed us that he had to go to eastern Canada immediately. Mr Shears would replace him while he was absent. Therefore, when the committee requires a report or information or the Custodian's opinion, the committee should get in touch with Mr Shears. Also, when the committee came up with recommendations regarding their principal policy, he wanted us to inform him as soon as possible.

We expressed our wish to inspect a selection of properties representative of those owned by Nikkei people before we came up with recommendations.

We asked Mr Shears to facilitate the inspection for us. We proposed to create a list of properties under the protection of the Custodian, and this proposal was accepted as well. After that we discussed the location of the office and decided to rent Room 1012 in the Royal Bank Building at 675 West Hastings St, Vancouver. After that, Mr McPherson and Mr Shears left the room. It was decided that:

1. Mr McMaster would be the deputy director.
2. The committee would be named The Advisory Committee on Japanese Properties in Greater Vancouver and for short, The Advisory Committee.
3. The property would be inspected at two o'clock the next day.

## Inspection of the Properties Owned by Nikkei People

*24 March:*

Judge Smith, Mr Jones, and Mr Kimura, with a guide from the Custodian, went to view stores and rental rooms around Powell Street. These were places already rented out through real estate agents, but they were generally humble and on the level of temporary dwellings. The situation was the same on Cordova Street. It seemed that there were a considerable number of places that required large sums spent on them to comply with city bylaws. It seemed impossible for such a small patrol of people to protect so many properties. Due to the war, the general public turned a blind eye to vandalism of empty houses. Vandals had grown increasingly bold, under the illusion that everyone approved of their conduct. It was easy to see that damages were increasing daily.

The Custodian received a request from the evacuees to send books that were stored in two places. They, being Hakujin, had been unable to read titles and get the requested books. We thought this would be an opportunity to see the properties as well, and all of us went to view them. On the second floor of a store it seemed someone had gained entry through a window. A ruined gramophone and records were strewn across the floor. The Custodian informed the owner, but nothing was stolen. Although it was reported to the police, the vandals have yet to be found. We proceeded to the United Church, where the belongings of believers were stored, and fortunately there had been no vandalism there. We were able to locate the fishing-related books requested.

Along the way, I asked if we could go to my acquaintance's house on Cordova Street. He had asked me to check on some flower vases he'd hidden

Figure M.13 A City of Vancouver inspector checks the beams of a dwelling at 437 Powell Street in 1942 as part of the city's campaign to force the sale of property. Kinu Uchida, listed on the title as the wife of a Japanese-Canadian merchant, had owned the building since 1905. Photograph courtesy of City of Vancouver Archives (CVA), 1184-1544. Jack Lindsay, photographer.

under the floorboards. When we got there, someone had already pried up the boards, and there was nothing there. Because the owner had carelessly used new floor boards, it had been easy for the thief to notice the variance. There was a similar case on Powell Street where the owner had hidden precious items in the ceiling and pasted over the cache with new wallpaper. Apparently, that had attracted the eyes of the thief.

At a store called Maikawa, two sales clerks, a man and a woman, were hired by the Custodians at the request of the owner to sell the remaining stock. They said there were hardly any customers coming to the store and almost all business was mail-order sales from removed Nikkei people. They locked up the store tightly at six o'clock, but they felt uneasy until they opened up the next morning and saw whether or not everything was safe.

## List of Real Estate Owned by Nikkei People

We received a list of real estate placed under the Custodian's jurisdiction, owned by removed Nikkei people.

| | premises, houses, empty stores, others | empty lots | total |
|---|---|---|---|
| A. City of Vancouver, north of False Creek | 193 | 15 | 208 |
| B. City of Vancouver, south of False Creek | 191 | 42 | 233 |
| C. North Vancouver and West Vancouver | 16 | 14 | 30 |
| D. Burnaby | 13 | 14 | 27 |
| Total | 413 | 85 | 498 |

Evaluation for tax purposes

| | premises | buildings | lots (empty) | total |
|---|---|---|---|---|
| A. | $257,847.00 | $481,917.00 | $6,265.00 | $746,029.00 |
| B. | $199,800.00 | $250,010.00 | $8,955.00 | $458,765.00 |
| C. | $9,461.50 | $19,210.00 | $3,965.00 | $32,816.00 |
| D. | $5,421.83 | $12,830.00 | $3,360.00 | $21.611.00 |
| Total | $472,710.33 | $763,967.00 | $22,545.00 | $1,259,222.00 |

The total tax amount for the above properties $45,464.20

There were 379 cases where Nikkei owners appointed real estate agents or lawyers. The Custodians were in the middle of creating cards for each of the 496 cases mentioned above. If we leave the over 400 pieces of real estate scattered over the city, as well as the movable assets stored in them, it is clear that the rate of loss and damage would be far more than under usual circumstances. We all agreed, unofficially, that there was no other way but to sell everything, although we would have to adjust the details. (Religious and educational materials should be exempt.)

*26 March:*

The Custodian requested our help to send a sewing machine from Steveston to some removed Nikkei people. There were Japanese tags attached to it that they couldn't read. They also wanted us to investigate whether or not the machine was in working order. This was outside of our jurisdiction, but we went to Steveston with permission to inspect a few other warehouses as well. The sewing machine was in the former Fishermen's Association building, and because a guard was stationed at the hospital section, there was no damage. However, furniture and boxes kept at the former daycare were all opened, and Japanese carpentry tools and Japanese dolls were strewn about the floor. We could not tell how much had been stolen and which stuff belonged in which box, and it seemed impossible to clean it up properly.

We went to the Buddhist Temple because we'd heard that someone had broken in through a window. It seemed to be simple mischief, and there were about five pots of ashes of the dead with their contents scattered. It was not unusual for Nikkei people to honour the dead collectively, so we told the guard to put the ashes into the large pot.

## Main Policy Decisions

*30 March:*

At eleven in the morning, we all gathered at the room of Justice Smith and decided the following:

1. Under the circumstances and in order to stop losses, we decided, in principle, to sell all property owned by the removed Nikkei people.
2. Regarding the sale of the above properties, there were a few points to be investigated further. Therefore, the sale details will be decided after we see the documents and hear the Custodian's views.
3. The sale of religious and educational properties shall be put off unless there

is a request or permission from the person responsible or a compulsory sale due to debt.

*7 April:*

At ten in the morning we all gathered at the room of Justice Smith. The Custodian requested us to deliberate urgently on three Nikkei properties next to a munitions factory. The sale contract had to be completed as soon as possible. According to city zoning, all three properties were in an industrial area. In the opinion of Mr Jones, "Once the city declares that the present houses are not fit for habitation, only a factory will be allowed to be built. The evaluation for tax purposes is based on a certain rational formula to be fair, but it's not necessarily the same as the market price."

Consequently, the Custodian wanted advice on the following points.

1. The buyer's price.
2. The evaluation of the real estate agent the Custodian is using for the Department of Enemy Property Disposal.
3. After deliberating on these prices, please advise us of a proper price.

We decided to have regular meetings every Wednesday at 10 a.m. in the private room of Justice Smith.

## Items under Deliberation

*14 April:*

At the weekly regular meeting, the Custodian and Mr McMaster, after deliberation, presented the following items to us.

A. The method of real estate sales

1. Advice on whether or not to adopt the tender system.
2. If yes, the method of advertising.
3. Deadline for tender?
4. Sale condition. Cash payment? In case of installment method, how big should down payment be? The terms of payment.
5. How to provide opportunity for prospective purchasers to survey the houses.
6. Listing with real estate agents?
7. How much should agent's commission be?

8. Is it possible to persuade Nikkei people to entrust their certificate of land title to the Custodian?

(Note: There was a note attached to this stating that the Custodian was already selling properties under the Department of Enemy Property Disposal through a tender method. They wish to do the same with the property of relocated Nikkei people.*)

B. Form of the catalogue and other items

1. Is it necessary to create a catalogue for the general public? If yes, in what form?

2. In this catalogue, shall we include properties under the Department of Enemy Property Disposal?

3. Should we create the catalogue according to districts and carry out separate tenders accordingly?

C. How to evaluate the properties

1. Evaluate individual properties?

2. Who shall we ask to evaluate?

3. Who will pay the cost of evaluation?

D. How to deal with existing rental contracts

1. Shall we give priority to renters in place at the time of sale?

2. How to deal with the expired rental contract?

E. How to dispose of the movable assets

1. Shall we employ the tender method? If yes, how to evaluate and decide on a minimum price;

2. Shall we employ the auction method with proceedings open to the general public? How do we allocate the auctioneers?

3. At auction, how to evaluate and decide on a minimum price?

4. How to share the auction costs (including the transportation of assets).

5. In the case of assets being in rental houses, shall we give priority of purchase to the renters?

* The work of the Custodian of Enemy Property was divided into two departments. One was responsible for the sale of property belonging to "enemy" owners – that is, owners in Japan or detained under the Defence of Canada Regulations (a small minority of property-owners). The second was responsible for the property of those formally designated "evacuees," uprooted and interned merely because they were of the "Japanese race." In early 1942, these departments had different policies regarding the sale of property without consent ("enemy" property could be sold, but "evacuee" property would be protected and preserved), but over time officials of the Custodian sought to extend the policy of forced sales to the second category as well. See Stanger-Ross and Landscapes of Injustice Research Collective, "Suspect Properties."

6. How to store religious objects or objects considered having sentimental value.

7. How about setting up a deadline for those who want to have their movable assets sent to them?

(Note: There was a note attached that in some cases the Custodian is renting Nikkei houses to store the movable assets, and in those cases they want to sell the movable assets before liquidating the houses.)

To the above items, we came up with general suggestions, and after discussion with Mr McMaster and Mr Shears, we deliberated further and added modifications.

A.

1. Yes to the tender method.

2. It is all right to advertise everything at the same time but to create separate deadlines in order to avoid market saturation and to maintain prices.

3. The terms the Custodian is using are all right.

4. An instalment method is acceptable, but judgment needs to be used according to individual situations.

5. Because the majority of Nikkei owners appointed agents, we will use them. In the cases where owners did not appoint agents, the Custodian will appoint them.

6. Not necessary.

7. The general standard rate.

8. Encouraging Nikkei people to entrust their certificate of land title to the Custodian will only increase their sense of alarm.

B.

1. Make a catalogue which includes listing headings to register the real estate, such as: the lot number; block; district; name of town; house number; building classification; appointed agent; etc. (However, real estate belonging to religious and educational institutions shall be excluded from the catalogue.)

2. The decision lies in the hands of the Custodian.

3. Yes.

C.

1. Yes.

2. The evaluation should be kept secret until the end of the tender; therefore, the Custodian should use surveyors already employed or, if necessary, make a careful selection from among them.

3. Pending.

D.

1. Impossible.

2. Houses with a completed contract shall be leased until the sale of the house. Those with uncompleted contracts shall be sold with the lease.

E.

1, 2, 3, 4, 5, and 6 are all pending.

7. (Pending.) However, at one time, the BC Security Commission was against sending movable assets to removed Nikkei people because there were no storage spaces, but now their storage facilities have gradually improved and they are capable of storing some movable assets. We would like the Custodian and Security Commission to now allow the sending of some of these movable assets.

*15 April:*

I went home by night train for a break, with permission from Justice Smith. My family had moved to Christina Lake but was still living in a hotel. I settled my family into a cabin at long last, returning to Vancouver early in the morning of 27 April.

## Special Deliberation regarding Lots Next to Munitions Factory

*28 April:*

The regular meeting was held. (The regular meeting of 21 April was postponed.)

The pending subject from 7 April, regarding properties adjoining the munitions factory, was debated. The Custodian provided us with the prices offered by companies wishing to purchase, as well as the price estimates of the realtor, Mr Douglas Reeve (from Johnson, Reeve and Watson). We came up with the following recommended prices.

| | 1 | 2 | 3 |
|---|---|---|---|
| Buyer's price | $1,100.00 | $1,400.00 | $800.00 (full payment) |
| Mr Reeve's estimate | $2,000.00 | $1,500.00 | $1,000.00 (full payment) |
| Our recommendation | $2,000.00 | $1,750.00 | $1,125.00 (full payment) |

THE NEW CANADIAN

An Independent Weekly for Canadians of Japanese Origin

Please be sure to include your former address as well as your new one when reporting a change of address

10¢ per copy | KASLO, B. C. | 40¢ per month | Saturday, April 17, 1943

nd Protest
Organize
vas Funds

...OCAN CITY. — A submission of ...st to Ottawa over the liquidation ...panese evacuee properties in the ...ic defense area was wired by the ...n Japanese Evacuee Property ...ers' Committee this week.

...working committee of two per...s each from the four Slocan ...tres, Lemon Creek, Popoff, Bay ...m and Slocan City was elected ...a meeting of property owner ...gates from these centres on ...il 8. They are Y. Shoji, T. Nam... from Bay Farm; Y. Nakagawa

# Test Case Receiving Support From Evacuees Across Canada

## Suggest Campaign To Raise Funds Definite Plans Nearly Complete Total Cost Likely Near $6500

KASLO, B. C., Apr. 17.—With property-owners in the interior housing projects taking a strong stand, it is expected that plans for the submission of a test case on the property issue before the Supreme Court of British Columbia will be definitely mapped out within a few days.

## Anglicize Japanese Names Oda to MacGregor, Watanabe To Miller In Hawaii

HONOLULU, T. H.—Petitions have been filed by about 2400 persons of Japanese descent in the territory with the governor's office asking permission to anglicize their names.

One reason advanced for the increase in name changes is that the

Figure M.14 The property disposal committee was unnerved by this 17 April 1943 article in *The New Canadian*, which explained the Japanese-Canadian legal challenge to the forced sale of their property, eventually decided in the Exchequer Court. As Kimura somewhat indirectly suggests, Japanese Canadians had received explicit assurance that their property would be preserved and protected in their interest. Image courtesy of the Multicultural History Society of Ontario (MHSO) and Simon Fraser University Library.

After the meeting, we moved into unofficial discussions, and I was asked my opinion of a newspaper article in *The New Canadian*.

When removed Nikkei people entrusted their properties, they understood that it was for the sake of safekeeping. They did not realize that, after their removal, the properties would be transferred to the Custodian by an order-in-council. Therefore, they rather entrusted their properties to lawyers or realtors, and some even neglected to report to the Custodian. Therefore, the Custodian will constantly face opposition to the forced sale of their properties.

From the Custodian's viewpoint, it is reasonable to sell the properties because they cannot protect them sufficiently. Howcvcr, it would be difficult to obtain comprehensive consent of all Nikkei people. If there is any basis for a legal challenge, Nikkei people would take this to the courts. The sooner the outcome of the legal challenge becomes clear, the easier the problem for the Custodian.

When we deliberated the possibility of encouraging Nikkei people to deposit land title certificates, I was allowed to put my opinion in the draft. From the beginning, I had an apprehension that such a legal challenge might occur.

*5 May:*

At our weekly meeting, we had no particular item for deliberation and listened to Mr McMaster's report.

1. Mr Shears held a meeting with representatives of major real estate companies on 3 May, and Mr McMaster participated as an observer.
2. The design of the catalogue is almost completed, and we are now making references to the Custodian's recording system. As soon as that is over, the catalogue will be sent to the printing shop.
3. The real estate card catalogue is also near completion.
4. The map showing housing lot numbers is completed.
5. Mr Shears goes to Winnipeg in two days to meet with Mr McMaster. He is going to write a newspaper ad as soon as he returns to Vancouver.

At two o'clock on the same day, there was a phone call from the Custodian saying they have a piece of registered mail from Kaslo addressed to me, via Christina Lake.

It was a letter from the Assembly of Nikkei Property Owners in Kaslo, advising me to resign. I had expected this would come, after the newspaper article, and reported the news to Justice Smith. We decided to discuss this matter at the coming weekly meeting.

*10 May:*

Mr K.W. Wright, counsel to the Custodian, wanted to meet with me regarding the partial right of possession of Mr Yamazaki, who has been in Japan since 1936.

"There is a property in Marpole under the three-part, joint equal ownership of Mr Kiyomitsu Yamazaki, Mr Jujiro Nishimura and Mr Daishiro Teramura. The unpaid taxes on this property have reached $66.40, by the present date of 1942. Mr Nishimura, with a letter of attorney from Mr Yamazaki, proposed that the Custodian release Mr. Yamazaki's one-third rights to him. Mr Teramura, the third owner, has passed away, and this made things complicated. Furthermore, since the property seemed to be a school, the Custodian supposed that these three people are likely to be trustees, therefore they are reluctant to release the property to Mr Nishimura." He asked me what I thought about the issue.

"I think that Mr. Nishimura is trying to release his ownership because the property will be liquidated as the property of an absentee owner or as part of an inheritance arrangement. I think what the Custodian is supposing is correct, but I shall consult with Mr Tsutae Sato and Mr Sadayoshi Aoki, both of them former principals of the Language School in Marpole, Vancouver, before the war. Please classify this Marpole Language School as a property belonging to an educational institute, and at the same time, take measures to stop the possible sale of the property by the city due to overdue taxes."

*12 May:*

At the regular weekly meeting, after approving the hiring of Mr Durkee as an assistant to Mr McMaster, we discussed the subject of Nikkei people protesting the forced sale of their properties and then referred to the letter advising Mr Kimura to resign. According to some opinions, once the Custodian is judged to have the function of selling properties for the sake of protection, there would be no reason for Mr Kimura to resign. He said, "First of all, I was not elected to be a committee member by Nikkei people, and it now turns out that they are not supporting my work and are, in general, against me. Under this circumstance, I should resign. If the Custodian is judged to have the function of selling properties, Nikkei people can elect a representative if necessary and then obtain government approval." He then requested to be released from the committee. However, the translated letter advising him to resign simply said, "Your continued position as a member, in the general opinion of your fellow countrymen, is considered to be untenable," and no threatening words were employed. Furthermore, the main mission of the committee, as well as the drafting of advertisements, had not been discussed yet. Therefore, it was decided that Justice Smith would hold onto Mr Kimura's letter of resignation for several days.

*19 May:*

Regular weekly meeting

Commercially zoned real estate had high evaluations for tax purposes, and accordingly, municipal taxes were also high. We have been studying how to lower taxes, and so we listened to Mr Jones's explanation.

A. The city tax evaluations are fair to property-owners and generally determined by a set formula with little modification over the years. These are not necessarily the same as the market price. (The market price is influenced by the general economy, the development of new areas, or improvements to roads and other facilities.)

B. Every fiscal year, the city, based on its budget, collects the mill rate of tax evaluation as municipal taxes. (That is to say, the evaluations are almost the same every year, but the mill rate can be changed.)

C. 1. Those who are unhappy with the evaluation can take necessary steps to revise their taxes at the court of revision within a certain time limit.

2. Those who are not satisfied with the result of the deliberation can apply for reconsideration to the board of assessment.

3. If that application is unsuccessful, including the options mentioned above, there can be an appeal to the provincial Supreme Court.

D. The maximum devaluation that can be obtained through the above mentioned three processes (or one of the processes) is determined by the city charter, and that must be within 10 per cent. That is to say, we can get a maximum 10 per cent tax deduction a year. Every property-owner has the right to devalue their property. On the other hand, if other owners do not like the devaluation of surrounding properties, they have the right to oppose and sometimes speak out against the move.

E. Some actions, such as a factory or a shopping arcade being built in the middle of a residential neighbourhood, negatively impact the properties in the larger vicinity. Owners can then collectively appeal to the city's court of equalization. In our case, the issue is simply one of devaluation. If some owners think there is an issue of compensation for the loss, they can appeal to the civil court.

After hearing his explanation, we acknowledged that the difficulty we are facing with properties in commercial and industrial districts lay with today's unusual circumstances; therefore, we decided to seek ways to further reduce taxes before submitting cases to the Custodian.

*20 May:*

I received another resolution, posted on the eighth, from the Association of Nikkei Property Owners in the district of Slocan advising me to resign. I asked Justice Smith to put my resignation on the agenda of the next regular meeting.

*24 May:*

Since it was a holiday, I received an invitation from Mr Charley Moore, our old neighbour before we moved to Christina Lake. I spent a half-day chatting about the good old days and was treated to his stepmother's, Mrs Barkley's, home cooking at lunch and dinner. It felt very nostalgic.

## The Liquidation of a Fraser River Farm

When I returned to my hotel, I saw Mr Yamaga. As soon as he saw me, he said, with a dead serious face, that he had finally decided to submit his resignation. Although he had been expecting challenges, he made up his mind to leave after seeing today's Advisory Committee decision. (It was a holiday.) They decided, by a majority vote and based on the Veterans' Lands Act retroactive to 1 January 1943, to approve the comprehensive, compulsory purchase of all properties along the Fraser River owned by Nikkei people. Consequently, the director of the Veterans' Lands Act would be collecting house rents, farmland rents, and crop fees. Mr Yamaga was bitterly disappointed with the complete lack of clarification regarding the evaluation of individual properties and the arrangement of the crop fee.

I heard that after the First World War, the government, based on an act similar to this one, created land for fruit farms in the southern Okanagan and sold the lots to returning soldiers and then sold the remainder to the general public. Therefore, I supposed that if there was any property remaining, it would be sold to the general public as well. However, this compulsory purchase happened during the war, and I had no idea whether this was happening through the lobbying power of the Veterans' Association or the will of the government.

In the middle of December 1942, soon after the establishment of the Nikkei Fishing Boat Disposal Committee, there was a proposal, through Mr Johnson, asking for special consideration of a few hundred fishermen veterans. I communicated through Mr Johnson that by the order-in-council we were obliged to treat every fisherman equally concerning sale contracts. He was requested to "Please contact and start negotiations as soon as possible with Nikkei owners or members of the Liaison Committee." Nothing much developed from this communication. Perhaps only a limited few were involved in this endeavour.

Figure M.15 Cabinet Minister Ian Mackenzie (right), pictured here with Col. Clyde Scott, was a key architect of the sale of Japanese Canadian–owned farms to the Veterans' Lands Act Administration, which he oversaw. Mackenzie had built his political career in opposition to Asian immigration. Reproduced with the permission of Library and Archives Canada (2016). LAC, HC-8922, 1939.

*26 May:*

Regular weekly meeting

The messages from the Custodian were as follows:

1. As a result of repeated negotiations, based on requests of relocated Nikkei people, eight houses have been sold up until today.

2. There are another seventeen houses which are being advertised for liquidation. Two of them have already sold, and the registration documents were being drawn up. The remaining fifteen houses were in the middle of negotiations.

3. The real estate catalogue was sent to the printing shop today.

Justice Smith said:

> The Order-in-Council PC 469, issued this January 19, 1943, clarified the right of the Custodian to sell the properties of Nikkei people, and there is no room for Nikkei people to stop this through the court of appeals. Also, it is clear to us how difficult it would be to protect over 400 Nikkei properties, including stores, houses, and other buildings. That is why we have approved the sales, to minimize losses. The committee was always trying to minimize Nikkei losses. You have been doing a great job, and your resignation will not improve the situation of Nikkei people. It would be more beneficial for you to postpone your resignation for a couple of weeks, at least, and participate in the drafting of advertising for the Custodian.

Because of this advice, I agreed to postpone my resignation until the next meeting, on 2 June.

*2 June:*

Regular weekly meeting (at the committee office)

The Custodian sought the committee's opinion regarding the following:

1. Is it necessary to increase the number of evaluators? Should we hire those who were recommended by Mr Reeve? (approved)

2. Regarding the advertising of properties, we should divide them equally into three and advertise 150 houses at a time, putting some time between the sale deadlines. (approved)

3. A list of real estate agents and lawyers appointed by Nikkei owners was presented, and a preliminary draft of the advertisement would be presented at the next regular meeting.

Drafting Real Estate Advertising

*9 June:*

Regular weekly meeting

A draft of real estate advertising through the Custodian's tender system was presented, along with two pages of a rough copy of the catalogue.

Following is the abstract of the advertisement.

1. The bidder must use one envelope per real estate bid. If a bidder wants to bid on several pieces of real estate, he must use separate envelopes.
2. When a bidder bids on several pieces of real estate using the alternative tender method, the Custodian will recognize only the real estate listed first and negate the others.
3. A 10 per cent deposit on each bid is required for the Custodian.
4. Every bid shall use an envelope addressed to the Custodian with "Tender for Real Estate – Catalogue Parcel No. …" clearly written on it.
5. The bidding can be done through full payment or on an instalment plan. In the case of an instalment plan, the bidder needs to come up with a minimum down payment of … with the remaining amount paid to … each year for … years.
6. The people with tenders shall calculate a necessary adjustment (for example, of taxes and rent) on the transfer document's date in the case of full payment and in the case of an instalment payment, on the date of the sale contract.
7. Real estate with a lease contract or encumbrance shall be a collateral condition.
8. Before handing over the transfer document, in the case of full payment, and the sale contract, in the case of an instalment payment, the Custodian reserves the right to cancel approval of tender and return the deposit.
9. The Custodian is not responsible for matters such as the location of the real estate, the condition of the structures, or the degree of improvements.
10. The deposits of unsuccessful tender applicants shall be returned to them.
11. The highest bid or any other bids are not necessarily accepted.

12. The bidding on properties in group A of the catalogue will be accepted by noon on July … 1943. The deadline for other groups shall be announced later. (Regarding real estate transferred to the Custodian to be sold, see the catalogue in the real estate agency offices in the city, and obtain the necessary information and suggestions.)

The Custodian sought the opinions of the committee regarding the following issues related to the above.

### Consultation regarding Sale Advertisements

1. The minimum amount of down payment and the maximum period of payment for the instalment plan.
2. Newspapers to place the advertisements in.
3. Number of times the advertisement will run.
4. The date the first advertisement will run and if it is necessary to post more than once.
5. The Custodian is thinking of setting the bidding deadline about 30 days after the posting of the advertisement. What do you think about this?
6. The Custodian thinks it desirable that the evaluator keep the evaluation a secret until the deadline. What do you think?
7. All the bidding shall be kept sealed until the deadline, to be opened in the presence of the Advisory Committee. What do you think?
8. As stated in the advertisement, on the envelope it shall be clearly written "Tender for Real Estate Catalogue Number … " but if the envelope is opened by accident because of the lack of this notation, we think it shall be returned to tender. What do you think?

After deliberation, the committee responded to the Custodian as follows.

1. In principle, the minimum down payment shall be 30 per cent, with the period of settlement within three years. However, depending on the state of the property, if it is necessary to increase the down payment and to shorten the period of settlement, an appropriate measure shall be taken accordingly.
2. Items 3 and 4 are within the discretion of the Custodian.
5. Approved.
6. Yes.
7. Approved.
8. Yes.

## Approval of Resignation

After that, Justice Smith accepted Mr Kimura's resignation and promised to send the telegram to the secretary of state.

(In the evening, Justice Smith invited Mr Kimura, Mr Jones, and Mr McMaster for dinner, and Mr Kimura went home by night train.)

## Part Six

# Recollections

In this part of the memoir, Kimura reflects more broadly on the history of racism in British Columbia and places the wartime policies within this larger frame. He urges readers to understand these recollections as a necessary context rather than an airing of grievances: "If readers think I am stirring up racial hatred, that would be the complete opposite of my intention." Here Kimura exonerates Prime Minister Mackenzie King for his decision to uproot and intern Japanese Canadians ("He must have been afraid that now, under wartime circumstances, someone might actually harm Nikkei people, and if such awful things were to happen, the Japanese military might take revenge on interned Canadian soldiers. I think that the prime minister, after deep deliberation, concluded to send all Nikkei people to a safe place as soon as possible") but continues to sharply criticize "anti-Nikkei propaganda" both before and during the war.

# Recollections

## Various Anti-Nikkei Campaigns

Ever since the Japanese arrived in BC, they have had to endure persistent anti-Nikkei campaigns. Aside from the olden days, in March 1938 a member of Parliament, who always took up absurd rumours and used them as material for anti-Nikkei campaigns, made a proposition to Parliament that they cancel as meaningless an existing gentleman's agreement with Japan. He said that the number of illegal Japanese immigrants exceeded the number of allocated immigrants.

In Vancouver City Council, despite the confirmation of legal advisers that this was an obvious abuse of power, a councillor came up with a proposal to "refuse the application of business licences from Toyojin." As well, there was a demand to create a law to "restrict the activities of Japanese merchants to within a Japanese clientele." Around the same time, city council took up the propaganda statement, "The majority of cod-fishing union members were Nikkei people, and they were trying to raise the price unilaterally." Council created a marketing committee, which held "public hearings" about the price of cod for a considerable length of time. Although the committee had invited many witnesses and spent large sums of money, the result was "nothing." It looked bad to bury this investigative report, so the committee, to save face, submitted it to the Ministry of Fisheries as a reference at the end of October. The ministry pointed out that four main judgments (discoveries) written in the report were lacking in reliability.

To restrict Toyojin's business licences, it was necessary to change the city charter. However, city council could not resist their unreasonable aldermen, and a draft of the amendment was tabled in the provincial Parliament in the middle of November. Part of their reasoning was that the ratio of licences issued to Vancouver Toyojin in 1937 was as follows:

| | |
|---|---|
| Boat-builders | 28.57% |
| Cleaners and dye factories | 53.47% |
| Dressmakers | 53.01% |
| Fish shops | 44.44% |
| Vegetable shops | 91.44% |
| Food stores | 19.82% |
| Laundry clerical workers | 89.58% |
| Laundries | 64.28% |
| Chicken meat and egg shops | 38.09% |
| Sewing shops | 29.59% |
| Peddlers | 55.32% |

The increase of licences issued to Japanese workers for the ten years between 1927 and 1937 was 74 per cent. For Chinese workers, there was a 34.7 per cent increase. I supposed that what they wanted to say was that they were an economic threat. (However, the most important statistical numbers, such as amount of production, volume of business, and number of employees, etc., were not there. Of course, they did not refer to the trades Toyojin were not engaged in or the occupations Toyojin were banned from.) Some members in the Private Bill Committee were sympathetic toward city council, but because it was clearly an illegal abuse of power, they could not possibly agree to the draft and refused the amendment on 23 November.

Seemingly plausible rumours were spread that Nikkei fishermen had special maps, much more detailed than those of Hakujin fishermen, or that Japanese Navy spies disguised as fishermen were snooping along the coast.

For Nikkei gill-net fishermen, things had been peaceful since 1929, but suddenly in April the boat-puller's licences (the so-called "partner's licences"), which were related to their fishing operations, were reduced by 40 per cent. (Since then, licence reductions continued yearly, with the licence completely abolished by 1941.)

The proposal to cancel the gentleman's agreement with Japan mentioned earlier was voted down in Parliament. The government, to prevent resubmission of the draft, appointed a board of review for illegal immigrants on 14 March. The meetings were held in strict secrecy in various locations in BC, with testimonies and names coming by mail. (In Vancouver, the meeting was held on 24 March 1938 in the Immigration Hall.) The chairman was Dr Hugh

L. Keenleyside from the Department of External Affairs. The members were Mr F.W. Taylor, district superintendent of immigration, and Inspector G.W. Fish from the RCMP.

At the same time, responding to a question in Parliament, the government announced that for eight years, from 1930 to 1937, they had sent back the following number of people to Japan as illegal immigrants.

| | |
|---|---|
| 1930 | 4 people |
| 1931 | 7 people |
| 1932 | 59 people |
| 1933 | 26 people |
| 1934 | 17 people |
| 1935 | 10 people |
| 1936 | 13 people |
| 1937 | 9 people |

In late December, a *Nisei* pioneer expressed his opinion that Nikkei people were congregated only along the west coast and somehow that put us in a disadvantaged position. He thought it desirable that we spread ourselves across Canada. Some of those who were professional anti-Nikkei campaigners abused this remark and started the propaganda, "See, the Japanese are planning to take over the entire economy of Canada."

## Board of Review Report on Illegal Entry

In the middle of January 1939, the board of review on illegal immigrants presented in its report to Parliament that the number of people who testified or reported illegal entry was unexpectedly small.

The following was an example of investigative results from about 100 Nikkei people.

| | |
|---|---|
| Voluntary return | 6 people |
| Sent home | 23 people |
| Residential permit | 4 people |
| Legal entry | 36 people |
| False report | 10 people |
| Residence unknown | 21 people |
| Total | 100 people |

Besides this report, the results of an investigation by the Department of Immigration and the RCMP were included. According to this result, before

1932 there were about 3,000 illegal entries in total. Among them, about 1,500 cases were related to interpreters at the immigration office, and the other 1,500 were reported by other sources, including people who had run away from their boats. The breakdown was as follows.

| | |
|---|---|
| Sent home | 161 people |
| Residential permits | 47 people |
| Voluntarily returned to Japan, afraid of arrest | 2,300 people |
| Residence unknown | 400 people |
| Total | 3,000 people |

There were very few illegal entries after 1932, and the report concluded that the number of illegal entries were miniscule. There was no evidence of the mass illegal entries they were being accused of. Even though the results of various investigations proved them innocent, persistent anti-Nikkei propaganda continued.

*28 February:*

A member of the BC Parliament submitted a written query: "There is a rumour that under the supervision of the Japanese Navy, installations for hidden oil tanks are being dug somewhere in the Queen Charlotte Islands. I wonder if the government has investigated this rumour or not, if so, I ask the government to announce the result." (This question was a friendly one, intended to stop the spread of irresponsible rumours.) Of course, the rumour was a false one, misinterpreting a trial mining dig. After that, there were people who spread the false rumour of a massive illegal entry operation based in the Queen Charlotte Islands.

A newspaper reported in late April that an alderman, who would be a candidate in the next election for the provincial Parliament, insisted on stopping Nikkei people from penetrating the fishing industry and again took up the issue of business licences with the city as if it were a huge problem. He came up with a set of unbelievable licence ratios and insisted that his intention was to maintain a high standard of living for Hakujin citizens, not to persecute Toyojin based on racial prejudice.

In early August, an alderman proposed that the city council attach covenants at the time of sales to properties the city owns (including residential lots) to stop them falling into the hands of Toyojin. By creating this covenant, regardless of whether it would be a civic trade or an auction, the covenant shall be inherited as a condition of the sale. By doing so, we would narrow the scope of the sales but protect them forever by making it impossible for Toyojin to own or rent them.

During deliberation, the legality of the eternal binding condition was questioned, and it was transferred to the Department of Law. It never surfaced again. Perhaps they realized that it could not be done. A week later, another alderman proposed that the council reject all new applications for commercial licences from Toyojin. Newspapers reported that the alderman had gone too far.

"If we make it clear to Toyojin that they have no opportunity to engage in commercial activities in our city, they will go home. I don't care whether the refusal of the licences is against international law or human morality. The duty of city council is first of all to serve the future welfare of the citizens."

This sort of proposal will never pass in council, but I suppose it was appealing to some segment of the population.

In the fall, by the order of Hon. George S. Pearson, commissioner of fisheries, the production of salted salmon was banned. Thus, salted salmon produced in Canada and exported every year to Japan disappeared. Chum salmon used to be used for the salted salmon, and now it was used for canning in order to increase food production. In a case like this, usually some kind of compensation was provided to the producers, exporters, as well as workers related to the industry. However, it seemed no such consideration was made in this case. The commissioner of fisheries also ordered the hiring, in the salt-cod factories, of more Hakujin or Dojin workers to render the number of Nikkei workers less than half. Thus, employment opportunities for Nikkei people were getting ever narrower.

According to a newspaper report, the November issue of *Liberty* magazine praised the State of California for noticing the yellow peril at an early stage and taking appropriate measures against it. In BC as well, many said that unless we considered excluding Toyojin from each industry, in three or four generations time it would be a Nikkei province. If we didn't solve it now, the solution would be more and more difficult. Therefore, even with the expense of it, somehow we must find ways to deport and get rid of them altogether in a few years. Let them prosper in their ancestral land. That is the only way to stop future disasters.

I don't think it is enough for some people to simply write in the abstract "persistent anti-Nikkei propaganda continued," so I have written some of the concrete examples so far. If readers think I am stirring up racial hatred, that would be the complete opposite of my intention. To avoid this sort of misunderstanding, I will simplify hereafter.

Both in 1940 and 1941, similar kinds of anti-Nikkei propaganda continued. Of course, there were considerable numbers of people who rightly argued to give proper rights to Nikkei people. However, news media preferred to report sensational material, appealing to the mood of the times. These moral people could not correct the distorted view of many in the general public.

## National Registration: Report of Dr Carrothers, etc.

In 1940, from 19 to 21 August, national citizenship registration of those over 16 years of age was held. All Nikkei people participated and registered themselves. This registration was about people over 16 years old and does not reflect the total population of Nikkei. However, in February 1937, Dr Carrothers investigated the issue of the Toyojin population for the Rowell–Sirois Commission, and according to this report the Nikkei population was as follows:

| | |
|---|---|
| 1936 | 25,886 people |
| 1937 | 26,288 people |

(Note: 1931 – 23,342, 1941 – 23,194, 1951 – 21,663)

And he added:

1. The numbers above were calculated on the basis of Provincial Statistic Bureau of BC information that the total population of Nikkei was 22,205 in 1931.
2. Recent immigration from Japan is miniscule, but the majority of immigrants are wives, so the birth rate is rising.
3. If we estimate the total population of Nikkei at the end of this century with the present rate of increase, it would reach 180,000. However, in reality it won't be that high because the birth rate will gradually decrease and on the other hand the death rate will increase.

(Note: If we take a look every ten years at the Canadian census, it is obvious how sloppy Dr Carrothers's assumptions are.)

The population of Chinese Canadians

1. On the basis of a 1931 population of 27,139, we estimated that they would reach 21,740 people by 1936.
2. In recent years, the entry of Chinese women was banned, and some old Chinese either went home or died from old age. Therefore, the rate of decrease in Chinese population was 25 per cent annually.

# Conservative Leader Says Japs Given Priority For Herring Licenses

VICTORIA, Nov. 1.—Twice during the course of his lengthy debate in the Legislature on Thursday, R. L. Maitland, K.C., leader of the official Opposition, touched upon the Japanese situation in this province.

In regard to Japanese within the province, Mr. Maitland stressed the duty of the government to see that this province was kept British "in ideals, in loyalty and in constitution.

"I feel that the time has come when we must insist," he said, "that no industries in this province be dominated by any foreign race.

"The fact that an organization of our own people should, when applying for a license to reduce herring, be made subject to Japanese requirements first, is something against which I protest with all the strength I have."

Hon. George H. Pearson, as commissioner of fisheries, rose to deny that any white company had ever had to await requirements of Japanese fishermen. Mr. Maitland insisted they had. The incident had happened at Steveston "two or three years ago," he said.

Later Mr. Maitland referred in slightly critical vein to Hon. W. J. Asselstine's attitude when copper shipments to Japan were very much before the public eye. The minister had given eight reasons, he said, to show that it was good business to continue the shipments.

"I say that there is no such thing as good business shipping any material useful in war to Japan at this time.

"It is the closest thing to suicide that I can conceive of."

Figure M.16 As Kimura indicated, racist rhetoric suffused public discussion in the late 1930s and early 1940s in British Columbia. In this 1 November 1940 *Vancouver News-Herald* report on provincial parliamentary debate, both sides posited white supremacy as a principle of fishing licensing. Courtesy of the BC Archives.

3.The Chinese population would be zero in fifteen years if we calculate it based on the above decreasing rate. However, in reality, the birth rate would gradually increase, preventing such a scenario.

In April of 1938, the Canada Japanese Association investigated the size of their population alongside their occupations. They announced the results as follows:

| | |
|---|---|
| Canadian-born | 13,143 |
| Naturalized citizens | 2,316 |
| Japanese nationality | 7,381 |
| Total | 22,840 |

There were some who investigated which result was more credible. Some thought the calculations of Dr Carrothers, based on the 1931 Bureau of Statistics records, might lack the number of Nikkei people who went home. However, around the time of the above-mentioned national registration, those who were enthusiastic in spreading anti-Nikkei propaganda quoted those two differing results. They condemned the results of the Canada Japanese Association as sloppy and those of Dr Carrothers as not credible and maintained that there were 30,000 Nikkei people, including illegal immigrants.

They claimed that Nikkei people educate their children differently in their language schools; therefore, they were not trustworthy.

"Don't enlist them in the military."

"Don't give them the honour of participating in military training."

"Watch out for their acts of spying."

"Check illegal immigrants, and send them home."

There was a great deal of noisy propaganda being spread.

## Standing Committee for Special Registration of Nikkei People

The government, with the intention of stopping the negative propaganda, promised in early November to hold a special registration in the near future. Members of the standing committee were appointed to oversee registration as follows:

| | |
|---|---|
| Chairman | F.J. Hume, mayor of New Westminster |
| Member | H.F. Angus, UBC professor |
| Member | F.J. Mead, assistant commissioner, RCMP |
| Member | M.F. Macintosh, Lieutenant General, MLA, BC |
| Member | A.W. Sparling, DSD, GSD, Military Dist. No. 11 |

(Special Note: On 19 February 1941, twelve Nikkei people were appointed by the government to the Standing Committee for Special Registration of Nikkei people.)

Prime Minister Mackenzie King issued a very careful statement.

## The Statement of Prime Minister Mackenzie King

In order to protect Nikkei people who are being unfairly treated, and at the same time to remove illegal Japanese immigrants if they exist in Canada, the government has decided to hold a special registration of Nikkei people. After consulting with Nikkei community leaders, a standing committee has been appointed to supervise this registration.

At the national registration held last August, the question "Whether this was a legal entry or not" was not included. This time we ask this question clearly and will issue certification cards which will verify the status of those who entered the country legally and those who were born in Canada. We hope that by doing this we will eliminate any suspicions for good. At the same time, the government will take measures to protect law-abiding Toyojin and their property from those who act selfishly, illegally, and are influenced by rumours and irresponsible opinions.

Under the current circumstances, we cannot say there is no possibility of undue incidents, and the government will put off for now the conscription of Toyojin into the military. We ask them to contribute to the country through other venues.

To deal with the issue of Toyojin creating turmoil in BC, we appointed the following people to be members of a special committee and had them review and analyze the issues. We have received a report from the following:

Lieutenant Colonel A.W. Sparling, DSD (Convener)

Dr. Hugh L. Keenleyside, Counselor, Dept. of External Affairs

F.J. Mead, Assistant Commissioner, RCMP

Sir George Sanson, Ex Commercial Counselor, British Embassy, Tokyo

There is a rumour in the street that in recent years many Toyojin are entering Canada illegally, but that is simply not true. We have received reports that whether they are immigrants or born in this country, the great majority of Toyojin citizens are completely loyal to Canada. The government shares this view. *The important issues concerning the Toyojin in the province of BC are based on wrong information, which unjustly attacks the loyalty and rectitude of Toyojin.* It is

> harmful to the public peace to have attacks, such as those of a few weeks ago, arousing public opinion. The government is satisfied that military and judiciary authorities are well prepared to deal with any possible disturbance. Therefore, the general public should understand that the government has made sufficient arrangements to deal with any situation.

Despite Prime Minister King's announcement, anti-Nikkei propaganda continued to be rampant in Vancouver.

At the end of January, because someone in city council persistently attacked Japanese language education, there was a meeting of enquiry to study educational policy and school conditions. Representing Japanese language schools, Principal Mr Sato, Chief Officer Mr Ishihara, and others attended the meeting. Some Nikkei representatives from the community also attended as observers. I heard that their answers and explanations were received favourably. (Note: The chairman of this meeting was Alderman Jones, who was appointed to be a member of the Advisory Committee on Japanese Properties.)

## Special Registration of Nikkei People

From 4 March 1941, a special registration was held under the supervision of the RCMP, first in Vancouver, then spreading to other places. After an investigation, white cards for Canadian-born Nikkei people, salmon-pink cards for naturalized Nikkei people, and yellow cards for those of Japanese nationality were given as certification.

The cards were carefully elaborated. On the front there was a photo of the cardholder, the date of registration, nationality, the seal of the RCMP, as well as the signature of the registration officer. On the back was the registration number, name, sex, occupation, age, height, weight, distinguishing characteristics, fingerprint, and signature of the cardholder. The polite, straightforward attitude of the staff made a very good impression on Nikkei people, especially the way they carefully wiped off ink after fingerprinting.

(Note: At this registration, they investigated family matters. Later on, I heard that the population of Nikkei stood at 23,427. This was the number reported to the government by the Special Registration Standing Committee.)

## The Outbreak of the Pacific War and the Removal of All Nikkei People

On 7 December, the Pacific War suddenly broke out. Fishing boats owned by Nikkei people, which had always been the target of anti-Nikkei propaganda, were impounded under the Naval Order of Impoundment in a relatively short period of time. Boat-owners cooperated, and crews went home safely through an arrangement with the RCMP. Later, a curfew was imposed on Nikkei people, and they could not go out after sunset. Their cars, hunting rifles, radios, cameras, and so on were temporarily confiscated by the police.

Anti-Nikkei agitators must have thought that this was a great opportunity to lift up nationalistic spirits. They drummed up the fighting spirit of the military, escalated anti-Nikkei propaganda, and intensified anti-Nikkei sentiment among the general public.

On the 25th, the British territory of Hong Kong fell. Before this fall, Canada had sent reinforcements where defence was generally considered to be militarily impossible. All survivors were captured as Japanese prisoners of war and sent to prison camps. I wonder what went through the mind of Prime Minister King seeing the parallel of Nikkei people in Canada and Canadian soldiers in Japanese camps.

Back in 1907, in spite of it being peacetime, a mob agitated by anti-Nikkei propaganda attacked and damaged Japan Town. The present prime minister, Mackenzie King, deputy minister of labour at the time, had a bitter experience investigating into the real circumstance of this riot. He must have been afraid that now, under wartime circumstances, someone might actually harm Nikkei people and if such awful things were to happen, the Japanese military might take revenge on Canadian soldiers. I think that the prime minister, after deep deliberation, concluded to send all Nikkei people to a safe place as soon as possible.

Due to the many years of anti-Nikkei propaganda, the general public everywhere was hesitant about receiving Nikkei people. (For the sake of simplification, I have not so far referred to this incident, but in July of 1939, someone politically important in Ontario called for the extradition of Nikkei people. Nowadays, Nikkei people can live safely anywhere, but in the beginning, when Nikkei people started spreading to the prairies and eastern

Canada, most places accepted them only temporarily to supplement the shortage of labour on condition of them returning to BC after the war.)

Except for a few cases, most Nikkei people accepted the Order for Removal of Nikkei people by the government, followed the instructions of the BC Security Commission, and gradually moved. On 31 October 1942, evacuation from the coast was completed. What warmed my heart during this move was the demonstration of mutual help among Nikkei people, who endured hardships in the places they were sent to. I was also deeply moved by the sincere efforts of young people.

Thus, most Nikkei people safely moved to the interior of BC, with a considerable number of families being sent to southern Alberta. Some Nikkei men who were sent to a road construction camp in the beginning somehow found a way to reunite with their families in their places of evacuation. Government staff in charge of the removal felt it was a job well done, but as a consequence of the removals, a lot of Nikkei properties were left in the hands of the Custodian.

Anti-Nikkei agitators took this opportunity to proclaim, maliciously, that all property belonging to Nikkei people should be disposed of to prevent their return to the west coast. They also said that they should all be sent back to Japan after the war whether they liked it or not and regardless of whether they were naturalized or Canadian-born. With these campaigns, Nikkei properties, on top of the damages incurred from being vacant, were suffering from theft and break-ins. The Custodian, in an effort to stop the increasing damages, concluded that there was no other choice but to liquidate them, an opinion he shared with the government.

The government, which had made every effort to ensure the safety of Nikkei people, now faced the issue of their properties. They debated the Custodian's proposal in a special cabinet meeting and decided to allow the liquidation due to the lack of an alternative. To minimize criticism toward liquidation sales by the Custodian, the government set up the Advisory Committee as an independent organization. That is the background to the events I covered in this article.

## The Condition of Nikkei Properties in an Area Heavily Populated by Nikkei People

According to the zoning bylaws, the areas where the properties of Nikkei people were tightly packed were as follows: (I think these zonings remain the same.)

1. In Alexander Street, the eastern half of the 100 numbers and the western half of the 200 numbers were commercially zoned. East of this was industrial zoning.
2. Powell Street was the same as Alexander Street.
3. East Cordova Street, the 100 numbers and the western half, the 200 numbers, were commercially zoned. East of them was industrial zoning.
4. In Hastings Street, numbers up to 300 were commercially zoned. To the east was industrially zoned.
5. The Fairview area was all industrially zoned.

Therefore, when someone demolished an existing building and tried to build a new one, he had to build conforming to the zoning or ask for an exemption of the zoning from the city. This was cumbersome. Or again, if we tried to sell a lot for a factory, under the circumstances when construction rates were down, that was not easy either. Among the old buildings, there were many that required repairs to conform under the Fire Prevention Act. In addition, buildings with rental contracts were shabby and appeared to be only temporary lodging quarters. To make things worse, under the circumstance of rampant anti-Nikkei propaganda trying to stop the return of Nikkei people, prices of the properties kept dropping. It was a very pessimistic state of affairs.

## Comment

As I mentioned previously, I resigned from the Advisory Committee position on 9 June, so I did not know the sale price of individual properties. It is not difficult to imagine that prices were generally far below what most Nikkei people had expected. That is to say, the underpinnings of their lives that they had worked so hard for, over long years, were to a great extent destroyed.

Concern about physical assaults was mitigated by virtue of the removal into camps. Losses from quick voluntary liquidations that didn't go through the Custodian seemed to amount to a considerable sum. Furthermore, they endured emotional pain and hardships in the places they were moved to.

There were very sad cases where mental worry and the result of enforced travel hastened death. There were cases of unexpected sudden death.

I would say that these miseries were the result of the war and the persistent campaign of anti-Nikkei agitators.

I heard from an elderly man that Mr Tomekichi Homma's* appeal to obtain the right to vote was not successful because of the constitutional Natal Act.† (Those who are not listed on the provincial voting lists do not have suffrage with the federal government of Canada.)

In May of 1936, four representatives of the Nikkei second generation, with a petition to present to the Parliamentary Election Committee, went to Ottawa to ask for change to the 1934 Election Act that would give voting rights to Nikkei people. They seemed to get a very sympathetic response and laid the foundation for voting rights, but that goal still lay in the distance.

As people actually encountered Nikkei people who had moved and spread all over Canada, they soon realized that past discrimination was unjust. They gradually came to know the true value of Nikkei people. The accumulated anti-Nikkei sentiment evaporated, and people became open and warm. The designation of BC's west coast as a defence region was abolished, and distorted public opinions were replaced by more generous ones. In the end, the BC provincial government gave voting rights to Canadian-born and naturalized Nikkei people.

The Canadian federal government followed suit, and consequently, it became possible for Nikkei people to engage in professions it was not possible until then to consider because of lack of voting rights. Nikkei people endured many sacrifices, but now paths for success have opened up in various fields.

* On 19 October 1900, Tomekichi Homma applied to Thomas Cunningham, the collector of voters for Vancouver, to have his name registered in his electoral district. Cunningham refused, based upon the 1895 amendment to the Provincial Voters Act that stated that "no Chinaman, Japanese, or Indian shall have his name placed on the Register of Voters for any Electoral District." Homma's ensuing legal challenge was part of a large, co-ordinated effort by naturalized Japanese immigrants in British Columbia to challenge the Provincial Voters Act. Although Homma won in the British Columbia courts, the BC government appealed to the British Privy Council. The Privy Council found that "[n]aturalized citizens of Asian descent ... were barred from voting not just in provincial elections but also in federal elections" and they "were also not allowed to hold public office or to serve on juries." Price, "Canada, White Supremacy, and the Twinning of Empires," 630; Geiger-Adams, "Writing Barriers into Law," 21, 31.

† In this context, Natal Act refers to the British Columbia immigration bills and acts of the late nineteenth and early twentieth centuries. The original Natal Act in South Africa was modelled on American Jim Crow legislation in Mississippi. The British Columbia Natal Act referenced here restricted voting rights, thereby barring people of Asian descent from voting in provincial and, therefore, federal elections. Price, "Canada, White Supremacy, and the Twinning of Empire," 632.

# Part Seven

# Property-Owners in Protest

At the end of his memoir, Kimura includes two telegrams urging his resignation from the Advisory Committee on Japanese Properties in the Greater Vancouver Area. Kimura brought these telegrams to the attention of the committee and sought to resign at the time, although he did not do so until the end of May 1943.

# Letters Advising Resignation from the Advisory Committee on Japanese Properties

In regard to the liquidation of properties and assets owned by Japanese, it is hereby recognized that your appointment in the Committee runs counter to the general public opinion of your fellow countrymen in Canada. We advise you to resign from the post as soon as possible.

April 26, 1943
To Mr. Kishizo Kimura
From the Assembly for Protecting Properties Owned by Japanese in Kaslo

(Envelope)
Examined By Censor
Japanese Property Owners' Association
Mr. K. Kimura
Forward to:
#1012 Royal Bank Building
Office of the Custodian
Vancouver, BC
Received May 5, 1943

Mr. Kishizo Kimura
Dear Sir,
I inform you that we had the following resolution at the General Assembly of Removed Japanese Property Owners in the Slocan District:
**Resolution**
Regarding the liquidation of the properties and assets owned by Japanese people, we consider that your acceptance of the Committee position runs counter to the general opinion of your fellow countrymen in Canada and we advise you to resign from the post as soon as possible.
The above resolution was adopted.

April 24, 1943
General Assembly of Removed Japanese Property Owners in the Slocan District
Mr. Kinosita

(Envelope)
Examined By Censor
Mr. Kishizo Kimura
c/o Patricia Hotel
Vancouver, BC
Received May 20, 1943

# *Commentaries*

Figure 1.1 Eiko Shinde (right), my mother, with a friend in Steveston, BC, 1930s. Here she posed in a fur-collar coat, one of the personal luxuries that she was forced to leave behind when she and her young family were uprooted and interned. From the private collection of Masako Fukawa.

I

# A Difficult Past: *Kodomono tame ni* – For the Sake of the Children

*Masako Fukawa*

"Why didn't you tell us? Why didn't you do something?" I was a twenty-year-old university student when I came across "They're Only Japs," Pierre Berton's article on the mass exodus of Japanese Canadians from British Columbia in *Maclean's* magazine.[1] Confused and dismayed, I confronted my parents when I returned home: "Why didn't you tell us?" My mother's response was: "We didn't want the children growing up bitter about things over which they had no control. *Shikataga nai*. It can't be helped." I turned to my father and asked, quite indignantly, "Why didn't you do something?" My father responded: "I did. I went on my boat and told the sailor, 'I'm Canadian. I'm taking my boat out.' He pointed his rifle and put the barrel on my chest." At that instant, my mother got up from the table, went to the adjoining room, and brought out a photo of a boy and a girl sitting on an upholstered bench in a photography studio. She pointed to my six-month-old brother and me at eighteen months and asked: "What good would it have done to have your father carted off to jail? We had you two to consider and your grandparents." I heard in their voices their sense of helplessness and hopelessness.[2]

My interest in the dispersal, dispossession, and deportation of Japanese Canadians is personal. I have been trying to uncover and to understand what my parents' generation wanted to forget. In my journey to discovery, I have developed educational resources for use in museums and public schools and have written about Japanese Canadians in the British Columbia fishing industry. I have interviewed Japanese Canadians who experienced the internment, the dispossession, and in particular the confiscation and disposal of their fishing vessels. Kishizo Kimura's memoir has reminded me that there are many voices and many stories in the Nikkei community and has led me to examine the impact of these events on my own family and that of my husband, who were farmers. Although they took place more than seventy years ago, and despite the fact that more than a quarter-century has passed since redress, there still lingers a great sense of sadness and incredulity that these events took place in Canada, a democratic country.

My maternal grandfather was an *Issei* (first-generation Japanese immigrant). He was born in 1885 in Mio-mura, Wakayama-ken, and immigrated to Canada in response to a call from his elder brother to join him in Steveston at the mouth of the Fraser River in British Columbia. He arrived in 1904 and worked as a "puller," or apprentice fisher. After fulfilling the three-year residency requirement, he applied for a certificate of naturalization, which he was granted in 1908. It declared my grandfather "a British subject entitled to all political and other rights, powers and privileges … [and] subject to all obligations … [of] a natural-born British subject … within Canada."[3] As a naturalized British subject, he was eligible for a fishing licence and was granted one each year until 1941 when it was suspended. On 7 December 1941, Japan bombed Pearl Harbor on the island of Hawaii in the United States. In response, Canada declared war on Japan. Under the War Measures Act, already in effect in Canada at this time, the federal cabinet had authority to carry out whatever acts it deemed necessary on the domestic front. My grandfather, along with all others of the "Japanese race," was treated as an "enemy alien." He had been living in Canada for thirty-eight years, thirty-five of them as a naturalized Canadian citizen.

Japanese-Canadian fishers became the first targets of the government's wrath. Within forty-eight hours of war with Japan, my grandfather's fishing licence was voided, and his cod boat was immobilized. He was ordered to take his boat (which was tied up in Steveston at the mouth of the Fraser River) upriver to the Annieville Dyke, where it was impounded with hundreds of other boats owned by Japanese-Canadian fishers. His boat, *Y.I.*, with a gas engine, was valued at $700, but British Columbia Packers Ltd bought it for just $443 in June 1942 while my grandfather was languishing in Greenwood, an internment camp in the interior of BC. With the loss of his boat, his livelihood was gone, and his financial investment was in ruins. The emotional cost to him cannot be quantified in dollars and cents. His boat was more than a piece of property. It was his companion, his refuge in stormy weather, his pride and joy, and a symbol of his success. A fellow fisher described the loss as "being cut off at the root. All those years of work – just gone."[4]

Kimura himself was not a fisher, but he had been working in the fishing industry since the 1920s and his memoir demonstrates that he was aware of

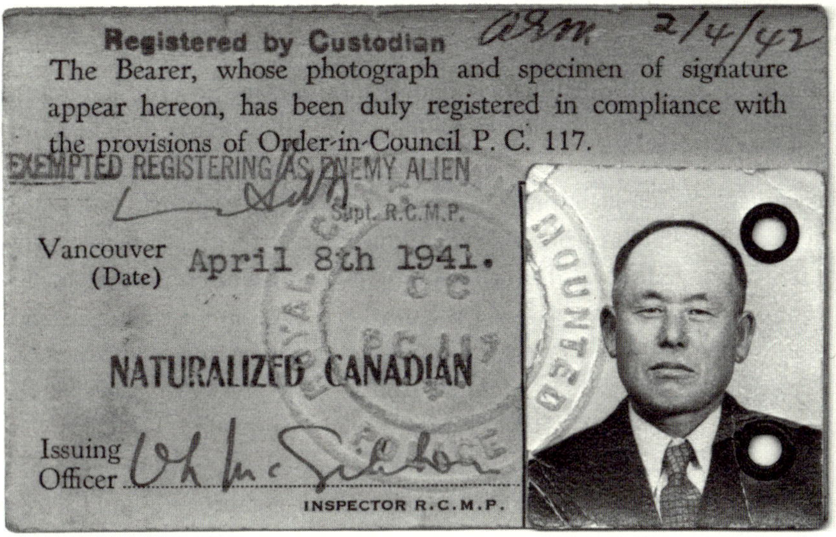
Registered by Custodian 2/4/42
The Bearer, whose photograph and specimen of signature appear hereon, has been duly registered in compliance with the provisions of Order-in-Council P. C. 117.
EXEMPTED REGISTERING AS ENEMY ALIEN
Supt. R.C.M.P.
Vancouver (Date) April 8th 1941.
NATURALIZED CANADIAN
Issuing Officer
INSPECTOR R.C.M.P.

Figure 1.2 Along with "all persons of the Japanese race," my grandfather was forced to register and to carry this identity card with him at all times. From the private collection of Masako Fukawa.

the strong attachment fishers had to their boats. When he was approached by Mr I for assistance with the sale of his boat, Kimura was sympathetic and wanted to help him get the best price. Mr I, however, "wanted to hand it over to someone kind and able to take proper care of it, without fussing over the price."[5] The same recollection also demonstrates the commitment of fishers to self-support. Mr I explained that the vessel was his "sole property," which had supported him all these years, and he wanted to give the money ($400) from the sale to the Compensation Board, since if he lost it, he would be destitute: "If I pay the Compensation Board now, I will continue to get my pension. That is much better and safer." The exact meaning of "pension" is unclear, but he was probably referring to the "maintenance allowance" that the federal government doled out at $100 a month from the sale of the internees' property and possessions and deposited in their bank accounts so that they could pay for their own upkeep while being interned.[6] "Old" as he was, Mr I did not want to become a burden to the government and as a consequence bring shame to himself, and more important, to his family.

In addition to their vessels, commercial fishers owned nets and fishing gear. For some, their investment in the equipment was greater than the cost of their boats. My grandfather, like most fishers, had put his nets and gear in storage at the end of the fishing season. They were being held at the Star Cannery net house to be readied for the 1942 season. He listed them on the form for the Custodian of Enemy Property, the government agency that had the responsibility to hold property "in trust" for Japanese Canadians who were required to leave the "protected area." It must have come as a shock to my grandfather to discover that "safekeeping" meant nothing. Correspondence with the Custodian over several years shows my grandfather inquiring about the whereabouts of his nets and gear. He and the government officials disagreed about the amount of gear that had been seized and debated the amount of money that was due to him.

Families lost their household possessions as well. Each adult was permitted to bring 150 pounds of goods with them to the internment camps. This meant that they could take only the bare necessities for daily living. They left behind their prized possessions and heirlooms rather than risk taking them to some unknown place. When my grandfather inquired about these "chattels," the officials of the Custodian responded by implying that my grandfather was not truthful, that he had "sold everything of value" before relocation, and that the balance of the goods was just "junk." Humiliated at being seen as dishonest and at his possessions being classified as "junk," my grandfather nonetheless pursued his claim with the Bird Commission, where he was further questioned.[7] It was not until 12 October 1950 that a settlement was reached, and he was awarded $410.90, minus legal fees of $3.77, the sum total of his life's work.

The cultural values of the *Issei* generation, to which my grandparents belonged, sustained them as they navigated the difficult pathways in their adopted country. The principal guide was the *ie*, or the "ideal" Japanese family system as defined by the Meiji Code of 1898.[8] The roles of each family member with their rights and obligations were clearly set out. It described how people ought to behave and was inculcated in children through six years of compulsory education. *Issei* transported the ideal to Canada but also adapted and changed it as a result of many factors: distance from Japan, the amount of direct contact with inherited traditions, the new environment, and exposure to new ideas and values, some of which were in direct conflict to what *Issei* believed ought to be. A prime example is the significance of the group to the *Issei* versus the significance of the individual in Canadian culture. According to Japanese tradition, family honour – not individual honour – was vital. Seniority within the family, and by extension in the community, demanded filial piety and respect; younger family and community members had obligations to elders because of their (the elders') experience and wisdom. Another concept of paramount importance for *Issei* was the continuation of the family. A childless family would adopt an heir, usually a male. When a female child was adopted, her husband would also be adopted to carry on the family line. The adopted son inherited the family name and wealth, and in return he was obligated to care for his adopted parents in their old age. Many challenges to this family dynamic were presented with the dispersal and dispossession of Japanese Canadians.

In 1942, my grandfather was in his late fifties, considered too old for road camp, and was relocated to Greenwood, a ghost town that housed the elderly men, women, and children in dilapidated buildings. Families were separated from the young husbands and fathers who were working and living in road camps. Even when they visited Greenwood, men were housed in a separate building, since they could not be accommodated in the same crowded rooms as the women and children, who also shared cooking and toileting facilities. Jobs were non-existent. My grandfather found work for a time as a janitor for the nuns who ran the Catholic school, but this was more as a volunteer than as an employee. He had no opportunity to rebuild his assets or to fulfill his position as patriarch of a household.

With two daughters but no son, my grandparents followed tradition by adopting my father when he married my mother. My father was a *kika nisei* (born in Canada but partially raised and educated in Japan).[9] He was born in Steveston in 1906 and taken to Mio village in Wakayama prefecture as a child. He graduated from high school and was waiting to enter business school when he was called back to Canada in 1923 because his father's sawmill on Gabriola Island had burned down, preventing his father from sending him remittances to continue his education. He returned to British Columbia and became a fisher. When he married into my mother's natal family, he became a *muko yoshi*, an adopted son-in-law. Traditionally, he would have taken on her family name so that it would not die out, but he did not: "because," he said, "we are Canadian and living in Canada."

The internment and dispossession prevented my father, too, from fulfilling his obligations to his family. With his boat confiscated and sold off, he had no means of providing for his family or for his adopted parents. He was in his thirties, and his prime working years were spent eking out a living in road camps, on a railroad gang, and in lumber camps so that the family could survive without becoming a "burden" on the government. The ban that prohibited Nikkei from working on Crown timber lands was lifted in 1943 by the federal government, which overrode the protest of the BC government because of the shortage of sawmill and logging workers.[10] My father became a "boss" at one of the lumber camps. He was in charge of several young *Nisei* men who were eager for employment and wanted to remain near their families in the internment camps.

My mother, left without any prospect of a family fortune being handed down from her father to her husband and to the next generation, felt an obligation to help create it. She was a teenager when she and her mother joined my grandfather in Steveston. She attended Lord Byng Elementary and worked as a house-girl in a Hakujin (Caucasian) household to learn English and Canadian customs. During the fishing season, she and her girlfriends followed the salmon runs, working in fish canneries in Steveston and other coastal communities. At the time of the dispersal, she was a young mother with two small children. In Greenwood, she used her skills as a seamstress and made and remade all our clothes and also did tailoring for others. She cooked in the lumber camp where my father worked and laboured in a hotel laundry in Grand Forks, taking the four children with her in the summertime. My mother was hard-working, independent-minded, and determined to lift the family out of poverty.

In doing research for our book, *Spirit of the Nikkei Fleet: BC's Japanese Canadian Fishermen* (my husband, Stanley Fukawa, studied the Japanese-language sources, and I worked in English), we were shocked to discover how pervasive and institutionalized racism was in the fishing industry. At the same time, we were awed by the tenacity, cooperation, and optimism of Japanese Canadians, who believed that their struggle and suffering to overcome discrimination would lead to a better future for their children. Disenfranchised in 1895, Nikkei were politically powerless. Their initial response was fatalistic. "*Shikataga nai*" (it can't be helped). However, *Issei* soon realized that they were at a tremendous disadvantage when they could not influence politicians and turned to the courts in 1900 in an effort to regain the right to vote. They lost their case. They were followed by *Issei* veterans who fought for Canada in the First World War. After much lobbying, they won the franchise, but only for themselves. The *Nisei* generation organized provincially in the 1930s and sent a delegation to Ottawa. Both generations were unsuccessful and re-

Figure 1.3
Yoshiharu Shinde, my father, was separated from his family and initially sent to a road camp in British Columbia. He lost his boat and livelihood and was forced to toil at a lumber camp (1943). From the private collection of Masako Fukawa.

mained politically impotent. Another world war and a half-century would pass before Japanese Canadians gained the franchise.[11]

Our book detailed long-standing discrimination in the fishing industry that created important precedent for the dispossession of my grandfather and father in the 1940s. The years between 1923 and 1930 were especially heinous for the Nikkei fishing community.[12] In 1922, a royal commission, referred to as the Duff Commission, was constituted to monitor and investigate the general state of the fisheries, but in reality it became the ways and means of achieving the "displacement of Japanese fishermen by white fishermen in the shortest period of time without disrupting the industry."[13] The key to controlling the fisheries was the issuing of licences, and hence reductions to Nikkei fishers were to continue annually until they were completely eliminated from the fishing industry. The response from the Nikkei fishing community was to pre-empt the government by deciding among themselves who should maintain their licence and who should give it up. Understandably, family responsibility was the primary consideration, and my grandfather survived the cut because he had a family to support. Coincidentally, my father returned from his studies in Japan to his birthplace at the height of these reductions and restrictions. Because he was single and without family responsibility, the community would not have approved a fishing licence being given to him. He was a *Nisei*, however, and that made him eligible for a puller's licence, and he was able to enter the fishery.[14] In addition to looking after its displaced fishers, two local Nikkei fishing associations sent delegations to Ottawa requesting more lenient treatment. When they failed, the local associations organized provincially and launched a legal challenge. The court case proceeded through the judicial system in Canada and to the highest court, the Privy Council in London, England, which ruled in their favour in 1929.[15] Their celebration, however, was short-lived, and the new era never arrived.

My view of Kimura's actions is shaped by my understanding of responses of fishers more generally to the onset of Canada's war in the Pacific. The bombing of Pearl Harbor was a shock to all Nikkei as it was to all Canadians. Nikkei fishers' pleas to be allowed to demonstrate their loyalty and their declarations to assist in the defence of the coastal waters were met with rejection.[16] They remained confident, however, that they would be treated fairly and would soon be back on the water. They cooperated with the round-up and impoundment of their vessels because they saw non-compliance as a sign of disloyalty. It was painful to watch their beloved boats being mishandled by the inexperienced sailors. Fearful that their boats would be completely destroyed if they were towed in the fierce December storm, Nikkei fishers from the Skeena, the west coast of Vancouver Island, and other fishing grounds navigated their own to Annieville on the Fraser River, unaware that they would all be sold off.

Kimura's effort to have the Nikkei fishers compensated for expenses incurred in the impoundment was not successful.[17] Fishers who navigated their boats from the Skeena did not have any time to inform their families or to take warm clothing or food. When they reached Steveston, they had to turn to relatives and friends for a bath, clean clothes, food, and a place to sleep. They also had to borrow money for their return trip home. Harry Yonekura, a *Nisei* fisher on the Fraser, says that after delivering his boat to be impounded, he had to hitch a ride with the Navy.[18] No provisions were available for Nikkei fishers prior to, during, or after the confiscation.

As the sole Nikkei representative on the Japanese Fishing Vessel Disposal Committee (JFVDC), Kimura was in a difficult position. He was knowledgeable about the community's struggle with racism, especially in the fisheries, since he himself was deeply involved in the industry. He was also aware that fishers were miserable with the sell-off of their boats and angry when they were sold without their consent.[19] In Part 4 of his memoir, he is addressing "the second and third generations," but I suspect it is intended more for *Issei* readers and asking for their understanding. It is written in Japanese. His detailed description of the procedures employed and the care with which he carried out his tasks seems to be saying that he dutifully carried out his responsibilities, something *Issei* would understand as fulfilling the demands coming from a higher authority. He chastises the younger generations, as *Issei* are expected to do, by bringing to their attention that *Issei* were "by no means ignorant or stupid." They fought discrimination, and yet throughout these difficult times, they remained law-abiding and proud of their heritage and made sacrifices in order to dutifully fulfill their familial obligations to those in Japan and in Canada. Kimura continues: Canadians recognized these qualities in the Nikkei fishers' behaviour during the war and as a "reward" were given the same rights as Hakujin and Native fishers.[20] He admits that there are those who disagree and insist instead that it was the granting of the suffrage that brought about the "sea change." The difference of opinion can probably be attributed to the generational and cultural differences between the generations.

The term "Nikkei" is used in the memoir and in this paper to identify people of Japanese origin, but for those in the fishing industry, their citizenship as "Canadians" is understood. It was of utmost importance. Proof of citizenship, either a certificate of naturalization as in the case of my grandfather or a birth certificate as in my father's, had to be presented to a fisheries official before a fishing licence was issued. Handwritten on these documents are the licence numbers, the dates issued, and the initials of the issuers. They also become the recorded history of the owner's fishing career. My grandfather first entered the industry in 1908 as a cod fisherman and continued without pause until 1941. My father wanted to be acknowledged as a "Canadian" and tried to go fishing during the ban but was stopped by a sailor armed with a rifle. Government documents, committee names, and communications omit "Canadian" when referring to Canadians of Japanese origin. I suspect that it was a deliberate act to perpetuate the myth that Nikkei are the "enemy" and "a security threat" lest some sympathetic non-Nikkei questioned the injustices being committed against their fellow Canadians.

Looking back on this history now, the government's duplicity is evident. For example, along with purported concerns with "national security," federal officials claimed that the confiscation and the sell-off of Nikkei fishing vessels were necessary to ensure food supply for the war effort. Kimura had experienced a similar government directive a few years earlier when the federal government prohibited the production of salted salmon and diverted the fish to canning in support of the war effort in Europe. If, as the government proclaimed, these drastic measures were necessary "to ensure food supply," why then were the "best" fishers being expelled and the newest vessels and equipment being disabled? Why ignore the military officials and the RCMP, who were confident that there was no national security issue with Japanese Canadians? If, as excellent fishers and farmers, Nikkei were allowed to remain in their occupations, they would have been in a position to contribute greatly to the war effort. Political ideology, wartime hysteria, and economic opportunism trumped logic, human decency, and democratic traditions.

The scope of this paper precludes any discussion of the decisions that led to the disposal of Nikkei farms in the Fraser Valley. Suffice it to say, their loss was devastating, and its impact has reverberated down through generations. Briefly, my father-in-law's farm was located in Mission City in the Fraser Valley. In 1929, he purchased ten acres of bush land with the savings from working in lumber camps for several years. His wife joined him in 1934 and laboured long hours alongside him on the farm and also carried on with the household chores. In 1942, they had eight acres in strawberries, raspberries, and rhubarb. The two acres of uncleared land was in heavy scrub with odd trees for fuel. On the farm was a ten-year-old house with a five-year-old addition, a bath house, three packing sheds, a rhubarb house, and a new garage with a 1941 Chevrolet truck. There was a well for water and electricity to the house.[21]

When given orders to leave the "protected area" before the end of April, my father-in-law hurriedly made plans to take the family inland before being forced into separation and exile to some place unknown. He approached a family acquaintance in Vernon to help him relocate to a place where he and his family could stay together. He did not want to be sent to road camp not knowing what might become of his wife and son. My mother-in-law was the only member of her family to immigrate to Canada, and she did not have any relatives here to turn to for support. Before departing, he leased his farm to Luke Guilfoyle from 1 April to 31 December 1942 for $400. The lease was extended to 30 September 1943. He left for the Hemsley Ranch in Cold Stream near Vernon, having taken care of his responsibilities as the patriarch. His family was intact, his farm placed in good hands, and with the rent from the lease he had the financial means to be self-supporting.

While adjusting to their new existence in a shack in Vernon, the Fukawa family received a series of devastating revelations. On 19 January 1943, the order-in-council granted the Custodian the right to dispose of Nikkei property in its care without the owner's consent.[22] It was rumoured that it applied only to unprofitable properties, and since his farm was cultivated and leased, he believed that it was safe from being sold. In the spring of 1943, however, as Kimura's Advisory Committee became active, it became clear that all real estate and personal property would be sold without the owners' consent. Then in June 1943, the committee from which Yamaga had resigned in disgust sold the rights to 769 Nikkei farms to the Veterans' Lands Act Administration. The Fukawa farm with decades of improvements and newly purchased equipment was sold without his consent. The capital from his property and possessions, including his shares in the strawberry co-operatives (the Pacific Co-operative and the United Farmers Co-operative Association), was put on deposit with the federal government, and he was forbidden to withdraw more than $100 a month.[23] Even if he had the capital, he was prevented from purchasing any land.[24] In a few short months, he went from an independent, financially secure farm-owner to a labourer in a stranger's apple orchard eking out an existence. Gone was the achievement of decades of hard work. Also gone was his son's inheritance.[25]

The removal and dispossession became the precursor of the expulsion of Nikkei from Pacific British Columbia and the exile of almost 4,000 from Canada. For some, such as cabinet minister from British Columbia Ian Mackenzie, the ultimate goal was the deportation of all Nikkei. Under the duress of their internment and dispossession, 10,000 had filed "requests for repatriation"; 3,503 among them were dependents whose parents signed for them. With the war over, an increasing number of Canadians began to recognize the injustices being perpetuated. Opponents of the deportation mounted a campaign to stop this unjust act, resulting in a groundswell of public opinion opposing "repatriation." The order was revoked in 1947 but not before 4,000 Nikkei had been shipped to Japan. Half of the deportees were Canadian-born. Ironically, at the same time, a Canadian was in the process of drafting the United Nations Declaration of Human Rights stating that the act of deporting citizens was a war crime.[26]

The Fukawa family almost became victims of this scheme, but they were allowed to revoke their "repatriation" request. My paternal grandmother was not so fortunate. She and her youngest son's family were casualties of the deportation. She had accompanied her husband and other relatives and relocated to sugar beet farms in Emerson, Manitoba, in order to keep the families together. While there, my grandfather passed away. When the order came to "voluntarily" choose between dispersal east of the Rockies or repatriation to Japan, my grandmother consented to be "repatriated." My parents were living miles away in Greenwood and not easily reached for consultation. She reasoned that she was a widow, elderly, destitute, and unemployable. There was nothing left for her on the west coast and no date as to when, if ever, they might return. On the other hand, the government offered incentives to those who chose to go to Japan. Their passage would be paid for, whatever capital still on deposit with the Custodian would be paid in full, and if they were lacking in funds, the government would pay a stipend of $200 each for adults and $50 for each child once they arrived in Japan.[27] My parents' pleas that she stay in Canada, their insistence that Japan was a suffering nation where disease, malnutrition, and starvation were commonplace, fell on deaf ears. The pull for an "*ie*," a physical "house," won out. My grandmother reasoned, "In Japan at least I have some land." My aunt and uncle, both *Nisei*, and their Canadian-born *Sansei* children, were duty-bound to accompany her. My uncle died of malnutrition before he could return to Canada.

This paper is an effort to put a human face on the dispersal, dispossession, and deportation by recounting the story of my family. It is a story shared by thousands of Nikkei who for decades were scapegoats for British Columbia's economic ills and then, in the 1940s, the targets of racist politicians who saw the war as an opportunity to rid the province of Nikkei by perpetuating the myth of "national security." Some of the losses were tangible and quantifiable while others were intangible, and the scars remain hidden even today. Having lived through a very difficult past filled with institutionalized racism and injustices perpetrated by their own country, what could make my grandparents and parents feel that they were now truly accepted as bona fide Canadians? For my grandfather and father, the granting of the franchise was a big step. Having fought and waited for half a century, they looked upon it as a privilege more than a right. They acknowledged the leadership of the Co-operative Commonwealth Federation party in gaining them the franchise and for their support during the internment years. In recognition and gratitude, *Issei* and *Nisei* fishers and farmers gave them their votes. For my grandfather, the turning point was the introduction of the universal old age pension in 1952 and the Guaranteed Income Supplement in 1967, which were for the benefit of all Canadians, including him. He now had an income to which all Canadians at age seventy became entitled. For my father-in-law, it was the introduction of the national hospital and medical care program in 1961. He reasoned that if Canada cared enough to provide hospital and medical care to all Canadians including himself, then Canada was a good country. For the mothers, a family allowance for each child under the age of sixteen removed some of the anxiety of providing for the children.

My father was still alive when I became active in the Redress Movement, and he used almost the same words as Kimura had to caution me about my involvement. "Don't protest so much. The younger generations do not know what it was really like." He added: "The people who perpetrated the wrongs are all gone. Don't burden future generations." On learning about my family's participation in the Ottawa rally, which included her granddaughter, my mother's reaction was to caution me with "the neighbours are talking" and not to bring any shame to the family. In 1988, when redress was won, my mother was the only one of the older generations in our family who was alive to celebrate its achievement.

In closing, I would like to share Mr M's story. He is in his nineties and a *kika nisei*. He was three years old when he was sent to Japan for his education and in 1936 returned to Steveston. He entered the fishery and in 1941 bought a new boat a few days before Japan's bombing of Pearl Harbor. Within forty-eight hours, he was ordered to take his boat from the west coast of Vancouver Island to Steveston to be impounded. Because the sales agreement was still being processed, he did not have the papers to show ownership. His boat was "lost." "I did not get to fish on it at all." Being young and single with no responsibility and "nothing to lose," he joined with others of the Nisei Mass Evacuation Group in protest against the separation of families as unnecessary and punitive. As anticipated, he was caught and thrown in jail in Vancouver. No charges were laid, and there was no trial. He and other *Nisei* detainees were put on a train and sent to Angler, a prisoner-of-war camp in Ontario, where he was incarcerated until exiled to Japan in 1946. He and his fellow *Nisei* prisoners were portrayed by government authorities as "militant resisters" who threatened peaceful relocation. They felt shunned by their own community as *gambari*, or "resister and troublemaker." What these *Nisei* wanted was justice, but incarcerated and left behind barbed wire by their own country as prisoners of war, they had nowhere to turn for mediation or representation. Mr M willingly shares his experiences and delights in telling stories of the antics they were involved in at the jail in Vancouver and at Angler. However, when I asked him, *How did you feel about what happened to Japanese Canadians?* his demeanor changed, and this jovial storyteller became agitated and indignant. "How do you think I feel?" I was taken aback at the unexpected outburst of emotion. I realized then that I had disrupted the carefully cultivated demeanor to the injustices that he still felt deeply. I had exposed his pain and bitterness, which had remained hidden for more than half a century. He expected me to know how he felt. I was expected to have observed and learned without being told.

My grandparents' and parents' generations have passed on, and the youngest *Nisei* are now in their late seventies. Those who lived in these difficult times will soon be all gone. Our ancestors believed that their actions were for the benefit of future generations, that their sacrifices and perseverance in times of physical hardships, political, and social injustices were endured for the sake of the children. Their mantra was *kodomo no tame ni*, meaning "for the sake of the children." We of this and upcoming generations are their children and have inherited our freedoms and respectability from them. Their journey was difficult, and they lived through it with dignity and decorum. It is incumbent on us to tell their stories not as victims but as survivors and fighters and to celebrate their spirit and their contribution to this country.

As Canadians, there are lessons to be learned from our difficult past as we meet the challenges present today and those that we will face in the future.

NOTES

1 Berton, "They're Only Japs."

2 Much of the family history that I relate in this chapter is drawn from conversations within my family, spanning from the early postwar period to the 1980s. Additional details are drawn from papers that have been preserved by the family, including correspondence with government officials.

3 See "Naturalization Act, 1914."

4 Marlatt, ed., *Steveston Recollected*, 59. Hideo Kokubu had three boats, but only one was sold and the other two just disappeared. He does not know what happened to them.

5 Kimura Memoir, 37. All references to Kimura's memoir will reference the page numbers of the manuscript as it appears in this book.

6 Adachi, *The Enemy That Never Was*, 261. Up to $100 a month could be drawn by evacuees for living expenses, with the condition that $260 per adult and $50 for each child be "reserved" for "post-war contingencies."

7 He appeared before the Japanese Property Claims Commission (Bird Commission) on 25 May 1948 in Grand Forks. The Japanese Fishing Vessel Disposal Committee (JFVDC) listed it as worth $431, one-half of its value. However, fishing vessels sold by the JFVDC were excluded from consideration by the Bird Commission.

8 Dore, "The Family."

9 Adachi, *The Enemy That Never Was*, 174–5. Adachi describes the *kika nisei* as being "essentially Japanese in temperament and personality" due to their training in Japan. He explains that they were seen by their *Issei* parents as superior to the *Nisei* in terms of their "adeptness in all the correct modes of traditional Japanese behaviour."

10 Ibid., 261.

11 Chapters 6 and 7 in Fukawa and Fukawa, *Spirit of the Nikkei Fleet.*

12 Meggs, *Salmon*, 120–31.

13 Harvey, "Litigating Racial Discrimination." This work is responding to the *In the Matter of a Reference as to the Constitutional Validity of Certain Sections of The Fisheries Act, 1914*, which was a set of questions posed to the Supreme Court of Canada regarding the extent to which what became known as the "oriental exclusion policy" should affect The Fisheries Act (and naturally, by extension, the Japanese-Canadian community, especially fishers). The BC Fisheries Commission (a.k.a. the Duff Commission) was chaired by William Duff, who was MP for Lunenburg, Nova Scotia, and included another MP from Nova Scotia and four MPs from British Columbia.

14 Yuko Shibata et al., *The Forgotten History of the Japanese Canadians: Volume I*, 8–9. Pullers or assistant fishers who did not require a licence prior to 1923 were now required to have one. This position was traditionally held by *Issei* before they fulfilled the three-year residency requirement to become a naturalized citizen.

15 Adachi, *The Enemy That Never Was*, 144–5.

16 *Marpole Richmond Review*, 14 January 1942.

17 Kimura Memoir, 29–31.

18 Harry Yonekura, interview by Masako Fukawa, 2002, Toronto.

19 Fukawa and Fukawa, *Spirit of the Nikkei Fleet*, 143.

20 Kimura Memoir, 57–8.

21 The Farm Appraisal Report of May 1942 assessed the land at $558 and the buildings

at $600 for a total of $1,158. The condition of the farm was described as "fully occupied, land in good tilth and free of noxious weed."

22 Sunahara, *Politics of Racism*, 106, 191.

23 Ibid., 110.

24 Ibid., 110–11. By 24 February 1942, no Nikkei could purchase land.

25 The Bird Commission awarded Fukawa $616.46 minus $35.66, which was paid to the Co-operative Committee on Japanese Canadians for legal fees. The net claim was $1,063 for the land and $300 for the truck. For one exception to the disposal, see Gill and Gill, "Zennosuke Inouye." Zennosuke Inouye was a World War I veteran who refused to sign over his farm. He wrote to the director of Veterans' Lands Act Administration in 1944, "I cannot refrain from resenting your action of taking away valuable property from a pensioned returned soldier of the last war who fought for Canada for the purpose of giving the same to another soldier who is returning from the present war." He petitioned furiously to regain his land, and in 1949 his property was restored to him. He was the only Japanese-Canadian veteran to recover his property from the Government of Canada.

26 Sunahara, "Deportation" and "Fighting Deportation," in *Politics of Racism*.

27 Ibid., 119.

2

# Kishizo Kimura and the Articulations of a Society Structured in Dominance

*Timothy J. Stanley*

> When you criticize, I would like you to investigate, face squarely, and consider the time period, the circumstances, situation, and environment that the *Issei* and some in the *Nisei* were placed in. I would like you to recognize that Nikkei people were rewarded for their struggle and finally reached the dawn of a new era after the war. With this understanding, I would like you to leap forward into various fields with self-awareness and self-respect.[1]

In the following, I propose a reading of the Kimura memoir that takes seriously Stuart Hall's idea that "race" is the articulation of societies structured in dominance rather than the embodiment of "real" biological or cultural difference or the epiphenomenon of more fundamental economic processes.[2] As such, racism is a structuring of dominance, and it is racism that produces "race" rather than "race" that produces racism.[3]

In offering this reading, I stand the usual way of reading historical documents on its head. Rather than reading the Kimura memoir outward as documenting surrounding historical events, I want to go from the outside in. The memoir shows how Mr Kimura is trapped in a racist structure of dominance whose manifestations have become so banal as to be unnoticed, precisely because dominance is not uniform or simply all one thing.[4] In effect, I want to see how the memoir *articulates* (i.e., voices) and *articulates with* (i.e., is consistent with) the structuring of dominance.[5] As such, I read it not as passively reflecting an external reality but rather as actively creating knowledge not just of the past and of the micro spaces of a society structured in dominance but with respect to ourselves as contemporary readers looking back.[6]

Here I find myself asking what I would have done if, like Mr Kimura, I had been asked to participate in the sale of the impounded fishing boats and even later of the seized property. Like him, I would have wanted the support of my community before agreeing to do so, but unlike him I have the advantage of knowing how things turned out. Part of the difficulty that Mr Kimura faced was that the entire process started slowly. He was initially invited to sit on a committee to manage the impounded boats; the idea of selling them off only emerged later, as did the forced removal of the racialized Japanese population from coastal British Columbia. But even when it became evident that the boats and other property would be sold off, in many cases without the owner's agreement, I also wonder what the other choice would have been: to withdraw and keep my hands clean or to participate in hopes of steering things, of softening negative impacts on my people or stalling for time until other choices arose. Especially if I have superior knowledge, do I not have a responsibility to participate? This is the dilemma of all go-betweens, of the people who make oppressive systems work by trying to soften their impacts when there really is no other choice. It is the dilemma that faces all of us who do not have the advantage of knowing how things will turn out.

The dominance witnessed by Kimura was the local product of a larger process through which people, originally from Europe, came to colonize the world. The invention of racism was integral to this project. European dominance differed from previous forms in that it was as much a cultural as a military, political, or economic project. As European imperialism developed, the imperialists sought actively to remake local knowledges in their own image, eliding and often actively erasing these knowledges.[7] By the late nineteenth century, through the triumph in the European world of what scholars like Jacques Barzun and Hannah Arendt came to call "race-thinking" but which we today might call racialization, and through the integration of this thinking into the disciplinary apparatuses of emergent colonizing state systems (i.e., through the development of racist state systems), the European-made world had come to be deeply structured along lines of so-called "race." Members of subject "races" were excluded from the dominating social systems or had their participation circumscribed, and members of the ruling "races" were included or licensed to be the dominant property-owners.[8] Indeed, Foucault argues that this racist structuring was the whole point of the disciplinary processes underlining the emergence of modern forms of governmentality.[9]

However, the resulting systems of racist and colonial dominance were highly dynamic systems and were neither solely the creation of people from Europe nor the creations of all Europeans. They established dominance

NOW, THEREFORE, pursuant to the authority conferred on the Commission, it is ordered as follows:

1. For the purpose of this order, and any subsequent orders of the Commission, unless the context otherwise requires:-

(a) "Persons of the Japanese race" means, as well as any person wholly of the Japanese race, a person not wholly of the Japanese race if his father or mother is of the Japanese race and if the Commissioner of the Royal Canadian Mounted Police by notice in writing requires him to register pursuant to Order-in-Council P.C. 9760 of December 16, 1941.

Figure 2.1 In its first formal order, on 20 March 1942, the British Columbia Security Commission defined "persons of the Japanese race." The uprooting and internment were part of the construction of racial dominance.

through hegemonic processes as much as through military force. Hegemony operated on metropolitan and colonized populations alike but often in different ways. While the local elites of colonized territories were often co-opted into these systems, dominance was continually resisted in larger and smaller ways. In specific times and places, specific practices consequently could be challenged, circumvented, or even ignored, while others might be forcibly imposed for a time and then only occasionally be enacted. At the same time, the defining categories of rulers and ruled created by these imperial systems were constantly slipping (as indeed they had to because they were not pre-existing natural divisions but invented ones). The either/or of racializations shifted as mixed populations, who cross back and forth between one category to another, emerged in many parts of the world and were defined in some contexts as part of the colonized group and in others as part of the colonizers.[10]

All of this was also very much a gendered system through which the dominant European gender, called in European civilization "men," came to dominate most activities. However, European women also played roles in colonization, often engaging in its cultural aspects even as they themselves were excluded from most aspects of men's dominance. Colonization even remade the gender systems of subject populations.[11] The results were complex, competing, and contradictory grammars of colonizing men and women in relation to colonized people, which enacted dominance in one dimension and subordination in another.

At the same time, not all Europeans engaged in colonizing violence, and not all colonized remained as such.[12] There were very different configurations of dominance in local spaces. A person who travelled, like the young M.K. Gandhi, might have found themselves subordinate in one location and dominant in another, offering resistance in one context and being the person to be resisted in still another. All of the categories at work, their imposed readings of particular bodies, changed with time and circumstance. People variously resisted, circumvented, or endured imposed categories and their consequences, bending them and making their boundaries ill-defined in practice. In order to maintain their dominance, members of dominant groups had to reassert or reinvent the framing categories of their dominance. This produced state systems whose complex articulations of one racialized category in relation to another or others came to be periodically re-articulated.[13] It also meant that the actual configurations of power at a given time were not necessarily sharply drawn but were uneven in their application, in their development, and in their effects on people in specific times and spaces. In effect, racisms developed unevenly.

During the late nineteenth and early twentieth centuries, the European project of colonizing the world came to be shared by people from Japan. A close ally of British colonial expansion earlier in the century, by the 1930s Japanese imperialism had become as brutal and as structured by racisms as its European counterparts. During the 1920s and 1930s, this included inculcation of belief in the superiority of the Yamato race. The resulting Japanese racism helps to explain aspects of its colonial, military, and other policies. This has led many scholars, beginning with the influential work of John W. Dower, to characterize the Pacific War as a "race war" waged by both the United States and its allies and by Japan.[14] One of the arguments for this view is that agents of the state systems of Canada and the United States treated their racialized Japanese populations markedly differently from other domestic populations whose origins were in enemy European countries.[15]

The construction of the racist dominance of English-speaking Europeans in the territory that Kimura writes about was integral to this project. It too had been centred on the conversion of other people's territories into European property. It too had been structured through the articulation of dominance by means of racialized categories. It too had created a state system that included or excluded people on the basis of how they were racialized.[16] In 1941–43, this creation was still a matter of living memory. For example, Won

Figure 2.2 Students of Vancouver's S-20 military school, 1945. The Canadian military was a site of both racial exclusion and integration. After barring Japanese Canadians from serving, the armed forces changed course during the last years of the war, recruiting them for intelligence work and transforming the military, in limited ways, into a site of racial integration. Front row, left to right: Takeo Nishimura, Louis Suzuki, John Fortin, Costello Sato. Back row: Jim McCardle, Ed Constantinedes, Hugh Langley, Merrilee Faulkner, Bob Henderson, Denise Church, John Arab, Bob Oikawa, Tage Wickstrom. (Jim Horiuchi). Nikkei National Museum (NNM), 2001.4.4.5.9.

Alexander Cumyow, often celebrated as the first Chinese Canadian, had been born at Fort Harrison, BC, in 1861 when British sovereignty extended little farther than cannon range of the Royal Navy or a few days march of the Royal Marines.[17] Only three years before Cumyow's birth, the main territory that Kimura writes about – what is today Vancouver, Steveston, and New Westminster – had been the unchallenged territory of the Musqueam and Kwantlen peoples. However, in the summer of 1858 all of this changed within a few weeks: several thousand gold-seekers invaded the Fraser River, and Colonel Moody's Royal Engineers surveyed the Lower Mainland, dividing it into a neat grid pattern of 160-acre plots for European resettlers.[18] By the end of 1858, the full disciplinary power of the most successful imperial system in history up to that point, supported by the most sophisticated military technology of the nineteenth century, the Royal Navy gunboat, had begun an inexorable process of remaking the territory of the Musqueam, Kwantlen, and other First Nations into the private property of Europeans.[19] As Cole Harris notes, through "the brutal application, episodic and public application of sovereign power," Anglo-European governmentality reordered bodies and their inclusions and exclusions within the territory.[20]

The creation of a regime of property and the exclusion of Indigenous peoples and Asians from this regime was central to this reordering. Following the establishment of the mainland colony of British Columbia in 1858, the colonial government began to set aside lands for the exclusive use of the Indigenous people. Despite Governor James Douglas's repeated injunctions to his officials to be generous in laying out these reserves, with the exception of those in the interior they tended to be small. In the Lower Mainland, more by coincidence than by planning, the reserves set aside worked out to an average of ten acres per family. At the same time, the remaining lands were divided into 160-acre plots for the pre-emption of Europeans and, at least in theory, of the Indigenous people and others as well. In 1866, the newly created colony of British Columbia reversed Douglas's land policy, which led to the breaking up of the larger reserves and the transfer of much of the best land to Europeans, while additional reserves were laid out based on the ten-acre-per-family rule.[21] It also adopted a land ordinance that allowed British subjects and those who took the oath of allegiance (i.e., in effect naturalized) to pre-empt land but specifically barred "Aborigines of this Colony or the Territories neighbouring thereto" from doing so without the consent of the governor.[22] This policy was reaffirmed by the Land Ordinance of 1870, which extended its provisions to "any of the Aborigines of this Continent."[23] Property was to be the monopoly of Europeans.

However, the dream of creating a territory of European property-owners faced another challenge. At the same time that people originally of European origins entered the territory and began converting it into their private property, another group entered who were largely indifferent to European hegemony and ultimately were seen as hostile to it by many of the European colonizers. These people were called "the Chinese," but at the time they called themselves many different things. Thus, the colonizers from Britain, the United States, and the Province of Canada extended bans on pre-empting land to so-called "Chinamen" while carefully keeping both "Chinese" and "Indians" out of the new state system that controlled this property regime, even though the latter were the majority of the population and the former may have been the next largest group.[24] The 1866 Land Ordinance also barred incorporated and unincorporated companies from pre-emption without the governor's permission. Since few people from China had enough capital to pre-empt on their own, and since most worked in groups and for companies and fewer still had the cultural capital to obtain the governor's permission, this measure in practice limited their pre-emption rights. Later legislation explicitly barred "Chinamen" together with First Nations people from pre-emption rights. For example, the 1874 Crown Lands Act required that pre-emptors or their agents occupy the land they claimed but barred "Indians or Chinamen" from being "agents."[25] Although people from China had voted in colonial elections and in the first election for the Legislative Assembly of the new Province of British Columbia, the third act of the BC Legislature barred "Chinamen" along with "Indians" from the provincial franchise.[26] In 1885, when John A. Macdonald was constructing a federal electoral regime based on maleness and ownership of property, he too ensured that both groups could not vote by excluding all people of "Mongolian or Chinese race"[27] from the franchise along with all First Nations living west of the Ontario–Manitoba border. He justified the measure on the grounds that the Chinese were a separate species from Europeans and that they were in danger of controlling the vote in British Columbia.[28] Meanwhile, popular racist violence and local action ensured that parts of British Columbia were not safe places for so-called Chinese, while under the federal Indian Act so-called status Indians were confined on reserve, their movements circumscribed by Indian agents. Speaking of the resulting apartheiding of British Columbia, Cole Harris observed, "racism was built into the landscape of settlement."[29]

As people from Japan and India entered the territory, they came into this racist structuring, and they too were subject to restrictions on the franchise and on property rights as well as to a social geography of popular and official racism. In the case of people from Japan, anti-Japanese measures were muted somewhat by imperial politics (Japan was Britain's ally from 1902 to 1923). All three groups of racialized Asians were subject to popular and government-organized racist violence of which the most spectacular incident was the 1907 anti-Chinese, anti-Japanese riot in Vancouver, an event directly inspired by those who had been carrying out the ethnic cleansing of the western United States.[30] By the early twentieth century, British Columbia was effectively an apartheided society, with racialized Chinese, Japanese, First Nations, and Anglo-Europeans living (with relatively few exceptions) in spatially segregated districts in which their children attended racially segregated schools and in which how someone was racialized determined his or her political and economic rights.[31]

This racist structuring had also been extended to the fishery. As Kimura notes, there were different quotas on the number of fish different groups could take, while different racialized groups performed different operations within the fishing industry. A commercial European fishery centred on salmon canning had replaced the original First Nations fishery of fishing weirs and coastal hunting. Thus, First Nations, European, and Japanese men operated the fishing vessels with racially homogeneous boats crews. First Nations women did the cleaning, gutting, and packing of the fish, while Chinese men prepared, soldered, and cooked the cans. Meanwhile, the capital involved in the fish plants was mainly European, although it did include some Chinese- and Japanese-Canadian entrepreneurs.[32]

However, despite its penetration into virtually all aspects of life in what had come to be called British Columbia, racist structuring was far from complete or always readily evident. People still established personal relations across the divides of "race" and culture. We can see this in the reaction of First Nations groups to the newcomers. During the 1858 gold rush, the Nlaka'pamux blocked Europeans from going up the Fraser Canyon, but they allowed the so-called Chinese to pass because the latter asked permission to enter and were careful to carry out their mining activities without destroying the land. For their part, the Musqueam established close ties with the Chinese market gardeners who leased their lands. By 1901, one-sixth of the conjugal relations involving racialized Chinese men in British Columbia were with First Nations women.[33] Some Europeans crossed over as well, of which the most celebrated example is James Teit, a Scot who collaborated with Franz Boaz but married into the Nlaka'pamux and helped to found the Allied Tribes of British Columbia, the first Native rights political organization in the province.[34]

This is the landscape that Kishizo Kimura is thinking back to: one in which there are official and popular racialized categories being enforced and enhanced by some people but being ignored by others, in which racialized categories slip but are being reinforced through power. Thus, following the outbreak of the Pacific War, Mr Kimura notes that members of the community were worried about their safety because of "the anti-Nikkei riots of 1907," a reference to the Vancouver anti-Chinese and anti-Japanese riot of 1907.[35] He also notes the work of "anti-Nikkei propaganda" and the efforts of the Vancouver City Council to restrict the business licences of Toyojin or Asians.[36]

Kimura himself articulates the racialized divides of British Columbia in the early 1940s. His manuscript refers to three groups in the fishery, "Nikkei 日系," "Hakujin 白人," and "Dojin 土人." For example, he points out that because of the provincial government's concerns over the food supply, the fishing boat committee planned to quickly release the boats to the "Hakujin and Dojin fishermen" but later notes that chartering the boats would be difficult, in part because "Nikkei fishermen would be anxious about the maintenance standards of Hakujin and Dojin fishermen."[37] Of the three distinct groups he identifies, only one is by means of a directly racializing term, "Hakujin," or "white people or person." "Dojin," or 土人 in kanji, literally a combination of the terms meaning "land," "territory," or "place" and meaning "man," "person," or "people," is probably best translated as Indigenous people. As such, it is a "race"-neutral, descriptive term. Similarly, "Nikkei," or 日系 in kanji as noted by the translator, means "Japanese lineage" and is an abbreviation for Nikkeijin 日系人, which I take literally to mean "people or person of Japanese descent."[38] Although these latter two terms are not necessarily racializations, his contrast of them to Hakujin 白人, uncontestably "white people," positions them as racializing categories paralleling the English-language racializations of "Japanese," "whites," and "Indians."

However, these categories are fluid on the ground and only become fixed through political processes. Thus, Mr Kimura notes that the term Nikkei refers to three different groups, each with potentially different loyalties and commitments to British Columbia and Canada. According to Mr Kimura, in 1938 the Canadian Japanese Association had estimated the Nikkei population as being comprised of the "Canadian-born," "naturalized citizens," and "Japanese nationality."[39] In 1941, the government maintained these categories when it registered all racialized Japanese, issuing differently coloured certificates to people depending on which of the three categories they belonged to: "white cards for Canadian-born Nikkei people, salmon-pink cards for naturalized Nikkei people, and yellow cards for those of Japanese nationality."[40] Although the 1941 registration symbolically "whitened" the Canadian-born, it also symbolically repositions those who retained Japanese citizenship as part of "the Yellow Race" and identified naturalized Japanese nationals somewhere between the two.[41] However, in singling out all people of Japanese origins for differential treatment by the government, it laid the basis for the uprooting and loss of property that followed.

The official identification of who is a member of a group and who is not has often been the historical precursor to more severe restrictions.[42] Such was certainly the case with respect to the only two other racialized groups required to register with the federal government – so-called "status Indians" (i.e., those recognized by the government as "Indians" under the 1876 Indian Act) and all persons racialized as Chinese under the 1923 Chinese Immigration Act.[43] From a bureaucratic perspective, the registration of the Nikkei, even if under three different categories, resolved the question of who was "Japanese" (i.e., it fixed the members of a racialized category and thus made possible their uprooting of the following year). As Mr Kimura notes, this uprooting began first with "all people holding Japanese nationality" and once preparations were made, followed with "not only naturalized Nikkei people, but *Nisei* [i.e., second-generation] who were born in Canada."[44] However, Mr Kimura seems unaware of the significance of the registration to the later uprooting. Instead, he celebrates it as giving the lie to the idea that there was a significant population of illegal immigrants among the Nikkei.[45]

But on the ground, this fixed and seemingly obvious racialized category did not necessarily translate into individualized forms of discrimination. Indeed, Mr Kimura demonstrates that even in the face of intensified official and popular racisms, people on both sides of the divide could and did maintain human connections. Shared social class, or at least cultural capital, contributed to this. Mr Kimura himself crosses over between included and excluded. Like his Anglo-European interlocutors, he too is a property-owner and entrepreneur (even if he was the manager of a co-operative rather than a capitalist in his own right). This gave him a social standing that appears to be not only unquestioned but welcomed. Thus, J.A. Motherwell, the fisheries inspector, approached him to represent Japanese Canadians on the fishing boat committee. Other members of the local elite, including fishing company executives and judges, subsequently accepted him. Apparently, he was a known quantity to key officials, which was why he was recruited. Social class could at times cut across other divides, as Paul Yee has argued in the case of Chinese businessmen and as Rolf Knight showed in the case of the Japanese Fishermen's Union.[46] Kimura's status was such that he could also consult with other community leaders. By and large, the fishing boat–owners themselves appear to have accepted him not only as someone of integrity but as someone of moral authority who could protect their interests. Unknown here are his relations within the broader *Issei* community. As Andrea Geiger has shown, this community included a larger number of outcast people from Japan, including people who were originally fishers.[47] Whether this is a factor at work in this case – i.e., whether Mr Kimura's family in Japan had a higher status to begin with or whether he shared the same status as most of the fishers – is beyond the scope of analysis here.

The reality that Mr Kimura is describing is one in which the lines between supposedly fixed racialized groups are not as self-evident as one might think. This is most evident when it comes to the problem of identifying the "Japanese" boats. The Navy had ordered that "Japanese" boats be impounded, but as Mr Kimura notes, racialized Japanese–operated boats were owned by "Canadian companies." The Navy still impounded these vessels, only to return them to their owners later. Some of the "Japanese"-owned boats were in the process of being sold to or bought from Hakujin, and the not insignificant legal question arose as to when such boats ceased to be in one category and became the other (i.e., when and under what circumstances the boats became subject to the impound order). Still other boats were jointly owned and even operated by Nikkei and Hakujin. Boats owned by Nikkei residents in Japan, whatever their citizenship, were considered "enemy property" and hence under the jurisdiction of the Custodian of Enemy Property and not the authority of Kimura's committee. A similar question arose as to what to do with the property "under the three-part, joint equal ownership of Mr Kiyomitsu Yamazaki, Mr Jujiro Nishimura, and Mr Daishiro Teramura." Mr Yamazaki had been in Japan since 1936, and his property was considered that of an "enemy alien" while the property of the other owners was not. In other words, on the ground, neat and self-evident racialized categories broke down and made little sense in practice. That the property was "Japanese" only makes sense if we understand that the term Japanese was a racializing and racist ascription that had little to do with actual ownership and might not have had much to with people's self-definitions: racializing because it divides and essentializes; racist because it excludes the actual everyday meanings that people make.[48]

Even though racialized categories hardened through the actions of the state system as the internment took place, the actions of state agents were not homogeneous. Rather, Kimura shows that the dispossession of racialized Japanese occurred, white supremacist dreams notwithstanding, not all of a piece but gradually, piece by piece. Hence, first the Navy orders the fishing boats to be impounded. But then the provincial government wants them to be out fishing to protect the food supply. The committee responsible for safeguarding the boats wonders whether leasing or selling the boats can best effect this. Meanwhile, many of the boats have been damaged (because of the way they were initially tied up), and dozens have sunk. These boats need to be repaired, but it is not immediately evident who should pay for the repairs. Nor does the uprooting occur all at once and it is indeed not complete until October 1942, six months after it started. Meanwhile, when one of the committee members, Commander Barney Johnson of the naval reserve, is ordered to report for active duty in Halifax, Mr Kimura organizes a farewell dinner for him, along with Judge Smith and other members of the committee, at a Japanese restaurant. Most of the boat-owners agree to sell in the end because they fear that their investments will otherwise be completely lost. They also need the money to support themselves and their families. Then there are the complexities of figuring out fair prices for the boats. Competing marine surveyors bring in different opinions, while some Hakujin buyers offer ridiculously low prices. Meanwhile, different elements of the Canadian state system are working, sometimes in harmony, sometimes in contradiction. Who will pay the expenses of the fishers who voluntarily brought in their boats and had to pay their own way to go home? After all, with the impoundment of their boats, they had lost their both their livelihoods and, in some of the more isolated communities, their means of transportation. Should it be the Navy because it ordered the boats impounded? Should it be the RCMP because they are responsible for the uprooting? After a few months, the Navy announces that it will no longer be responsible for the boats. Who then should pay for the civilian security guards who replace those of the Navy? The mandate of the committee is transferred to the Custodian of Enemy Property, not because the boats are technically enemy property but because there is no other entity that is equipped to do the job of taking care of them. Mr Kimura himself is told that he and his family can remain in Vancouver, but he chooses not to because his son cannot go to school. But the federal government did not have the jurisdiction to order the exclusion of racialized Japanese school children from the provincial school system; this is something that provincial and local officials had decided. Meanwhile, one of the boats ordered impounded is given a reprieve

Figure 2.3 An integrated classroom including Japanese-Canadian children at Strathcona School in East Vancouver, circa 1925. Kishizo Kimura's son, Edmund Kimura, who attended the nearby Hastings School, remembers such classrooms as the sites of seamless integration in the diverse neighbourhood. Interview with Jordan Stanger-Ross, 4 March 2015. Nikkei National Museum (NNM), 2014.14.2.2.23.

of several months because it is needed to ferry children to school. And so the Kimura memoir goes, cataloguing the minutiae of the creation of dominance, showing that it is a system being created piecemeal and in an ad hoc way. One small step follows another until racialized Japanese people no longer own any boats and they all have been removed from the coast. The manuscript does not describe the brutality of racist exclusion, yet it does articulate the banality of racist exclusion at every turn.[49]

However by 1943, when he is asked to return to the coast to assist with the forced sale of the property, no racialized Japanese people remain, and it is unknown if or when they will return, so the question arises of what to do with their property. Like the fishing boats, this property is at risk. The responsible authorities do not have the resources to preserve and protect it, so they decide to sell it off. However, unlike in the case of the fishing boats, the

Figure 2.4 Teen Town Dance group portrait, New Denver, BC, 1949. During the internment era and its immediate aftermath, mixed social spaces persisted in some interior BC communities despite the inherent violence of racialized internment.

dispossession of real estate is being carried out over the objections of the Japanese-Canadian owners. Several Japanese-Canadian groups accordingly ask Kimura to resign from the committee, which he does before any property is actually sold.

By this time, the ethnic cleansing of the west coast is complete. Even the Japanese-Canadian veterans of the First World War who obtained their Canadian citizenship and the right to vote by fighting for the country have been removed. The racialized category that was earlier contested is now unquestioned; to be racialized as Japanese is not to live on the coast. The racialized exclusion from the west coast has become universal. Shortly, there would not even be any "Japanese" property left. There are no Japanese restaurants to mark Mr Kimura's departure, so Judge Smith hosts a dinner and Kimura goes "home" to Christina Lake, where he is grateful that his family no longer lives in a hotel but has a cabin of their own.

But even at this moment when the exclusion of racialized Japanese people is complete, people still find place for human connection. This includes not only organizing dinners for departing co-workers but also using holidays to get together with old friends and neighbours. On the Victoria Day holiday marking the birth of the British monarch who reigned when the Empire was at its height, Kimura takes a break: "24 May/Since it was a holiday, I received an invitation from Mr Charley Moore, our old neighbour before we moved to Christina Lake. I spent a half-day chatting about the good old days and was treated to his stepmother's, Mrs Barkley's, home cooking at lunch and dinner. It felt very nostalgic."[50]

Hegemony enters into the most banal of human connections.[51] Mr Kimura is also unable or unwilling to assign any blame to the government or its officials for what happened to the Japanese Canadians. In the end, he is interested in being included in the Canadian state, not assigning it responsibility for destroying Japanese-Canadian society on the west coast. Rather, the situation is the fault of the anti-Japanese propagandists who stirred up hatred, which forced the government to "protect" racialized Japanese people. He convinces himself that Mackenzie King ordered the removal of Japanese Canadians because he was concerned for their safety in the face of popular anti-Japanese sentiments. He argues that like the royal commissioner who settled the claims of damage to Japanese Canadian–owned property following the 1907 riot, King knew first-hand the danger of popular violence. Thus, he is careful to reproduce King's 1941 statement requiring the registration of racialized Japanese people even though they were "loyal Canadians": "[T]he great majority of Toyojin citizens are completely loyal to Canada. The government shares this view. *The important issues concerning the Asians in the province of BC are based on wrong information, which unjustly attack the loyalty and rectitude of Toyojin*."[52]

Part of this "wrong information" was King's own belief that there is a sizable group of "illegal" Japanese immigrants, which registration was supposed to establish (in the end, it proved the opposite). Registration also created two thoroughly racialized categories, those who were Japanese and had to register and those who were not Japanese and did not have to register. But as Kimura notes, "the anti-Japanese propagandists" had a field day. That King was pandering to a racist vote in British Columbia and using the apparatuses of the state system to organize racializations into racist exclusions is something that Kimura cannot fathom. In Mr Kimura's world, there are kind, respectful people and those who are deeply prejudiced. To him, Japanese Canadians needed to show that they were in fact loyal citizens who conformed to the desires of the government because they knew it had their welfare at heart. Indeed, consolidating this explanation appears to be the principal motive behind his narrative: not so much to apologize for the government but to show the *Nisei* (second generation) that internment and the forced sale of property was not black and white, that the *Issei* (first generation) too resisted but, more important, deliberately restrained themselves to prove that they too were in fact "good" Canadians.

Kimura's own account is shaped by his self-admitted desire to show second- and third-generation Japanese Canadians that the first generation were not just hapless victims of racism, forcibly relocated and their property forcibly lost. Rather, they actively fought for their rights before the war through court cases, lobbying campaigns, and above all through the links they had built to others in British Columbia. As he told his imagined *Nisei* and *Sansei* readers, in the end Japanese Canadians had reached "a new era" because they had shown themselves to be loyal Canadian citizens and had won over the broader public to their cause. He notes: "[c]ommon sense among the general public no longer condones anti-Japanese practices, and I believe there is no room for anti-Japanese propaganda." He attributes this change to "the behaviour of the Japanese-Canadian fishermen who created such an atmosphere by following the law, making sacrifices, and cooperating with government policy during the war." For Kimura, this change is not due to the extension of voting rights to Japanese Canadians. Instead, "[i]n reality, Nikkei people in general raised their profile with the Canadian general public by demonstrating their diligence, pleasant character, law-abiding spirit, and patience toward past discriminatory treatment, and these formed the basis whereby Nikkei people were granted suffrage."[53] Thus, for Kimura, the details of which boats were sold under what circumstances matter, since they show this "diligence," "pleasant character," "law-abiding spirit," and "patience."

In Kimura's view, racism, which he identifies as being the root of anti-Japanese feeling and hence of the forced relocation, is the result of "propaganda," of prejudices and badly intentioned individuals. Racism is overcome through endurance, through not striking back, and perhaps above all by maintaining productive, civil, and mutually respectful relations wherever possible. Thus, Kimura emphasizes that not all relationships between "Japanese" and what the manuscript calls Hakujin fisherman were hostile. Some were co-owners of fishing boats. Japanese-Canadian fishermen worked closely with Anglo-European-owned canneries to the point where the cannery-owned boats they operated were impounded in the belief they belonged to the "Japanese." He himself organizes dinners celebrating the departures of the non-"Japanese" members of the committee. Even in the second part of his narrative, after it has become clear that the Custodian of Enemy Property was selling Japanese Canadian–owned property over the protests of the Japanese Canadians themselves and after he has resigned from working with the Custodian in person, his time in Vancouver ends with a dinner at the invitation of Justice Smith and including Mr Jones and Mr McMaster, three officials he had long worked with, before he took the night train "home" to the Christina Lake relocation camp.[54]

Thus, for Kimura, racism is an individual phenomenon that through "public opinion" and unscrupulous individuals comes to contaminate state policy. Racism is not the fault of Canada or of all Canadians, while Japanese Canadians themselves can "leap forward" because they had overcome the past. Racism is no longer tolerated, largely because people like him acted in a civilized and righteous manner. For Kimura, the legitimacy of the Canadian state and its officials is never in question. This is also very much the narrative of someone who is trapped in his own present in which the outcome is not known and in which it makes sense to try and steer things so that worse consequences do not arise from already difficult situations.

The problem with this explanation for racism is that it both articulates and articulates with racialized dominance. The racist state is not seen to be at work in structuring racism. Rather, its actions serve as a kind of wallpaper whose patterns are so often repeated to the point of banality that the essential violence on which it is predicated, of which removal of Japanese Canadians is an expression, goes unrecognized.[55] Mr Kimura cannot name this racist structuring of dominance, even as he describes it. Ethnic cleansing has come into existence despite the kind and thoughtful actions that Kimura has reported: the care taken of the seized fishing boats in the end, the RCMP officers who recover one family's treasure buried in their backyard, the apparently cordial working relations that Kimura celebrates. Even the local anti-Japanese propagandists were indulging in reproducing a larger discourse that justified their own colonization of the territory (the idea that it should somehow naturally be theirs and not that of Japanese Canadians, let alone of the First Nations) and were reproducing the much larger cultural pattern of racialized exclusion that was at the heart of the Pacific War.[56]

However, Kimura's memoir also articulates the human consequences of dislocation. He notes that so-called Japanese fishermen bought and sold fishing licences as well as boats, since a boat without a licence was valueless and the government controlled the number of fishing licences held by racialized

Japanese (through no less a person than J.A. Motherwell). Although he does not say this, even if the boats were sold at a fair price, the sudden end of the Japanese-Canadian fishery wiped out the value of these licences.

When he comes to the 1943 property sales, he notes with the characteristic understatement of a survivor,

> It is not difficult to imagine that prices were generally far below what most Nikkei people had expected. That is to say, the underpinnings of their lives that they had worked so hard for, over long years, were to a great extent destroyed. Concern about physical assaults was mitigated by virtue of the removal into camps. Losses from quick voluntary liquidations that did not go through the Custodian seemed to amount to a considerable sum. Furthermore, the dispossessed endured emotional pain and hardships in the places they were moved to. There were very sad cases where mental worry and the result of enforced travel hastened death.[57]

If anything, as we know, this was an understatement of the actual financial, psychological, and cultural costs, costs that continue to have intergenerational effects, not only for the *Issei* and *Nisei* who lived through the experience but through the multiple generations that grew up surrounded by a vast rupture in their family's lives and who have had to struggle to recreate community.[58] It is also an understatement of the actual costs for Kimura himself. Like thousands of others, he lost his life's work, his community, while he and his family were uprooted and had to start over. However, he also appears to have lost his position within the community that led him to play this role in the first place. The go-between's dilemma is that he or she may make a system of dominance work and even succeed in blunting some of its effects, only to be crushed by it in the end.

So what does all of this mean for the idea that I started with: that race is an articulation of dominance and racisms are systems of dominance that produce race? I think the Kimura memoir shows how, in practice, fluid categories become hardened and absolute through the agency of the state understood as both the actions of the state system and the overarching narratives that, as Philip Abrams wrote many years ago, make the state "a bid to elicit support for or tolerance of the insupportable and intolerable."[59] Here it is important to note that Kimura's own humanity shines through, showing that it is possible to establish connections to others across the deepest of divides. This in some ways makes Kimura's account profoundly anti-racist.

It also shows that, as we confront structured dominance, the central dilemma of our lives is that we ourselves are caught up in it. There is no place where we ourselves escape it. Nor is overcoming dominance a simple act of individual will. And specific forms of dominance become more and less intense for reasons that have very little to do with the immediacies of our own lives. At the same time, dominance does not fall from the sky. It is created and recreated by human beings. I write this paper on the unceded traditional territory of the Algonquin people about events happening half the world away on the unceded traditional territories of the Musqueam, Kwantlen, and other Indigenous peoples. I write in a language that has obliterated those of the Indigenous peoples of these territories as part of the very processes that I am critiquing. I write in the era of redress and urgent calls for reconciliation while the very dominance that enables the stuff of my life silences the lives of Indigenous peoples, a call for redress today made around residential schools but that in many ways began with the first successful redress movement, that of the *Nisei* and *Sansei* whose narrative Mr Kimura anticipates.[60] Like Mr Kimura, I too take Victoria Day off to visit old friends. But like Mr Kimura, I ask what other choice there is other than to participate in the structure of dominance, to resist or steer some of its enactments in the hope that the consequences will be less so that in the long run inclusions replace exclusions and so that the categories that articulate (with) dominance become inarticulate.

NOTES

1 Kimura Memoir, 58. All references to Kimura's memoir will reference the page numbers of the manuscript as it appears in this book.

2 Hall, "Race, Articulation and Societies Structured in Dominance," 305–45.

3 Stanley, *Contesting White Supremacy*. That "race" is a consequence and not a cause of dominance has been long held by certain scholars. See Barzun, *Race*. I place *race* in scare quotes to problematize its naturalness in contemporary discourse and to highlight its constructed nature.

4 For further information on banal racism, see Grant and Stanley, "Reading the Wallpaper"; Ahmed, *On Being Included*; Montgomery, "Banal Race Thinking." The idea of banal forms of dominance comes from Hannah Arendt via Michael Billig. See Arendt, *Eichmann in Jerusalem*, and Billig, *Banal Nationalism*.

5 For further discussion on the concept of articulation, see Slack, "Theory and Method of Articulation in Cultural Studies"; Winant and Omi, *Racial Formation in the United States*; Grossberg, ed., "On Postmodernism and Articulation." The concept of articulation allows exploration of a contingent set of social relations, key to the dynamics of racism.

6 Hall, *Representation and the Media*; Hall, "Work of Representation."

7 For a historically informed overview of theories of imperialism, see Young, *Postcolonialism*. For discussion of the remaking of local knowledges and their effects on the cultures of the colonizers, see Cohn, *Colonialism and Its Forms of Knowledge*; Stoler, *Race and the Education of Desire*; Mackenzie, ed., *Imperialism and Popular Culture*; Said, *Orientalism*.

8 See Goldberg, *Threat of Race*; Goldberg, *Racial State*; Arendt, "Race-Thinking before Racism"; Allen, *Invention of the White Race*. For a historical example, see Barzun, *Race*. For discussion of racialization, see Fanon, *Black Skin, White Masks*.

9 Michel Foucault, *"Society Must Be Defended."*

10 For more on the historicity of racial categories, see Stanley, *Contesting White Supremacy*; Beasley, *Victorian Reinvention of Race*; Young, *Postcolonialism*; Hannaford, *Race*; Ignatiev, *How the Irish Became White*.

11 For example, see Perry, *Colonial Relations*; Pickles, *Female Imperialism and National Identity*; Perry, *On the Edge of Empire*; Ware, *Beyond the Pale*. I borrow the concept of gender systems from Barlow, "Politics and Protocols of *Funü*"; Barlow, "Theorizing Women"; and Pascoe, "Gender Systems in Conflict."

12 For examples of colonization from the point of view of specific individuals, see Haig-Brown and Nock, eds., *With Good Intentions*. On the complexity of responses to colonization, see Lutz, *Makúk*.

13 Winant and Omi, *Racial Formation in the United States*.

14 Cameron, "Race and Identity"; Dower, *War without Mercy*. See also Price, *Orienting Canada*.

15 Takaki, *Double Victory*.

16 Key work on the construction of British Columbia as a colonized territory includes Harris, *Making Native Space*; Harris, *Resettlement of British Columbia*. For more on the construction of European dominance in relation to First Nations, see Lutz, *Makúk*; Perry, *On the Edge of Empire*; Tennant, *Aboriginal Peoples and Politics*; Gough, *Gunboat Frontier*; Fisher, *Contact and Conflict*. For accounts of colonization articulated by First Nations historians, see Carlson, ed., *Stó:lo-Coast Salish Historical Atlas*; Wa and Uukw, *Spirit in the Land*; Drake-Terry, *Same as Yesterday*; Fraser Basin Council, *Bridge between Nations*. For information on the exclusion of Chinese, see Stanley, *Contesting White Supremacy*; Harris and Galois, "Population Geography," in Harris, *Resettlement of British Columbia*, 137–60.

17 See Stanley, "Strong Poetry of Won Alexander Cumyow."

18 See Harris, "Making of the Lower Mainland," in Harris, *Resettlement of British Columbia*, 68–102.

19 Gough, *Gunboat Frontier*.

20 Harris, "Making of the Lower Mainland," in Harris, *Resettlement of British Columbia*, 101–2.

21 On pre-emption, see ibid., 85–8. On the reserve policy and its changes during the colonial period, see Tennant, *Aboriginal Peoples and Politics*, 26–52, and Harris, *Making Native Space*, 17–69. On the ten-acre rule, see Tennant, *Aboriginal Peoples and Politics*, 42–4.

22 "An Ordinance to Further Define the Law Regulating the Acquisition of Land in British Columbia (Pre-emption Ordinance, 1866)."

23 "An Ordinance to Amend and Consolidate the Laws Affecting Crown Lands in British Columbia (Land Ordinance, 1870)."

24 Harris and Galois, "Population Geography," in Harris, *Resettlement of British Columbia*.

25 "An Act to Amend and Consolidate the Laws Affecting Crown Lands in British Columbia," 10.

26 See "An Act to Make Better Provision for the Qualification and Registration of Voters," 18. The lieutenant governor refused to sign the legislation into law on the grounds that it interfered with the federal jurisdiction over "Indians." However, the federal government ruled that the legislation did not do so. It was consequently re-enacted in time for the second provincial election.

27 Canada, House of Commons, *Official Report of the Debates of the House of Commons*, 1885, 1,582.

28 Stanley, "'Aryan Character of the Future of British North America.'"

29 Harris, "Making of the Lower Mainland," in Harris, *Resettlement of British Columbia*, 102.

30 Price, *Orienting Canada*; Adachi, *Enemy That Never Was*; see also Pfaelzer, *Driven Out*.

31 Stanley, *Contesting White Supremacy*; Stanley, "'Carrying into the Schools.'"

32 Newell, *Tangled Webs of History*; Newell, *Development of the Pacific Salmon-Canning Industry*; see also Knight, *Indians at Work*; Muszynska, *Cheap Wage Labour*.

33 Barman, "Beyond Chinatown." On close Chinese–First Nations relationships, see also Jorgenson, "'Into That Country to Work.'"

34 See Wickwire, "Teit, James Alexander."

35 Kimura Memoir, 6.

36 Ibid., 87.

37 Ibid., 5, 8.

38 Matsuki Masutani, "Translator's Note," in this volume, lxi. Although Mr Masutani translates 日系 as "Japanese lineage," Japanese descent or Japanese ancestry is closer to

the original kanji or Chinese. The term 人 can be singular or plural and can mean "man" in the sexist idioms of the nineteenth and early twentieth centuries, "human(s)," "person," or "people."

39 Kimura Memoir, 93–4.

40 Ibid., 96.

41 See Keevak, *Becoming Yellow.*

42 Snyder, *Black Earth*, 185. Snyder's brilliant synthesis of recent research on the Holocaust repeatedly demonstrates that racialized categories are constructed in both popular imagination and through government action. In the case of the Jews of eastern Europe, identification of who was Jewish, and hence of who was to be murdered, was based less on people's religious practices or ethnic self-identifications than it was on the ideological constructs of the Nazi regime. For example, in the logic of what Snyder calls the Nazi myth of Judeo-Bolshevism, all Jews were communists and all communists Jews. Thus, following the invasion of the Soviet-occupied territories of eastern Europe and then of the Soviet Union proper, all that members of the Soviet Communist Party had to do to escape being murdered themselves (i.e., to prove that they were not communist) was to murder "a Jew," regardless of whether their victims had been a member of the party. This enabled members of the NKVD (the predecessor of the KGB) and the Soviet police to collaborate in the Holocaust.

43 In the case of First Nations, see Dashuk, *Clearing the Plains*, and Truth and Reconciliation Commission of Canada, *Canada's Residential Schools.* On the Holocaust, see Snyder, *Black Earth.*

44 Kimura Memoir, 17.

45 Ibid., 92–6.

46 Yee, "Sam Kee"; Knight and Koizumi, *Man for Our Times.*

47 Geiger, *Subverting Exclusion.*

48 Even from the point of view of official Japanese definitions, who was Japanese and who was not was not as straightforward as racist discourse represents. For example, at the time of the dispossession of racialized Japanese in British Columbia, the Japanese government considered people of Chinese origins living in Taiwan as "Japanese."

49 See Arendt, *Eichmann in Jerusalem.* The processes and the consequences of the ethnic cleansing of racialized Japanese from the west coast are infinitely less brutal than what occurred during the Holocaust in Europe, and it would cheapen the memory of either event to compare them directly or to suggest that the actions of their engineers were at all equivalent. Nonetheless, the Kimura manuscript's focus on the minutiae of the creation of racist exclusion is disturbingly reminiscent of Hannah Arendt's account of the minutiae of Adolph Eichmann's engineering of the Holocaust and hence of the banality of evil.

50 Kimura Memoir, 79.

51 Ed Kimura and Doris Kimura, interview by Jordan Stanger-Ross, 4 March 2015, Vancouver. In an act of neighbourliness, Mrs Barkley also appears to have stored the personal belongings of Mr Kimura and his family throughout the war.

52 Kimura Memoir, 95. Original emphasis.

53 Ibid., 54.

54 Ibid., 84.

55 Grant and Stanley, "Reading the Wallpaper."

56 Cameron, "Race and Identity"; Dower, *War without Mercy*.

57 Kimura Memoir, 100.

58 For example, see Tateishi, "Inevitable Antiracist Educator."

59 Abrams, "Notes on the Difficulty," 79.

60 See Truth and Reconciliation Commission of Canada, *Honouring the Truth, Reconciling for the Future*.

# 3
# Resistance and Accommodation to Racism and Discrimination

*Vic Satzewich*

While the academic analysis of racism and resistance to racism in Canada offers many rich insights into the motivations behind policies that institutionalized racist discrimination and how racism has been experienced, Kimura's memoir supports another line of inquiry that has been pursued less often but is arguably just as important as the above two. In many cases, institutional authorities in Canada, including politicians, government bureaucrats and administrators, and police and security service officials, sought out, found, and/or recruited individuals within ethnicized and racialized communities to help implement discriminatory policies and laws. In addition, institutional authorities often took advantage of political and ideological divisions within ethnicized and racialized communities by co-opting some individuals and groups to help monitor the activities of, and repress, others within the same community. Not only did these individuals appear to collaborate willingly with the repressive apparatus of the state, they often sought out and used the state to undermine co-ethnics, advance their own interests, and settle old scores within the broader collectivity. How are we to interpret the actions of those individuals and groups within ethnicized and racialized communities who appear to have cooperated and collaborated with institutional authorities to carry out their racist and discriminatory projects?

In this chapter, I seek to offer a typology of types of collaboration with the state and examine the question of how we ought to interpret the actions of those individuals, like Kimura, who assisted institutional authorities in implementing a legally sanctioned injustice. Though Kimura seemed to be a willing participant in the Fishing Vessel Disposal Committee, does his participation count as collaboration with racist authorities or as a particular form of resistance to racism, or can it be considered a combination of both collaboration and resistance? Taken in broader context, Kimura's actions are not that unusual. There are many other examples of individuals who appeared to collaborate with institutional authorities in carrying out various types of racist and discriminatory actions. The bulk of this chapter examines some of these other instances, including cases of early and mid-twentieth-century collaboration on the part of First Nations, Chinese Canadians, and Italian Canadians. I conclude with some thoughts about Kimura's cooperation. In so doing, I suggest that Kimura's actions are best characterized as a hybrid strategy, or what I call *collaborative resistance*, insofar as he opted to cooperate with institutional authorities seemingly as a way to help combat the long-established fear, distrust, and racism directed toward Japanese Canadians.

## Resistance, Collaboration, and Consent

One of the dominant narratives within Canadian writing about the historical experiences of racialized communities tends to focus on the many forms of racism, discrimination, and injustice heaped on members of those communities by politicians, various levels of government, labour unions, business associations, and members of civil society.[1] This line of inquiry examines the many ways that institutional authorities and various elites understood and constructed "race" difference and how those constructions of difference became transformed into full-fledged racism and various forms of institutionalized discrimination.[2] Discriminatory polices ranged from the overt, such as the Chinese Immigration Act of 1923, which barred virtually all people of Chinese origin from migrating to Canada until 1947; the thinly veiled Continuous Journey Regulation, which discriminated against potential immigrants from India without actually naming Indians as the object of exclusion;[3] to the so-called "polite racism" of the 1908 gentleman's agreement between Japanese and Canadian authorities that sought Japanese government assistance in limiting Japanese migration to Canada following the anti-Japanese and Chinese riot in Vancouver in 1907.[4]

Another important narrative focuses on how members of racialized communities experienced injustice and racism and fought the various forms of discrimination they were subject to. As Jordan Stanger-Ross and Tim Stanley both point out, just as there are many different forms of racism, so too are there many forms of resistance to racism.[5] Anti-racism can take the form of public instances of protest: letter-writing, petitions, marches, strikes, and blockades targeted at institutional authorities. Constance Backhouse's work

*Colour Coded: A Legal History of Racism in Canada* documents in rich detail how members of racialized communities fought various forms of racially discriminatory laws, regulations, and policies in the courts.[6] Other historians and social scientists have focused on the various forms of collective protest over discrimination, social exclusion, and unjust working conditions faced by ethnic and racialized minority workers.[7]

Anthropologist James Scott argues, though, that resistance can also take less visible, hidden forms. In *Domination and the Arts of Resistance*, Scott's interest is in "how we might more successfully read, interpret, and understand the often fugitive political conduct of subordinate groups."[8] Resistance to oppression, Scott notes, can of course take the form of open rebellion or public protest. But he also argues that resistance can also be subtler and can involve "subterranean" actions ranging from anonymous attacks on the property of dominant groups, poaching, foot-dragging, ingratiation, character assassination, to shunning. Analyzing resistance in a small Malaysian community, he argues that in situations laden with power, those who are subordinate variously make use of disguise, deception, and indirection while maintaining an outward impression of willing, even enthusiastic consent. He studies the micro-interactions between those who possess seemingly little political or economic power and those who are socially, economically, and politically dominant. In so doing, he makes a distinction between what he calls the "hidden" and the "public" transcripts of interaction. The hidden transcripts need to be read as part of the "infrapolitics of subordinate groups," by which he means to "designate a wide variety of low profile forms of resistance that dare not speak in their own name."[9] In challenging the apparent binary between collaboration and resistance, Scott also argues that in many cases, individuals and groups who appear to actively collaborate with institutional authorities in carrying out repressive and discriminatory policies are actually engaged in subtle forms of resistance. They use apparent collaboration and consent as a way of undermining and challenging the racism, discrimination, and inequality that they and members of their community are subject to.

Though Scott argues that collaboration with institutional authorities can be a form of resistance, his analysis identifies an important conceptual problem involving how we go about differentiating between collaboration as a form of hidden resistance and collaboration as active, self-interested consent on the part of those who want to advance their own interests in relation to co-ethnics or the dominant group itself. In other words, how are we to measure and assess the extent to which collaboration bleeds into resistance and the extent to which collaboration can lead to long-term, positive change for a community subject to intense racism and discrimination? This is, in part, why Kimura's memoir is so interesting. In a way, Kimura's memoir constitutes one of those hidden transcripts, now made public, that give us a window into the complex issues of collaboration and consent. Was his collaborative resistance a consciously chosen strategy at the time that events were unfolding, or was it a way in which he used memory and his memoir to justify and explain his actions many years later?

## Racial Domination and Collaboration

As many analysts of the history of Western colonialism have recognized, colonial domination was expensive and difficult to organize.[10] Though structured around ways to extract resources from various regions of the world for the benefit of the mother country, colonial officials and their government masters were almost always worried about the economic bottom line. For colonial authorities, the economic benefits of colonialism needed to outweigh the administrative costs of organizing the domination. Colonial rule was also fragile because colonial agents of domination could not be everywhere at the same time. In order to effectively organize their control and domination, European colonial officials often relied on assistance and collaboration from the ranks of those who were subject to their domination. We know that historically, whether it was in East Africa, West Africa, the Caribbean, or Asia, both British and French colonial policies, with their emphasis on indirect rule, tried to use local elites and to incorporate traditional political institutions into their structures of domination.[11] Though British and French approaches to indirect rule were somewhat different, elements of their approaches were similar insofar as they variously involved favouring or promoting some ethnic, tribal, or religious groups in the expectation that they would act as agents of social control over other colonized groups or as a way of dividing and conquering the colonized population to further solidify their domination.[12] Thus, it was not unusual for members of groups who were targets of racism and discriminatory treatment to become incorporated into the structures of colonial domination. This helped to legitimize the domination but also helped to drive wedges within communities so that they could be better manipulated and controlled.

At the same time, colonial domination was also orchestrated on the basis of the notion of "the rule of law." As explained by David Groff in the context of colonialism in Africa, "the establishment of some reasonable facsimile to the rule of law was both an ideological and practical imperative. Ideologically, the rule of law was necessary both because of the positive dictates of the two countries' liberal traditions and the need to defend the colonial enterprise against rhetorical attacks of domestic critics and vociferous members of the nascent African petty bourgeoisie."[13]

Though he recognizes that the rule of law was needed to "facilitate colonial commerce and promote the establishment of capitalist productive relations … it is clear that the idea of the rule of law in a colonial context served primarily as a means of external legitimation."[14] Groff analyzes the case of Kwame Kangah of Assikasso, of the Ivory Coast, and describes him as "a long time French collaborator in the region" in the early twentieth century. He argues that individual Africans could advance their own personal interests by exploiting both the clientelistic relationships inherent in the colonial situation and the colonizers' own need to uphold some semblance of the rule of law as a means of establishing the legitimacy of their imperial enterprise.[15]

The history of indirect rule in these other colonial contexts is not irrelevant for the understanding of how the Canadian state managed its relations with ethnicized and racialized groups in this country. Canada, of course, was formed as a colony first of France and then of Britain, and it only slowly shed its status as a colony over the course of the late nineteenth and early twentieth centuries. At the same time, as Canada became more independent from Britain, it never had external colonies where Canadians, with the sanction of the Canadian state, sought to exploit the resources of another region outside of its borders. But Canadian authorities did organize a process of internal colonialism that sought to exploit the resources of First Nations, and until the mid-twentieth century, Canada's political and economic elites very much identified with Britain, and many members of the bureaucratic elite in this country had ties to the United Kingdom.[16] Thus, Canadian authorities were no doubt familiar with British colonial tactics in other countries and adapted and modified those tactics in order to dominate and control both First Nations and those ethnicized and racialized groups who immigrated to Canada during the late nineteenth and early twentieth centuries and whose presence was defined as a threat to social stability. That domination was also organized through the notion of "fair play," which reinforced the colonizers' sense of moral superiority.[17] First Nations, along with many immigrant, ethnic, and racialized groups in Canada, experienced repression at the hands of the state in Canada. And, in the context of that repression, there were a number of ways in which members of ethnicized and racialized communities cooperated with the state and participated in their own domination. In the remainder of this chapter, I consider the meaning of three forms of "collaboration": collaboration in the context of internal colonialism; collaboration as a reflection of class conflicts within ethnic and racialized communities; and collaboration as way to settle political scores within an ethnic community.

## Collaboration and Cooperation in the Context of Internal Colonialism

Even though Canada did not have external colonies, it does nonetheless have a history of internal colonialism. The history of Canadian authorities' efforts to civilize, assimilate, and control First Nations is now well known, as are its classed, gendered, and generational dynamics.[18] Residential schools were established to resocialize First Nations children and transform them into ideal typical Europeans.[19] Farming in First Nations communities was promoted as a way of instilling capitalist economic values and a Protestant work ethic in communities, and homemakers' clubs were organized for First Nations women after World War II to teach them ideal typical forms of European domesticity.[20] Various religious and cultural practices were also targeted for repression, including the Sun Dance on the prairies and the Potlatch on the northwest coast of British Columbia.[21]

But colonization also involved efforts to transform Indigenous political structures and bring them into line with British understandings of how communities should be governed and represented. Prior to European contact, Indigenous governance structures varied across groups. In some communities, power and authority were shared based on particular sets of skills or expertise; in some, women had considerable influence over decisions that affected the community as a whole.[22] These traditional systems of rule became objects of concern on the part of the Canadian state, in part because they did not conform to Euro-Canadian understandings of how patriarchal power should be organized within communities. Not unlike Britain's efforts to orchestrate regimes of indirect rule in its own colonies, the federal government, via the Department of Indian Affairs, instituted a policy of limited indirect rule in communities by forcing the election of chiefs and councillors. In the 1876 Indian Act, Section 61 stated that

> at the election of a chief or chiefs, or the granting of any ordinary consent required of a band of Indians under this Act, those entitled to vote at the council or meeting thereof shall be the male members of the band of the full age of twenty-one years; and the vote of the majority of such members at a council or meeting of the band summoned according to their rules, and held under his instructions, shall be sufficient to determine such election, or grant such consent.[23]

The Indian Act also outlined the terms of office for chiefs and councillors, and the government could depose a chief or councillor on the grounds of "intemperance, immorality, dishonesty and incompetence."[24] The Department of Indian Affairs, via their resident Indian agents, kept a close watch on the activities of chiefs and councillors and did in fact depose leaders both for committing social indiscretions and for their too active opposition to the imposition of government policy.[25] Federal legislation gave the minister of Indian affairs the power to disallow any policies or laws passed by the council if they were deemed to be contrary to government policy.

While there was indeed resistance to what became known as the elective system of governance in some First Nations communities, and while it was often the focus of political conflict within communities, it was nonetheless imposed in many communities across the country.[26] The elective system remains in place today despite efforts in some communities to return to more traditional forms of governance. Some communities have dual forms of governance, with traditional systems of governance operating in conjunction with (and sometimes in opposition to) the elective system.

That the Department of Indian Affairs wanted to incorporate First Nations people into structures of their own domination should come as no surprise. Following the tried and tested practice of indirect rule developed in other colonial contexts, Canadian authorities recognized that effective control over, and assimilation of, First Nations could not occur without the support of some individuals and groups within that community. Moreover, the fact

Figure 3.1 David Laird, 1876. Minister of the interior from 1873 to 1876, Laird presided over the development of the first Indian Act, which sought to use elected chiefs and councils as part of a strategy of rule. Library and Archives Canada. LAC, 1936-270 NPC.

that some individuals stood for election and wanted to hold onto their positions once elected is not unusual. But the motives behind individuals' willing participation in this system of colonial domination were complex, and until further research is conducted on those leaders who participated in the imposed, Euro-Canadian system of governance, we can only speculate about their motives for involvement. Some may have sought the privileges that the office of chief or councillor afforded. Along with social status, the material benefits included a new suit of clothes and a few dollars per year. Though seemingly trivial in nature, some may have sought out these positions for these rather modest material and status-related benefits. Some may have participated in the state-imposed elective system because it brought them closer to control over other band-based collective resources, which could then be distributed to friends and relatives in the community to extend patron–client relations within their communities.[27] Others no doubt participated in the system because they wanted to do the best they could for their communities and try to represent their community's interests to colonial authorities. As Edmund Danzinger argues, in some cases, "Chiefs and councils … manoeuvered skilfully and doggedly to advance the welfare of their people in the face of paternalistic Indian Department and aggressive white developers … Walpole Island politicians, for example, became increasingly adept at managing their own affairs and dealing with the federal government."[28] In this way, collaboration was, for some First Nations leaders, a form of resistance, and they saw their participation in the elective system as one way to exercise opposition to the colonial project and colonial agents. A mix of factors likely motivated some.

At the same time, some contemporary assessments by First Nations commentators of historical and contemporary participation in such colonial imposed structures are particularly harsh. Howard Adams refers to such leaders as "Uncle Tomahawks,"[29] and Taiaiake Alfred argues that participation in, and collaboration with, Euro-Canadian imposed governance structures is a form of co-optation that has had long-term negative consequences for First Nations as a whole. According to Alfred,

> The co-optation of our political leadership is a subtle, insidious, undeniable fact, and it has resulted in a collective loss of ability to confront the daily injustices, both petty and profound, of Native life. Politically and economically, all Native people are in a vulnerable position relative to the superior power of the state. This is the reality that all must cope with. But individual people respond to this unjust power relationship in different ways. Some actively contend with the state; others cooperate with it. These people rationalize and participate actively in their own subordination and the maintenance of the Other's superiority. They become co-opted.[30]

These contested interpretations of the meaning of "collaboration" on the part of First Nations leaders are, as we shall see, not irrelevant to Kimura's case.

## Resistance and Accommodation among Targeted Ethnicities: Class Conflicts within Ethnic and Racialized Communities

Though First Nations were an internal colony, other ethnic and racialized groups who migrated to Canada were also targets of government oppression and discrimination. Not unlike the case of First Nations, many immigrant groups were considered suspect minorities and were deemed problematic from the point of view of the long-term reproduction of Canada as a white society. Subject to competing and contradictory forces that, on the one hand, saw employers define them as good workers and useful sources of labour while on the other, the white working class and many politicians saw them as unfair competitors in the labour market and as undesirable as future citizens, many ethnicized and racialized immigrant groups were targets of government repression.[31] As a result, Canadian political elites were often conflicted about the presence of certain ethnicized and racialized communities in the country. They were interested in facilitating capital accumulation and satisfying the demands of employers for cheap labour, but they were also nervous about losing working-class political support and changing the character of Canada as a "white man's country."[32] Opposition to various ethnicized and racialized groups was ideologically grounded in various types of racism and in many cases was accompanied by discriminatory legislation to control the entry into, and activities within, Canada of those groups.

Though the ideological racism that defined groups as "other" often tended to not differentiate between individuals who were of different class origins or gender, in some cases class advantage trumped racialized disadvantage. Some members of racialized communities were able to evade racist exclusions because of their class background. Before the introduction of the Chinese Immigration Act in 1923, Chinese merchants (along with diplomats, tourists, and students) were excluded from the requirement to pay the head tax upon arrival.[33] Moreover, members of these categories continued to be allowed entry to Canada after the imposition of the Chinese Immigration Act, which put a stop to all Chinese working-class immigration to the country. According to Anderson, it was believed that merchants "would contribute capital and trade arrangements to Canada's development" and, though not equal to similarly situated white immigrants to Canada, they nonetheless faced fewer restrictions when landing in Canada.[34] Even if immigration policy did not differentiate between different socio-economic classes within racialized groups, in many cases there was nevertheless often de facto class diversity within those communities. Individuals who migrated to Canada occupied specific positions in productive relations in their home country. Some occupied socio-economic positions in Canada similar to the ones they did back home, while others were able to achieve some level of upward mobility after having lived and worked in Canada for several years. Thus, some members of communities came to Canada with working-class or peasant backgrounds and ended up in working-class positions or as farmers in Canada. Some moved up and started and ran their own businesses.[35] Some employed the labour power of co-ethnics, while some acted as economic brokers between mainstream and minority communities. As a result, immigrant and ethnicized communities were rarely completely homogeneous in terms of their class composition. These social class differences were significant, in part, because they led to complex ways in which those who were in positions of relative socio-economic advantage interacted and cooperated with the state and with broader white business interests, and at times they resisted or accommodated themselves to state-led discrimination.

Even though it is often thought of as a relatively homogeneous racialized community in Canada at the end of the nineteenth and early part of the twentieth century, the Chinese-origin population of the country was in fact internally stratified along class lines. That is, there were at least three social classes within the Chinese-Canadian community in the early years of the twentieth century. First, the vast majority of the Chinese-origin population in the country was made up of individuals who sold their labour power for wages.[36] In terms of traditional political economy, they were racialized members of the working class.[37] Many sold their labour power to white business-owners involved in railroad construction, mining, and agriculture, but others sold their labour power to business-owners who were also of Chinese origin. Some Chinese immigrants occupied what political economists term "petit bourgeois" positions in Canadian society. They were small-scale entrepreneurs who owned their own businesses and perhaps employed two or three others, usually co-ethnics, in businesses such as laundries, restaurants, and market gardening. The social origins of the Chinese entrepreneurial class are complex. Some working-class Chinese immigrants were able to escape the uncertainties of and discrimination in the mainstream labour market by starting businesses of their own. In many cases, they employed small numbers of co-ethnic Chinese as a way of carving out a competitive economic niche for themselves. But there was also a third social class within the Chinese Canadian community, and they consisted of relatively well-off merchants and capitalists who employed larger numbers, usually of Chinese workers but sometimes also white workers. Some merchants came to Canada with considerable wealth and started large-sized businesses in this country, while others worked their way up.[38]

Though the racist public and government rhetoric directed toward the Chinese-Canadian population at the time did not often distinguish between workers, merchants, and larger business owners, the everyday realities of life within Chinese-Canadian communities was structured by class differentiation.[39] Moreover, this class differentiation is important, because it shaped the diverse forms of resistance and accommodation to racism and state-imposed discrimination. At one end of the response to racism were those efforts by Chinese business-owners to challenge discriminatory legislation in the courts. Constance Backhouse documents in considerable detail a legal challenge to the Saskatchewan government's 1912 Act to Prevent the Employment of Female Labour in Certain Capacities, or what was known more colloquially at the time as the "White woman's labour law."[40] In 1924, Yee Clun, a Chinese-Canadian restaurateur, applied to the City of Regina for a licence to hire white women in his restaurant, arguing that since the supply of new Chinese immigrants had been cut off a year earlier, he could not find enough staff. When his request was turned down by the city councillors, he sought a judicial review of the decision. In so doing, Yee Clun hired a white lawyer to challenge the legality of the law in the province. The provincial judge who heard the case ruled that Regina's law was discriminatory and deemed the council's decision to not grant him a business licence invalid and unlawful.[41]

Chinese-Canadian legal challenges to discriminatory legislation were not out of the ordinary. Lisa Rose Mar and Kay Anderson describe a number of cases in which Chinese-Canadian entrepreneurs who owned various types of business enterprises in Vancouver's Chinatown in the late nineteenth and early twentieth centuries challenged racist legislation in the courts.[42] According to Anderson,

> the firm of Jun Kee took the city to the BC Supreme Court in 1897 to claim for damages wrought by fire lit by the then city engineer. The engineer had been ordered by council to destroy a row of cabins in the vicinity of the firm's property. A Lee Chung appealed to the city in

Figure 3.2 Yip Sang (1890s) and other prominent merchants amassed fortunes mediating between Chinese labour and the Canadian state. University of British Columbia Rare Books and Special Collections, The Wallace B. Chung and Madeline H. Chung Collection 0217522.

> 1890 for compensation for his eleven hogs, destroyed by the health inspector on the alleged grounds they had "hog cholera." The city paid Lee Chung $50. In 1899, the lawyer for Sam Yuen applied for an injunction restraining council from burning a building of his that had been condemned [by the health inspector].[43]

Indeed, the volume of litigation brought forward by Chinese-Canadian entrepreneurs in British Columbia at the turn of the twentieth century was so large that in 1901 Robert Marrion, Vancouver's health inspector, said that "[t]he Chinese appear to be made for litigation."[44]

But the reaction of Chinese business-owners to racism and state-imposed discrimination went beyond explicit resistance via the courts. In some cases, there is evidence that Chinese business owners shared in, and helped to reproduce, some of the racist rhetoric directed at co-ethnics and helped to reproduce Euro-Canadian understandings of social problems and issues, particularly those within more poverty-stricken, "deviant" parts of Chinatown. In Vancouver, groups of merchants joined together to add their voices to the broader white concerns that Chinatown was being overrun by "prostitution" and other types of "vice." Some also shared the growing state concern over the presence of opium dens as a destructive force within the community. For example, even though city council ignored it, in 1906 the Chinese Board of Trade submitted a petition protesting "the unimpeded movement of prostitutes" into two streets in Chinatown in language that Anderson notes was "not far removed from the most traditional of white Christian mission ministers in Chinatown."[45] As their petition explained, "[i]t is our desire to have our children grow up learning what is best in Western civilization and not to have them forced into direct contact with its worst phases."[46] In another case, Chinese-Canadian merchants formed an anti-opium league of their own and sent a petition to Ottawa to ask that the federal government to "decisively exercise its authority and powers to prohibit the importation, manufacture and sale of opium into Canada so that the social, physical and moral condition of both Chinese and Europeans may be vastly improved."[47]

What is interesting about these latter forms of resistance is that in many ways they were based on the same ideological concerns of white authorities and played on and reproduced the same racist images that were articulated in broader white society by newspapers, politicians, and social reformers. In some ways, this kind of resistance indirectly helped to lend legitimacy to white concerns that these activities were in fact real problems in need of a solution.

In other cases, Chinese Canadians acted as ethnic brokers between the broader white and Chinese-Canadian communities.[48] The activities of these brokers between the late nineteenth and mid-twentieth centuries are analyzed more fully by Lisa Rose Mar in *Brokering Belonging: Chinese in Canada's Exclusion Era, 1885–1945*. Though their roles shifted and evolved over this time, her work shows how Chinese-Canadian brokers sometimes used racist policies like the head tax to further their own financial advantage. In other cases, they downplayed racist policies and undermined others' resistance to racism, such as the opposition to school segregation in Victoria in the early 1920s, in order to curry favour within the circles of white institutional power.[49] The activities of these Chinese-Canadian entrepreneurs and brokers suggest that "collaboration" with the state is not always a form of what Scott would describe as hidden resistance.[50] Instead, it points to alignments of class interests that cut across racialized boundaries and the use of institutionally racist policies as a way of furthering one's status and socio-economic interests.

## Collaboration and the Settling of Old Scores

A third form of collaboration with the state in the first half of the twentieth century involved groups using the state to settle old scores within the community of co-ethnics. In this instance, Italian Canadians are an instructive case when it comes to examining the complexity of the response to racism and discrimination.

During World War II, about 600 Italian Canadians were interned because of the federal government's fear that at least some Italian Canadians were fascist supporters and hence might side with Italy in its war against the Allies.[51] Operating under the auspices of the Defence of Canada Regulations (DOCR), which allowed authorities to "deprive people of their liberty, without normal safeguards of charges under the Criminal Code, legal counsel, habeas corpus, and a 'day in court,'"[52] the Royal Canadian Mounted Police played a key role in identifying those who were deemed to be threats to the safety and security of Canada. The RCMP's concern about Italian Canadians and their support for fascism was evident even before the war. As Reg Whitaker and Greg Kealey argue, the internment of Italian Canadians was carried out by not only monitoring the Italian language press in Canada,

> but, much more important, sources were developed within various Italian communities around the country, which yielded increasingly detailed reports in the late 1930s. The RCMP found especially useful a network of informants from the communities. Willing collaboration was fairly widespread, perhaps reflecting anti-fascist sentiments and resentment against some of the Canadian leaders enlisted by the Italian diplomats, in other cases, involving more mixed motives.[53]

As one RCMP official put it at the time, "[e]ssentially … the Canadian government interned those whom the Italian community told it to arrest."[54]

Clearly, the internment of Italian Canadians during World War II was carried out with the help of Italian Canadians. This was also true of Japanese-

Canadian internment, where Etsuji Morii cooperated with the British Columbia Security Commission in order to help control potential resistance to the evacuation.[55] Though Morii did not sell out members of the Japanese-Canadian community to the authorities, he did seem to be able to use his position as a broker to mollify the process of internment for himself and his supporters.[56] The motives behind some Italian Canadians' collaboration with the state are no doubt complex and likely stem from personal rivalries, business competition, and regional and political-ideological differences within that community.[57]

In Hamilton, some resented the negative attention that fascist activity brought to the community that was already under threat because of longer-standing feelings of "Italophobia."[58] Besides the stereotype of Italian Canadians as "blackhanders" and "bootleggers," the English-language press in Hamilton in the 1920s and early 1930s equated them with organized crime. According to Cumbo, in that city the internment remains "a highly sensitive subject, the uncertain and often confused role played by informants during the war resulted in intra-group tensions and recriminations lasting to this day."[59]

## Kimura: Collaboration, Resistance, or Collaborative Resistance?

One of the striking aspects of the Kimura memoir is the glimpse he provides into the public transcript of those who were responsible for the confiscation and sale of property. His detailed account of meetings, conversations, and the process of impoundment adds depth and texture to this sad episode in Canadian history. One of the things that stands out in this public transcript is the care authorities seemingly took to make it appear that they were dealing with Japanese Canadians and their property in a fair way and on the basis of the rule of law. Establishing the Fishing Vessel Disposal Committee, the various advisory committees on Japanese Canadian–owned properties, and a dispute resolution process to deal with instances when Japanese Canadians felt their vessels were undervalued speaks to the sense of fair play that the authorities thought they were engaged in. Though operating in a highly discriminatory framework and setting, government officials still seemed to feel that they ought to treat Japanese-Canadian fishing boat–owners fairly, especially when it came to determining the price at which their boats were sold. This is evidenced by the establishment of the Liaison Committee to represent Japanese-

Canadian fishing boat–owners, the hiring of certified appraisers, and the establishment of an appeal mechanism in cases when a price could not be agreed upon. Further, it is notable that final purchase price was based on a negotiation between buyers and sellers, at least until the spring of 1942 when the government decided upon a "forced sales plan." Though clearly in an unequal bargaining position, Japanese-Canadians owners were not initially presented with a take-it-or-leave-it approach to the determination of the value of their fishing boats. Again, in the highly racialized context of the time, it is conceivable that the state could have taken other paths, far less fair, in its dealings with Japanese-Canadian fishing boat–owners. "Fair play" in an unfair context was, as noted earlier, a central element of British and French colonialism around the world. Canadian authorities seem to have inherited the ideology of fair play from their British forefathers, even though the initial decision to confiscate and sell property was far from fair. By claiming to be dealing with Japanese Canadians fairly, authorities no doubt further solidified their belief that even in the context of heightened wartime tension, they were still reasonable, morally superior agents taking a difficult but principled stance on what they perceived as a threat to the security of the country.

The Kimura memoir is also notable for the brief glimpses it provides into Kimura's own motivations for involving himself in the Fishing Vessel Disposal Committee and the ways in which Japanese Canadians responded to state-led oppression during wartime. Part of the memoir can be conceived in what Scott describes above as a hidden transcript of resistance. Though some boat-owners no doubt considered resisting this policy, it does not appear that many engaged in outright resistance, and in several places in his memoir he seeks to refute allegations that Nikkei fishermen hid fishing nets and other equipment before giving up their boats to authorities.[60] Kimura emphasizes the orderly, peaceful way in which fishing boats were brought to government yards for safekeeping before sale but also highlights the limited choices that Japanese-Canadian fishing boat–owners faced in this context. Kimura interprets the orderliness of the processes as a reflection of Japanese-Canadian fishermen's commitment to the Canadian war effort. By cooperating with the quick transfer of ownership, they ensured that their boats would be used productively by the new white owners to help "ensure the food supply."[61] This cooperation, Kimura claims, resulted in long-term changes in broader Canadian opinions of Japanese Canadians. As Kimura suggests, "I think these are meaningful points because they could *make the Canadian general public rec-*

*ognize that Nikkei Canadians carried out their responsibility as Canadian citizens* in spite of extremely difficult circumstances."[62] Because the process of confiscation was so orderly, Kimura speculates that Japanese Canadians gained the trust and respect of other Canadians and were paid back by a reduction in everyday racism that they faced after the war. In their case, cooperation with institutional authorities could be considered a form of hidden resistance to racism.

But can the same be said of Kimura's cooperation with institutional authorities? There is little evidence that he used his position to favour his friends or disadvantage certain Japanese-Canadian fishermen with whom he might have had conflicts or disagreements before the war. His cooperation does not seem to have been motivated by a desire to settle old scores within the community, as was the case with Italian Canadians who collaborated with the authorities in the internment of suspected fascist supporters. As Jordan Stanger-Ross points out, Kimura and his family did derive some personal benefit from participating in the work of the liquidation committee.[63] He and his family were relocated to a "self-support camp" where internees had greater control over their living conditions, and he was allowed to travel to restricted areas of the province during his work for the committee. These seemingly modest material and status benefits were no doubt significant, but it is not clear whether they fully explain his decision to cooperate with the authorities in the dispossession process.

Instead, his collaboration with institutional authorities seems to have been more akin to that of First Nations leaders who tried to make the best of a bad situation and who took on positions as chiefs and councillors in an effort to try to mediate relationships between the state and the targeted racialized community. In so doing, he was adopting an approach that can be characterized as a form of collaborative resistance in which cooperation with institutional authorities can help to lead to the breaking down of racism and discrimination. Though it is unclear whether his initial decision to cooperate in the disposal of property was motivated by a desire to prevent the same kind of "mob"-led violence that was directed against Japanese Canadians during the 1907 Vancouver riots, he did nonetheless invoke this concern in his memoir.[64] Notably, he also gave a rather charitable interpretation of Prime Minister Mackenzie King's decision to uproot Japanese Canadians from their homes. According to Kimura, King "must have been afraid that … under wartime circumstances, someone might actually harm Nikkei people, and if such awful things were to happen, the Japanese military might take revenge on interned Canadian soldiers. I think that the prime minister, after deep deliberation, concluded to send all Nikkei people to a safe place as soon as possible."[65] In the highly charged racist circumstances of the time, collaboration in order to avoid further racist hostility and physical violence coming from the Canadian public was not necessarily an unreasonable choice. Given that members of the community had lived through extreme violence and racist hostility only a generation earlier, his concern over avoiding a repeat of the 1907 riot was probably an accurate assessment of the fears at the time.

Though he does not explicitly say so, he was probably also referring to his own involvement with the liquidation committee when he said that "by following the law, making sacrifices, and cooperating with government policy during the war," Japanese-Canadian fishermen created an atmosphere in postwar Canada that "no longer condones anti-Nikkei practices."[66] In an effort to counter presentist interpretations of his and other's actions during the war, and to address subsequent criticisms directed toward his generation (and indirectly toward him personally), he pleads for a better understanding of the constraints that the community was facing at the time and for the long-term positive consequences of collaborative resistance: "When you criticize, I would like you to investigate, face squarely, and consider the time period, the circumstances, situation, and environment that the *Issei* and some of the *Nisei* were placed in. I would like you to recognize that Nikkei people were rewarded for their struggle and finally reached the dawn of a new era after the war."[67]

Though the reasons for the subsequent postwar economic success of Japanese Canadians are complex,[68] his and others' collaborative resistance ought to be considered as part of the mix.

## NOTES

1 Henry and Tator, *Colour of Democracy*.

2 Porter, *Vertical Mosaic*; Satzewich, *Racism and the Incorporation of Foreign Labour*; Bolaria and Li, *Racial Oppression in Canada*; Anderson, *Vancouver's Chinatown*.

3 Johnson, *Voyage of the Komagata Maru*.

4 Bolaria and Li, *Racial Oppression in Canada*.

5 Stanger-Ross, "Telling a Difficult Past"; Stanley, "Why I Killed Canadian History"; Stanley, *Contesting White Supremacy*; Bonnett, *Anti-Racism*.

6 Backhouse, *Colour-Coded*.

7 Lambertson, "'Dresden Story'"; Avery, *Reluctant Host.*
8 Scott, *Domination and the Arts of Resistance.* See p. 17 specifically for commentary on successfully understanding the political conduct of subordinate groups.
9 Ibid., 19.
10 Brett, *Colonialism and Underdevelopment in East Africa*; Crowder, *West Africa under Colonial Rule*; Crowder, "Indirect Rule."
11 Crowder, *West Africa*; Crowder, "Indirect Rule."
12 Crowder, "Indirect Rule."
13 Groff, "Dynamics of Collaboration," 147.
14 Ibid.
15 Ibid., 146–7
16 Porter, *Vertical Mosaic*; Frideres and Gadacz, *Indians of North America.*
17 Mar, *Brokering Belonging.*
18 Satzewich and Wotherspoon, *First Nations.*
19 Miller, *Shingwuak's Vision.*
20 Carter, *Lost Harvests.*
21 Pettipas, *Severing the Ties That Bind.*
22 Dickason, *Canada's First Nations.*
23 Quoted in Voyageur, *Firekeepers of the Twenty-First Century*, 4.
24 Satzewich and Mahood, "Indian Affairs and Band Governance."
25 Ibid.
26 Walls, *No Need of a Chief for This Band.*
27 Boldt, *Surviving as Indians.*
28 Danziger, *Great Lakes Indian Accommodation and Resistance*, 198.
29 Adams, *Tortured People.*
30 Alfred, *Peace, Power and Righteousness*, 73.
31 Satzewich and Liodakis, *"Race" and Ethnicity in Canada.*
32 Roy, *White Man's Province.*
33 Anderson, *Vancouver's Chinatown*, 58.
34 Ibid.; Mar, *Brokering Belonging.*
35 The class position of farmers and small business–owners is the subject of debate, particularly when it comes to historical analysis where individuals could simultaneously sell their labour power for wages and own some productive property. Some Marxists and neo-Marxists consider farmers and small business–owners as part of the petite bourgeoisie. See, for example, Darroch and Soltow, *Property and Inequality in Victorian Ontario*, and Marsh, *Great Transformation.*
36 Li, *Chinese in Canada*, 84.
37 Miles, *Racism & Migrant Labour.*
38 Li, *Chinese in Canada.*
39 Mar, *Brokering Belonging.*

40 Backhouse, *Colour-Coded.*
41 Ibid., 169.
42 Mar, *Brokering Belonging*; Anderson, *Vancouver's Chinatown.*
43 Anderson, *Vancouver's Chinatown*, 88.
44 Ibid.
45 Ibid., 99.
46 Ibid.
47 Ibid.
48 Mar, *Brokering Belonging.*
49 Ibid.
50 Scott, *Domination and the Arts of Resistance.*
51 Iacovetta et al., eds, *Enemies Within.*
52 Whitaker and Kealey, "A War on Ethnicity?," 128.
53 Ibid., 133.
54 Ibid.
55 Sunahara, *Politics of Racism.*
56 Ibid.
57 Cumbo, "'Uneasy Neighbours.'"
58 Ibid., 104.
59 Ibid., 100.
60 Kimura Memoir, 13–14, 52.
61 Ibid., 52.
62 Ibid. (emphasis in original).
63 Stanger-Ross, introduction to this volume and "Telling a Difficult Past."
64 Kimura Memoir, 6, 97.
65 Ibid., 97
66 Ibid., 54.
67 Ibid., 58.
68 Hawkins, "Becoming a Model Minority."

# 4

# Citizen Beings, Being Citizens: Reflections on Japanese-Canadian Experiences in War and Peace

*Laura Madokoro*

I was very young when my maternal grandmother passed away. I have no personal memories of her, but I do treasure the stories recounted by my parents, aunts, and uncles. I know that Miki Madokoro (née Kimoto) was warm-hearted and generous. She was an outgoing individual who struck up conversations with anyone and everyone – a trait inherited by my Aunt Marlene and my Uncle Bud. I also know that when my family was interned during the Second World War, eventually making their way east to Toronto, she became a die-hard Leafs fan and that my grandfather famously cheered for anyone but her team of choice. Other than these few tidbits, I know little of Miki Madokoro. There is even less in the way of material memories.

One of the few items to survive the passage of time is my grandmother's citizenship certificate. The certificate is about 10.5″ x 7.5″ and is embossed with ornate red filigree. The weight of the paper is thick and surprisingly heavy; it feels important. The certificate is all the more surprising because, as it shows, my grandmother was born in Steveston, British Columbia, in 1918. She was a "natural-born" Canadian.[1] At first glance, therefore, it seems that there was no reason for her to possess such a certificate.

I was reminded of my grandmother's certificate, and its obscure and unexplained origins, as I read through Kishizo Kimura's memoir. Although Kimura does not talk about citizenship explicitly, his memoir is rife with references to the citizenship of Japanese Canadians and that of 白人, Hakujin ("white people" or "Caucasians").[2] As such, Kimura's memoir offers the opportunity to explore the nature of citizenship in Canada during and after the Second World War. More personally, the memoir rekindled a dormant

Figure 4.1 *Above and opposite* Canadian citizenship certificate, Mary Madokoro. From the personal collection of Laura Madokoro.

interest in finding out how and why my Canadian-born grandmother came to have a certificate of Canadian citizenship.

Citizenship certificates in Canada are a relatively recent form of official documentation. From 1868 to 1947, persons could be naturalized as British subjects and received certification to that effect.[3] After the passage of the Canadian Citizenship Act, the government began to issue formal citizenship certificates such as my grandmother's. In 1954, the same year she applied for her "large" citizenship certificate, the so-called "miniature certificate" came into existence. These smaller certificates were wallet-sized and bore the bearer's photograph and signature on the reverse side. As historian P. Davis observes, the miniature certificate was more effective at proving status and identifying the bearer, and so the larger certificate evolved "as an increasingly symbolic document for ceremonial purposes."[4] The idea of my grandmother's citizenship certificate serving a ceremonial or symbolic purpose in the performance of citizenship informs the analysis in this chapter of the gulf between the social experience of citizenship and the legal status of citizen.

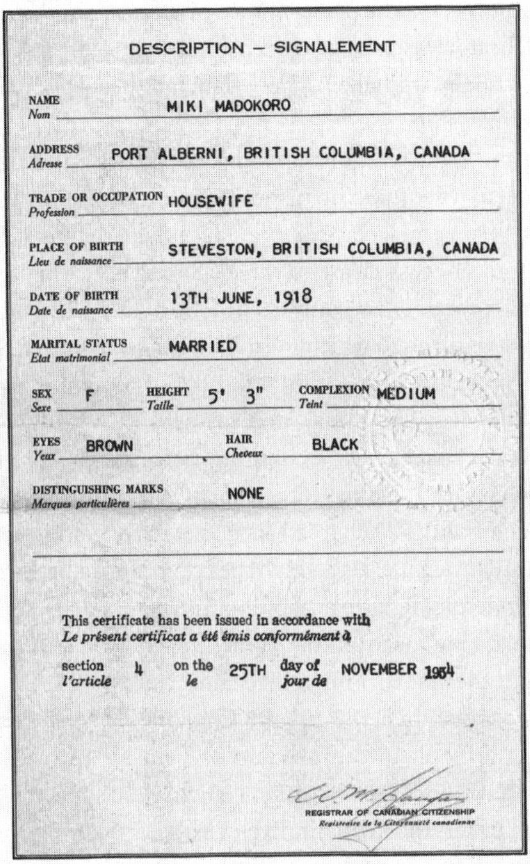
DESCRIPTION – SIGNALEMENT

NAME / Nom: MIKI MADOKORO

ADDRESS / Adresse: PORT ALBERNI, BRITISH COLUMBIA, CANADA

TRADE OR OCCUPATION / Profession: HOUSEWIFE

PLACE OF BIRTH / Lieu de naissance: STEVESTON, BRITISH COLUMBIA, CANADA

DATE OF BIRTH / Date de naissance: 13TH JUNE, 1918

MARITAL STATUS / Etat matrimonial: MARRIED

SEX / Sexe: F HEIGHT / Taille: 5' 3" COMPLEXION / Teint: MEDIUM

EYES / Yeux: BROWN HAIR / Cheveux: BLACK

DISTINGUISHING MARKS / Marques particulières: NONE

This certificate has been issued in accordance with
*Le présent certificat a été émis conformément à*

section / *l'article* 4 on the / *le* 25TH day of / *jour de* NOVEMBER 1954.

REGISTRAR OF CANADIAN CITIZENSHIP
*Registraire de la Citoyenneté canadienne*

To this end, the chapter revisits the many ways that Japanese Canadians experienced citizenship during the internment and postwar years. It considers the numerous passing references to citizenship in Kimura's memoir and notes the evolution in his thinking about the Japanese-Canadian experience of citizenship as a kind of relationship, in contrast to his assumptions about the normative experience of Hakujin Canadians. As part of this process, the chapter considers how Kimura inadvertently communicates differences between the experience of social citizenship, as theorized by T.H. Marshall, and the legal status of citizen. In the case of Japanese Canadians confronted with internment and property dispossession, these differences led to words and actions that amounted to the performance of citizenship that reified the inclusive and celebratory aspects of citizenship in an effort to claim the identity of citizen, while marginalizing how they had been disappointed by the legal status of citizenship.[5]

In thinking about the relationship between history and performance, the historian Kathleen Wilson distinguishes between theatrical and social performances. The former take place on the stage where the intended and actual audiences are more or less clearly defined. Social performances or performances "as social practice," by contrast, function "as both optic and event: a methodological lens through which meanings can be conveyed." They are also an act of cultural transfer, an embodied form of "creating, preserving and transmitting" knowledge, memory, and history."[6] "Indeed," Wilson writes, "performance often enacts what a community imagines to be the most important to its survival." It is therefore critical, Wilson contends, to consider performance "as a politically charged social practice."[7] While appealing, this call fails to illuminate what exactly might be considered a performance. There is a real danger in reducing historical events and actors to mere performances and performers, taking away all that is integral to their beliefs and actions. Was my grandmother performing citizenship by applying for a certificate? Did the act serve to secure her status as a Canadian citizen? As scholars have noted, it is very difficult to capture and present an authentic experience in-text. In what anthropologist Norman Denzin describes as a "crisis of representation," he observes, "[q]ualitative researchers can no longer directly capture lived experience." In other words, lived experience is a chimera, one that exists only in the "social text written by the researcher."[8] Experience and texts are mutually constituted so that "real-life experiences are shaped by understandings gained from participating in the performances of others – performances turned into texts."[9]

This chapter works from the premise that the notions of lived experience and performance are deeply intertwined. It foregrounds the possibility that within the context of social and legal citizenship strictures, certain actions take on the tincture of performance when they may, in fact, simply be part of the lived experience of citizenship. The debates on performance and lived experience inform the analysis that follows, especially Denzin's conclusion that there is a "mystery of experience" with "no secret key that will unlock its meanings."[10] Specifically, the notion of performing citizenship, distinct from an individual's social experience of citizenship, serves as the framework for understanding the unsolved mystery of Miki Madokoro's citizenship certificate. Using this framework, I argue that through actions that simultaneously operated as performances of citizenship, Japanese Canadians sought to move beyond the disappointment of their social experience as citizens to insist upon all the promises that legal citizenship status entailed.[11]

## On Citizenship

Legal citizenship status refers to the civil status of a citizen as the member of a state. Legal citizenship entails both rights and responsibilities. Even before the 1947 Citizenship Act, early citizenship law in Canada referred to the obligations of both government and citizen. For instance, the 1914 Naturalization Act stated: "A person to whom a certificate of naturalization is granted … shall, subject to the provisions of this Act, be entitled to all political and other rights, powers and privileges, and be subject to all obligation, duties and liabilities, to which a natural-born British subject is entitled or subject."[12]

Legal citizenship can also be considered a kind of promise, reflecting mutual hopes and aspirations of what these rights and responsibilities will produce beyond the legal strictures of citizenship. Governments, for instance, hope that citizens will be loyal in a spontaneous and passionate way, beyond the laws requiring loyalty and outlawing treason. They invest in the education of their citizens in order to encourage this loyalty.[13] Meanwhile, governments are expected to protect the rights of citizens, including the right to vote and hold office, and to assist citizens in need outside of the country. Both parties undertake to fulfill these responsibilities in various ways, informed by the hopes and aspirations inherent in the citizenship compact. This is the nature of the promise inherent in the legal status of citizenship.

In Canada, citizenship legislation historically outlined the means by which citizenship could be obtained or revoked. The "right to citizenship," for instance, currently belongs to people born in Canada or to those who meet established criteria, such as the children of Canadian citizens born outside the country.[14] Others may apply for citizenship.[15] Such are the building blocks of citizenship legislation. Recent scholarship has shown that far from being a cold, legal category in which membership depends on adhering to prescribed regulations, citizenship is a dynamic experience. For example, Glenda Simms, in her work on racialized citizenship in Canada, argues that "citizenship is not only a legal definition; it is testimony to how one is treated in a given society."[16] Scholars of the Japanese-Canadian experience emphasize how associations of "alienness" and "foreignness" served to marginalize the Canadian-born Japanese (Japanese Canadians) and normalize "the identity of a Canadian citizen as white" prior to, during, and to some extent after the Second World War.[17]

Citizenship matters profoundly to our understanding of Japanese-Canadian experiences. It matters as a marker of belonging and as evidence of the state's excesses in interning and deporting Japanese-Canadian citizens, acts described by Pamela Sugiman as "violation(s) of the rights of citizenship."[18] Beginning in 1942, the federal Liberal government interned some 22,000 Japanese Canadians, including 13,909 Canadian-born citizens, purportedly for national security reasons, though other factors, such as racial animosity in British Columbia, were important considerations.[19] In 1946, 3,964 citizens had their citizenship revoked and then were deported as part of efforts to reduce the size of the Japanese-Canadian community in Canada.[20] Other rights, including choice of residence, social welfare benefits, and equality in education – all rights held in the promise of legal citizenship – also proved illusory during the war and in the immediate postwar period.[21] As historian Ken Adachi observes, the internment of Japanese Canadians east of the Rockies involved so many restrictions it was "tantamount to being prisoners on probation, enjoying none of the rights of citizenship such as acquiring or leasing property and launching businesses."[22]

Yet even in this moment of crisis, or perhaps precisely because of the intensity of such a time, Japanese Canadians remained hopeful that the promises inherent in the formal status of citizen would protect them. When the partial evacuation from the coast was announced in January 1942 (in which all Japanese male nationals, aged eighteen to forty-five, were to be removed from the coast by 1 April 1942), most Japanese Canadians took the decision "in a reasonable spirit, pending further detail of the orders." According to Adachi, "[m]ost Japanese accepted the fact that certain restrictions and interferences with civil rights had to be assumed 'as willingly and cheerfully as possible.'" They took comfort in the fact that the "policy of 'partial' evacuation had drawn a distinction between aliens and citizens, thus putting a premium upon citizenship 'as something distinctly worth having.'"[23] The move to a total evacuation erased such sentiments.

Despite their disappointment in the promise of citizenship, Japanese Canadians and their supporters framed their opposition to internment processes in terms of equality and citizenship status. A *Nisei* letter to the BC Security Commission, for instance, declared:

> we request you to remember that we are British subjects by birth, that we are no less loyal to Canada than any other Canadian, that we have done nothing to deserve the break-up of our families, that we are law abiding Canadian citizens, and that we are willing to accept suspension of our civil rights – rights to retain our homes and businesses, boats, cars, radios and cameras. Incidentally, we are entitled as native sons to all civil rights of an ordinary Canadian within the limitations of Canada's war effort.[24]

Such appeals were dismissed. Even after the war, full citizenship rights remained elusive. Japanese Canadians remained disenfranchised in British Columbia (and therefore federally) and were barred from returning to their homes on the west coast until 1949.[25] Even Japanese Canadians who enlisted during the Second World War in a powerful performance of citizenship and loyalty ultimately referred to themselves as "second-class citizens."[26] Crucially, the treatment of Japanese Canadians as self-described second-class citizens galvanized community leaders and supporters to campaign for full citizenship rights as well as equality of treatment under the country's immigration laws.[27]

The wartime violations and the rights held in the promise of legal citizenship status became a powerful rallying point for many Japanese Canadians. Notions of citizenship were central to the campaigns for a bill of rights in Canada and redress, and their results had a profound impact on how participants understood themselves as Canadian citizens.[28] In 1988, when Prime Minister Brian Mulroney apologized on behalf of all Canadians for the wartime internment and property dispossession of Japanese Canadians, he stated, "Nearly half a century ago, in the crisis of wartime, the Government of Canada wrongfully incarcerated, seized the property, and disenfranchised thousands of citizens of Japanese ancestry." Wes Fujiwara, one of the leaders in the fight for redress, recalls: "After the settlement happened, someone asked me: 'How do you feel now that redress has happened?' I told that person I felt as if a huge weight had been taken off my shoulders, a huge weight that had been there for more than 40 years. I no longer felt like a second-class citizen. I felt like a first-class citizen for the first time."[29] In Fujiwara's words, we see the manifestation of the social qualities of citizenship. There was no formal category for second-class citizens in Canada, yet until redress was achieved, this was how Fujiwara felt. His experience reflected his social experience of citizenship, and like that of the Japanese-Canadian veterans, it was very different from his legal status in the country.

The idea of citizenship as a social experience gained prominence as a result of the work of British sociologist T.H. Marshall. In 1949, Marshall advanced the notion of "social citizenship" in a lecture titled "Citizenship and Social Class." In exploring the relationship between capitalism, equality, and citizenship, he identified three different types of citizenship: civil, political, and social. From Marshall's perspective, civil citizenship encompassed the "rights necessary for individual freedom," including "liberty of the person, freedom of speech, thought and faith, the right to own property and to conclude valid contracts, and the right to justice." Political citizenship constituted "the right to participate in the exercise of political power, as a member of a body invested with political authority or as an elector of the members of such a body." Social citizenship involved a whole range of rights, "from the right to a modicum of economic welfare and security to the right to share to the full in the social heritage and to live the life of a civilised being according to the standards prevailing in the society."[30] It is the notion of social citizenship that is most pertinent to the discussion that follows, for Marshall completely ignored the question of race in his analysis. Yet for Japanese Canadians, race was at the centre of the tensions between the promise of legal citizenship and their social experience as citizens. The records left by Kishizo Kimura and Miki Madokoro open up the space to contemplate different citizenship experiences and performances, distinct from national narratives of belonging and inclusion, or what Mona Oikawa calls, "nation-building and citizen constitution."[31]

## Kishizo Kimura: Citizen Reflections

Kishizo Kimura came to Canada with his adoptive parents in 1911. Eleven years later, at the age of twenty-three, Kimura applied to be naturalized. It was therefore in his capacity as a naturalized Canadian citizen that Kimura served on the Advisory Committee on Japanese Properties in Greater Vancouver. Although his entire memoir could be read as a citizen's deliberate rendering of the past and a testament of decisions made, certain passages are more pronounced in this regard. For example, the section titled "To the Second and Third Generations" is clearly intended to provide an account of the wartime events to younger generations to whom Kimura wished to explain his actions and those of other *Issei*. This, in and of itself, is revealing of a certain aspect of the social experience of citizenship in wartime – namely, of citizenship as a kind of burden. At a time when the loyalty of citizens is questioned in extraordinary ways, the need to prove and perform citizenship becomes paramount, particularly for those groups who are the subject of suspicious scrutiny.[32] *Nisei* professions of loyalty, especially after the bombing of Pearl Harbor, reflected the pressures they felt to prove themselves as loyal citizens. Kimura's address to younger generations hints at a similar desire to prove himself in the face of suspected criticism. More pertinent to this chapter, however, are the specific references to citizens and citizenship as they shed light on Kimura's different conceptions of Japanese-Canadian and Hakujin citizenship experiences and reflect the normalization of Canadian citizens as white.[33] This normalization, in turn, points to how Japanese Canadians performed citizenship beyond their legal status in order to convince the state, and Canadian society generally, to meet their expectations of what social and legal citizenship embodied.

While Kimura makes a number of explicit references to citizenship in his memoir (detailed below), there are also some noticeable absences. In particular, there is no direct mention of citizenship status in relation to his work on the advisory committee. As a member of the committee, Kimura was a broker, negotiating the sale of Japanese Canadian–owned property and mediating between various parties. He therefore played a critical role in representing the Japanese-Canadian community to the authorities who were pursuing the sale of property. Yet Kimura regularly failed to reference the citizenship status of the Japanese Canadians whose property he was handling. For instance, Kimura recalls, "the property of Canadians or naturalized citizens who resided in enemy countries would sometimes be treated as enemy property." He notes that the "Custodian has already disposed of a few properties, based on a request from removed Nikkei (Japanese lineage) and, with the cooperation of the BC Security Commission, are sending a hundred dollars a month until the account is exhausted." The citizenship status of these Nikkei is unknown. Were they Canadian-born? Naturalized? It is unclear, and perhaps Kimura did not think it was relevant. On other occasions, however, Kimura is more explicit. This is especially true in his recounting of Japanese-Canadian citizenship experiences in relation to those of Hakujin Canadians.

Kimura mentions citizenship far more frequently in the context of the Japanese-Canadian experience than that of Hakujin Canadians. More critically, when Kimura does discuss the citizenship of Hakujin Canadians, it is always in direct reference to the Japanese-Canadian "other." For example, Kimura recounts how newspapers "praised the well-planned government preparations for the mass landing of Nikkei people" in Alberta and Ontario and how "another newspaper report emphasized the protection of Nikkei." Kimura notes further that there were also reports that "*Japanese* crews" would be "locked in, at temporary housing." According to Kimura, "these reports had the effect of calming down citizens' minds, preventing misplaced war hysteria."[34] Significantly, the citizens who need calming are the citizens of "white Canada." In these passages, the citizenship of Japanese Canadians is completely erased.

On other occasions, Kimura draws attention to racist views that facilitated the internment of Japanese-Canadian citizens. Such views had the power to completely undermine the protections embodied in the legal status of citizen, and Kimura captures this phenomenon in his memoir. He writes,

> A newspaper reported in late April that an alderman, who would be a candidate in the next election for the provincial Parliament, insisted on stopping Nikkei people from penetrating the fishing industry and again took up the issue of business licences with the city as if it were a huge problem. He came up with a set of unbelievable licence ratios and insisted that his intention was to maintain a high standard of living for Hakujin citizens, not to persecute Toyojin [Oriental] based on racial prejudice.[35]

According to Kimura, the alderman declared, "If we make it clear to Toyojin that they have no opportunity to engage in commercial activities in our city, they will return to Japan. I don't care whether the refusal of the licences is against international law or human morality. The duty of city council is first of all to serve the future welfare of the citizens."[36] In this case, the alderman's mention of "the future welfare of the citizens" referenced the welfare of white citizens only. The harsh power of the alderman's words, repeated in Kimura's memoir, disrupted the possibility of Japanese Canadians as citizens.

As a result, the idea of performing citizenship in order to prove that Japanese Canadians deserved this legal status, and the protection implied, emerges in a number of passages in the memoir, including in Kimura's discussion of what Japanese-Canadian fishermen experienced after 1942.

Kimura suggests that although all "Nikkei immigrants have suffered from the anti-Nikkei movement since they landed in the province of BC," this was "especially" the case for Japanese fishermen. Kimura writes, "Although they were all naturalized citizens, they suffered from continuous, severe exclusion practices. The number of fishing licences was limited, and moreover, the licences themselves were limited by discriminatory conditions." After the war, however, Kimura understands that the laws had changed and were no longer "anti-Nikkei" and that the remaining limitations were only intended to increase revenues. He observed:

> common sense among the general public no longer condones anti-Nikkei practices, and I believe there is no room for anti-Nikkei propaganda. It was definitely the behaviour of the Nikkei fishermen who created such an atmosphere, by following the law, making sacrifices, and cooperating with government policy during the war. There might be some people who insist that this is "because Nikkei people received suffrage," but it is too simple to conclude that it is a matter of course that naturalized citizens and Canadian-born citizens have suffrage. In reality, Nikkei people in general raised their profile with the Canadian general public by demonstrating their diligence, pleasant character, law-abiding spirit, and patience toward past discriminatory treatment, and these formed the basis whereby Nikkei people were granted suffrage.[37]

In this instance, the behaviour of Japanese Canadians is being assessed, not by fellow citizens but by an anonymous body referred to as the "general public." A similar passage appears later in the memoir when Kimura discusses Dr Carrothers's investigation into the issue of the Asian population in Canada for the 1937 Rowell–Sirois Commission (on dominion–provincial relations). What concerned Kimura was the "rumour in the street that in recent years many Toyojin are entering Canada illegally, but that is simply not true."[38] He insisted that this conception was based on "*wrong information, which unjustly attacks the loyalty and rectitude of Toyojin.*"[39] He continued,

"It is harmful to the public peace to have attacks, such as those of a few weeks ago, arousing public opinion. The government is satisfied that military and judiciary authorities are well prepared to deal with any possible disturbance. Therefore, the general public should understand that the government has made sufficient arrangements to deal with any situation."[40] Again, Kimura refers to "public opinion" and the "general public," erasing the urgency attached to discussions of citizens (Japanese Canadians and Hakujin alike) in the later context of wartime internment and dispossession. In the case of the Rowell–Sirois Commission and pre-war sentiment, it is an anonymous public and not Hakujin citizens who are assessing their Japanese-Canadian neighbours.

Perhaps in Kimura's mind, citizenship united people during peacetime and divided them during the war. At the very least, his choice of language reveals a certain degree of ambivalence about the rights and responsibilities of citizenship. This ambivalence is particularly pronounced in Kimura's discussion of Japanese-Canadian veterans. He writes: "After coming home from the war, they acquired Canadian citizenship and the right to vote. However, they were not exempt from the impoundment order, and their boats were liquidated. They, as well, had to follow the order for removal of all Nikkei people from the coast."[41]

In actual fact, the men who served were naturalized Canadians. When they returned home, they fought for and eventually obtained the right to vote in 1931, but in Kimura's understanding, they also acquired citizenship. The conflation between franchise and citizenship is telling on this occasion, for it suggests that even though Kimura understands that franchise is only part of the citizenship conversation (see quote beginning "common sense among the general public," above), he places a premium on the franchise rather than on legal citizenship status. More than the status itself, it is the promise of what it represents – such as full participation as political subjects – that matters. His observation that the veterans were "not exempt from the impoundment order" acknowledges the limits of legal citizenship, limits that, in the case of Japanese Canadians, were reinforced by the social experience of citizenship. The gulf between the two could precipitate a performance of citizenship, a phenomenon that Kimura identifies in his memoir.

When the actions of the Canadian state during the war drained citizenship of value, Kimura observes that Japanese Canadians replenished the empty vessel by behaving as model citizens. Of the Japanese-Canadian fishermen "giving up their boats and cooperating promptly to release the boats to go out fishing," Kimura argues that their response should be made into "meaningful points because they could *make the Canadian general public recognize that Nikkei Canadians carried out their responsibility as Canadian citizens* in spite of extremely difficult circumstances."[42] In this passage, Kimura points to how Japanese Canadians should behave in order to fulfil their responsibilities as Canadian citizens, pointing to the performance of citizenship as an identity claim rather than a legal status. It was a performance born of deep inequity.

Throughout Kimura's memoir there are hints of the uneven power dynamics at play during the internment and dispossession of Japanese Canadians. In his written expressions and his choice of examples, Kimura inadvertently shows that Japanese Canadians had to perform their citizenship status, while citizenship was the normative experience for Hakujin Canadians. The idea of Japanese Canadians having to perform as citizens frames my exploration of why and how Miki Madokoro, a Canadian-born woman, sought a certificate of Canadian citizenship almost a decade after the war's end.

## Miki Madokoro: Acts of Citizenship

In *The Year of Finding Memory*, Judy Fong Bates writes of her father's tragic suicide and the pain and unanswered questions triggered by his sudden death. Pointing to the power of material history, Bates recounts how her desperate feelings were further complicated when she discovered her father's Canadian citizenship and head tax certificates in a box under his bed. She writes, "I took a deep breath and lifted more letters out of the box … Toward the bottom of the box, on top of some Kuomintang government bonds, was his Canadian citizenship certificate, dated 25 July 1950."[43]

Similarly, in *Bittersweet Passage: Redress and the Japanese Canadian Experience*, Justice Maryka Omatsu recounts comparable feelings upon discovering her own father's official papers. She recalls:

> In preparation for his death, my father, always the accountant, had organized his papers and balanced his finances. All his worldly and prized possessions fit into one drawer. Going through his wallet, I found his plastic Canadian citizenship card, his Hamilton senior citi-

> zens transit card, and – tucked away in a back compartment and neatly folded – his worn World War II government-issued "enemy alien" identification card, complete with his photo and thumb print.[44]

Significantly, for Omatsu, it was her father's numbered identification card, which identified him as an enemy alien, that evoked the greatest feeling: "During the war and for a time after, all JC were legally required to carry these numbered identification cards. They had to produce them upon request by police and government officials. Sitting on his bed, with his lifetime spread out around me, I felt anger and sadness upon seeing that tattered document – anger at the government that had "tattooed" my father and sadness for the man who had always lived in fear."[45]

My reaction to my seeing my grandmother's citizenship certificate for the first time was less momentous; I considered it an interesting curiosity, and it was not until I began to think about Kimura's references to citizenship that I began to wonder about the origin of the certificate. Like the documents conserved by Judy Fong Bates's father, the simple fact of the certificate's survival seemed to hint at it having some kind of value. My grandmother did not, for instance, retain the registration card she was required to complete and carry in 1941. Yet there was no other surviving information to explain how my grandmother felt about obtaining a document that proved her legal status as a Canadian citizen. Indeed, during her lifetime it seems that she simply kept it tucked in a drawer. It was my grandfather who, after her death, "put it with his important papers."[46]

Other relatives expressed surprise that she had the certificate. For instance, my great-aunt (also Canadian-born) had no such certificate.[47] None of my grandmother's surviving children recall her talking about citizenship. As my Uncle Dennis reminded me,

> neither Mom nor Dad were very demonstrative about the whole evacuation, internment and resettlement. We did not sit around the dinner table hearing stories about that time. The whole attitude was "shigata ga nai" – it can't be helped, so let us just get on with what we can make of our lives. And, in my opinion, they did very well raising five children in a country that still really regarded them as second-class citizens.[48]

I think that my uncle is right, that in many ways legal citizenship did not matter to my grandparents, who had other preoccupations. Still, I do think that citizenship, as a social experience, must have mattered to my grandmother in some capacity. The evidence for this rests, ironically, with her application for a document to prove her legal status as a citizen. After all, why would a Canadian-born woman have a citizenship certificate? Did she need it? Or did she want it? My suspicion is that even if the certificate was obtained as a result of the most mundane bureaucratic processes, its preservation – first by my grandmother and then by other relatives – ascribes value to the notion of being a citizen, especially when an individual, and a family, have been disappointed by the promise of citizenship.

According to statistics from Citizenship and Immigration Canada, almost 20,000 citizenship certificates were issued to Canadian citizens in 1954. This pales in comparison to the 58,711 issued a year later and the 95,462 issued in 1957.[49] The reasons that so many citizens applied for certificates remain unclear. So too do the various reasons that people, and their descendants, preserve such documents, though it is possible to speculate on motives in both cases. These motives might include a bureaucratic reason such as an application for a passport or a driver's licence that requires proof of identity. Citizenship certificates might similarly be preserved as evidence or as symbolic proof of belonging.

Over the course of researching my grandmother's citizenship certificate, I discovered one other citizenship certificate belonging to a Japanese Canadian. Unlike my grandmother's, which had been relegated to safekeeping in a drawer and then a file of "important papers," this one was preserved at Library and Archives Canada. It belonged to Anno Makishi, who is generally recognized as the first Okinawan to settle in Canada. He arrived in BC in 1903 and farmed in the province before moving to Alberta. Makishi was naturalized in 1907 and worked as a fireman in the coal mines near Drumheller before returning to farming. He passed away in 1965.[50] Among his archival fonds, one finds what my grandfather would have called "important papers," carefully labelled and carefully preserved in acid-free folders. These papers include copies of his Japanese passport and Canadian Citizenship Certificate No. 169274, issued 6 July 1954. Makishi's certificate is different from my grandmother's. It was issued under a different series (Series A), and the certificate clearly states that the certificate is being "Issued under the Canadian Citizenship Act." The information on the back is also slightly different.

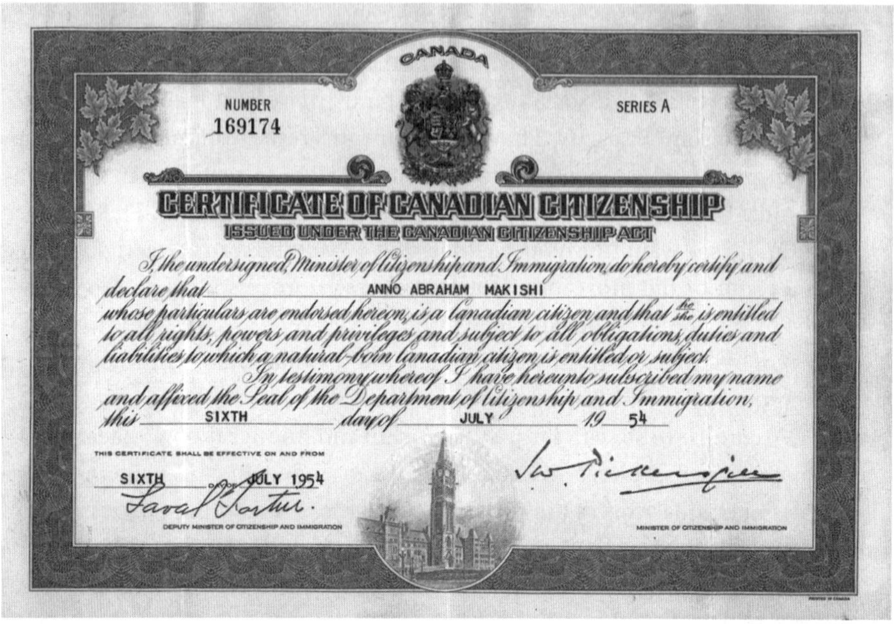

CANADA

NUMBER 169174

SERIES A

CERTIFICATE OF CANADIAN CITIZENSHIP

ISSUED UNDER THE CANADIAN CITIZENSHIP ACT

I, the undersigned, Minister of Citizenship and Immigration, do hereby certify and declare that ANNO ABRAHAM MAKISHI whose particulars are endorsed hereon, is a Canadian citizen and that he/she is entitled to all rights, powers and privileges and subject to all obligations, duties and liabilities to which a natural-born Canadian citizen is entitled or subject.

In testimony whereof I have hereunto subscribed my name and affixed the Seal of the Department of Citizenship and Immigration, this SIXTH day of JULY 1954

THIS CERTIFICATE SHALL BE EFFECTIVE ON AND FROM

SIXTH DAY OF JULY 1954

DEPUTY MINISTER OF CITIZENSHIP AND IMMIGRATION

MINISTER OF CITIZENSHIP AND IMMIGRATION

Figure 4.2 *Above and opposite* Canadian citizenship certificate, Anno Abraham Makishi. Citizenship certificate for Anno Makishi © Government of Canada. Reproduced with the permission of Library and Archives Canada (2016). LAC, Anno Abraham Makishi fonds, MG 30, C115, Vol. 1.

Though the preservation of this certificate at Library and Archives Canada imbues the document with significance, it is unclear why Makishi obtained a citizenship certificate. The fact that he was naturalized, rather than Canadian-born, may have played a part in his decision to obtain formal documentation attesting to his legal status. In my grandmother's case, the story is complicated by the fact that she was Canadian-born.[51] At first, the most plausible explanation was that she was travelling and needed it for a passport application. She may even have needed it to cross the border. But this seems unlikely. My aunt was only one year old when my grandmother applied for her certificate and does not believe my grandmother travelled abroad that year or any time immediately afterwards.[52]

When I asked experts in the field about my grandmother's certificate, they thought she might have been one of the Canadians deported to Japan after the war. Professor Victor Ujimoto of Guelph University was surprised that a Canadian-born woman was in possession of a citizenship certificate. So too was historian Patricia Roy. Both suggested that the only reason she would

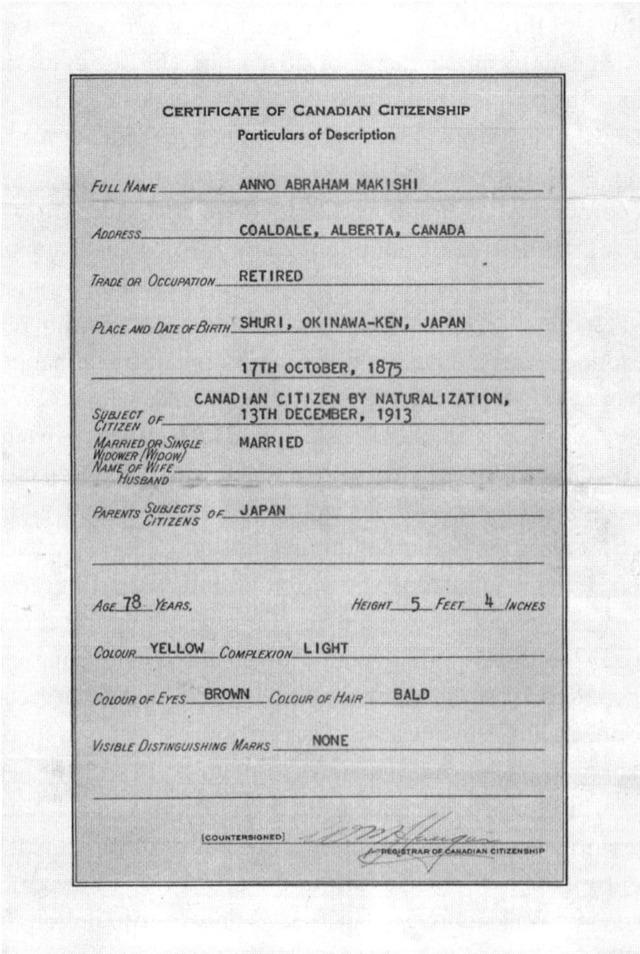

CERTIFICATE OF CANADIAN CITIZENSHIP
Particulars of Description

FULL NAME ANNO ABRAHAM MAKISHI

ADDRESS COALDALE, ALBERTA, CANADA

TRADE OR OCCUPATION RETIRED

PLACE AND DATE OF BIRTH SHURI, OKINAWA-KEN, JAPAN

17TH OCTOBER, 1875

SUBJECT / CITIZEN OF CANADIAN CITIZEN BY NATURALIZATION, 13TH DECEMBER, 1913

MARRIED OR SINGLE / WIDOWER (WIDOW) MARRIED

NAME OF WIFE / HUSBAND

PARENTS SUBJECTS / CITIZENS OF JAPAN

AGE 78 YEARS, HEIGHT 5 FEET 4 INCHES

COLOUR YELLOW COMPLEXION LIGHT

COLOUR OF EYES BROWN COLOUR OF HAIR BALD

VISIBLE DISTINGUISHING MARKS NONE

(COUNTERSIGNED) REGISTRAR OF CANADIAN CITIZENSHIP

have sought a certificate was if she had been deported to Japan and had subsequently returned to Canada. As Ujimoto explained, "many Canadian born 'citizens' were given a forced choice to 'return' to Japan or to be interned east of the Rockies. Many children didn't have a choice but to 'return' with their parents to their place of emigration if their parents decided to return to Japan. This resulted in citizenship being stripped, but the irony was that being born in Canada didn't confer the same citizenship rights to all people."[53]

My grandmother was not a deportee. Still, as I researched her history, the case of the deportees came to underscore why so many Japanese Canadians, including perhaps my grandmother, felt the need to claim their identities as

Canadian citizens through the performance of words and acts that disguised the poverty of their social experience of citizenship. The case of the deportees also hinted at the complex history surrounding a single document, for, read another way, the certificate also appears as concrete evidence for someone whose status as a citizen had been profoundly undermined.

The deportation of natural-born Canadians to Japan (a country they had never known) stands as a low point in the promise of Canadian citizenship, for it marked an occasion when citizens were stripped of their rights as well as their legal status as citizens.[54] The decision to pursue citizenship revocation and deportations emerged from a debate about what should happen to interned Japanese Canadians after the war, and it coincided with the drafting and introduction of the Canadian Citizenship Act. There was deep tension between the two. As historians Patricia Roy, Jack Granatstein, Masako Lino, and Hiroko Takamura observe in *Mutual Hostages*, "[i]n Parliament, BC members warned against using the proposed Citizenship Act to allow Japanese to evade deportation."[55] At the same time, they note, "Canadians at the time were unusually conscious of citizenship; the first Citizenship Act was due to come into effect on 1 January 1947. Many editors urged the government to cancel the orders as acts of racial discrimination which contradicted the new concept of Canadian citizenship."[56] While leaders of the Japanese community protested that "legal barriers on their movement were inconsistent with the new Canadian Citizenship Act," politicians in British Columbia, most notably Ian Mackenzie (himself a naturalized citizen and member of Parliament for Vancouver Centre), opposed their return to the province.[57] In December 1945, cabinet therefore decided to give Japanese Canadians two options: to move east of the Rockies or to go to Japan. These limited options served a secondary purpose, that of a loyalty test.[58] Those who chose Japan over dispersal were later considered disloyal.

Church leaders, academics, journalists, and certain politicians (such as members of the Co-operative Commonwealth Federation) were outraged by the deportations, and there is some suggestion that their protests, including court challenges, influenced the politically sensitive prime minister, Mackenzie King.[59] Nevertheless, the government pursued its plans for citizenship revocation and deportation. These plans received a considerable boost in February 1946 when the Supreme Court ruled that the proposed deportations were legal, except for those of dependent women and children. The following summer, five boats carrying 3,964 people of Japanese ancestry were sent to

Japan. Despite the court's ruling, this figure included 2,000 Canadian-born persons, one-third of whom were dependent children under the age of sixteen who were ostensibly going to Japan voluntarily.[60] When the federal government apologized for the internment and announced the redress package in 1988, it recognized the deportations as a wrong, using the language of expulsion and deportation rather than the misleading term that had described the initial removal of natural-born Canadians, *repatriation*.[61]

The case of the deportees provides evidence of why many Japanese Canadians took extraordinary measures to speak the language of citizenship and perform as citizens, paradoxically lending import to the very legal status by which they had been disappointed. The case of the deportees, along with the tensions between social and legal citizenship captured in Kimura's memoir, led me to think of my grandmother's citizenship application as a kind of performance, especially after my efforts to find out about her application for a certificate produced little of substance. Her case file, preserved at Citizenship and Immigration Canada, revealed only mundane transactions, suggesting there was nothing exceptional about her application.[62] She applied for her certificate on 12 March 1954 in Port Alberni, where she lived. Her application includes reference to her birth in Steveston, British Columbia, in 1918, her marriage to Yoshio Madokoro, her occupation as a housewife, and her then four children. Her application was processed under Sections 4(1)(A) 34(1)(i) of the 1952 Citizenship Act.[63]

Section 4(1)(A) defines a Canadian citizen and states: "A person born before the 1st day of January, 1949, is a natural-born Canadian citizen, if he was born in Canada or on a Canadian ship and was not an alien on the 1st day of January, 1947."[64] Section 34(1)(i) states: "The Governor in Council may make regulations generally for carrying into effect the purposes and provisions of this Act, and in particular with respect to the following matters: ... the manner of proof of Canadian citizenship and the extension of certificates of citizenship." In other words, Miki Madokoro's application was processed based on her status as a Canadian citizen and her ability to prove this status. Her case file suggests that her birth certificate served as proof.

Nothing in the file hints at the larger motives behind her application. Perhaps, as Judy Fong Bates's recollections imply, there was something appealing about having a tangible proof of citizenship. Or perhaps the document was required for some bureaucratic transaction. We just do not know. We can speculate, however, based on Kishizo Kimura's insights into the social experience of Japanese Canadians, that the performance of citizenship in a quest to assert a citizen identity was an important aspect of the wartime experience. Miki Madokoro's certificate evokes the possibility that it remained an important feature of the postwar period as well.

## Conclusions

Miki Madokoro received her citizenship certificate seven years after the federal Liberal government passed the Citizenship Act, establishing a category of national citizenship distinct from British subjecthood. Prime Minister Mackenzie King, speaking at the first citizenship ceremony as a "citizen of Canada," declared citizenship to be "the highest honour a nation can confer upon an individual who has not been born into this heritage." On behalf of "all Canadians," he "welcomed" those who received certificates on 3 January 1947 "into the full enjoyment of the rights of Canadian citizenship," noting that "without citizenship, much else is meaningless."[65]

My grandmother may have heard King's comments, broadcast nationally on the CBC, but I wonder if they meant anything to her. She was a Canadian citizen by birth, but this status failed to protect her and her family against removal from their home in Tofino and the loss of thousands of dollars of property during the Second World War. I wonder if King's words rang hollow, given the fact that she continued to be denied the right to vote at the time of his speech and that she and her family were prohibited from moving back to British Columbia until 1949, two years after King spoke about citizenship in the national broadcast. Or perhaps she held out hope for the promise of citizenship and shared King's belief that Canada's "new conception of citizenship" would "bridge the gaps created by geography and racial dissent." I wonder.

In a symbolic gesture, King received the first Canadian citizenship certificate. Yet the significance of my grandmother's citizenship certificate has proved more elusive. Why did a Canadian-born woman need or want a citizenship certificate? What did it mean to her? Was it a testament to her status as a Canadian citizen? Was it something akin to the symbolism of the prime minister receiving the first Canadian citizenship certificate? Or was it intended to serve as protection against any possible future violation of rights of the kind she had experienced during the war?

We will probably never know the answer to these questions. Reading Kishizo Kimura's memoir, however, hints at a possible explanation for why she submitted an application for a citizenship certificate in 1954. Kimura's subtle references to different forms of citizenship reveal how Japanese Canadians performed various kinds of citizen-behaviour in order to move beyond their impoverished experience of social citizenship and the unfulfilled promises of legal citizenship in Canada. In Kimura's memoir, citizenship is treated as the normative experience for Hakujin Canadians, while Japanese Canadians appear in constant negotiation with their citizenship status and the disappointment it provoked. Relatedly, my grandmother's certificate evokes an attempt to secure the full potential of both social and legal citizenship in Canada, an aspiration that she may, or may not, have achieved in her lifetime.

The preservation, and survival, of Miki Madokoro's citizenship certificate raises questions instead of providing answers. It does not tell us whether or not she was a proud Canadian citizen or whether the promises of citizenship were ever fulfilled in her mind, disappointed as they were during the Second World War. The certificate's survival does, however, provide a window through which to view and reflect upon the Japanese-Canadian citizenship experience. Crucially, this window encourages an interrogation of the meaning and significance of formal legal citizenship status and how it intersects with the lived experience of social citizenship, resulting in actions that take on the hue and character of citizenship. To suggest that citizenship is lived as well as performed is not to detract from the value of citizenship; instead, the interconnected nature of lived and performed citizenship points to the historically contested nature of citizenship in Canada, a contest that continues in the present day.

NOTES

1 "Natural-born" is the official term used in the 1947 Citizenship Act.

2 The term 白人 or Hakujin is difficult to translate. Literally translated, it means "white person," but this translation loses some of the relational and contextual significance of the term Hakujin. The translator has therefore decided to retain Hakujin in the translated text. I agree with this decision because it affirms my own inclination, in keeping with the language employed by critical race scholars in Canada, to use the original, Hakujin, and its reference to whiteness, in my analysis of Kimura's memoir. See, for instance, Razack, *Race, Space and the Law*.

3 The first naturalization law in Canada was passed in 1868 and related to the status of British subjects within the dominion. Canadian citizenship status, as such, was introduced in the 1910 Immigration Act in an effort to distinguish British subjects born in the country and those arriving from outside the country.
4 Davis and Lafrance, *History of Naturalization and Citizenship Certificates*, 17.
5 Clarkson, *Room for All of Us*. Clarkson has been at the forefront in the production of celebratory narratives of citizenship that emphasize inclusion and belonging. Clarkson and John Ralston Saul are founders and co-chairs of the Institute for Canadian Citizenship. See also Clarkson, "Belonging: The Paradox of Citizenship." There is an echo of this in Patricia Roy's work on the postwar period: "In preparing a presentation for the Royal Commission on Bilingualism & Biculturalism in 1964, the Japanese Canadian Citizens' Association declared, 'we are for the multi-cultural society where a Canadian citizen is recognized as a national of Canada.' For both the Japanese and the Chinese, citizenship had trumped ethnic or 'racial origin.'" Roy, *Triumph of Citizenship*, 309.
6 Wilson, "Introduction," 376. Wilson cites the work of Diana Taylor, "Scenes of Cognition," 365.
7 Wilson, "Introduction," 377.
8 Denzin, *Interpretive Ethnography*, 3.
9 Ibid., 33.
10 Ibid., 36.
11 The work of organizations such as the Japanese Canadian Citizens' Association (JCCA) is beyond the scope of this chapter. Nevertheless, it is important to recognize that the JCCA, in its role as a broker between Japanese Canadians and Japanese nationals and the federal government, played a critical role in advancing the possibility of citizenship for these individuals. It did this by translating manuals on "How to Become a Canadian Citizen" into Japanese and advocating on behalf of people who were facing revocation, had lost their naturalization certificates, or were applying for citizenship for the first time. See Japanese Canadian Citizens' Association (LAC), MG28-V1, Vol. 9, File 19, 36–8. The JCCA also gave critical weight to the substance of Canadian citizenship by speaking to the language of rights and equality outlined in the act. Ibid. Moreover, through its efforts at promoting citizenship, it drew the attention of the federal government. A memorandum dated 28 June 1950 to Mr Foulds, the director of the Citizenship Registration Branch, noted, "one of the objectives of the Association has apparently been to encourage young Japanese Canadians to relinquish their sentimental ties with Japan and to adapt themselves as quick as possible to the Canadian way of life." The association's efforts to assist the return of those deported to Japan were also noted.
12 "Naturalization Act, 1914."
13 See McLean, "Education, Identity, and Citizenship."

14 "Citizenship Act."
15 Ibid.
16 Simms, "Racism as a Barrier," 333.
17 Oikawa, *Cartographies of Violence*, 9.
18 Sugiman, "'These Feelings That Fill My Heart,'" 80.
19 Adachi, *The Enemy That Never Was*, 414.
20 "Repatriation of Persons of Japanese Race; Revocation of Status; Loyalty Commission," Cabinet Conclusions, 15 December 1945, LAC, RG2, Privy Council Office, Vol. 2637, Item 6371.
21 Roy, *Triumph of Citizenship*, 211.
22 Adachi, *The Enemy That Never Was*, 258.
23 Ibid., 231.
24 Miki, *Redress*, 67.
25 Japanese Canadians were denied the franchise in British Columbia, rendering them ineligible to vote in municipal and federal elections as well. During the war, it was thought that as they were relocated east, they might get to vote in federal elections, but the government passed a bill in 1944 that prevented those who were ineligible to vote in the previous election from doing so in the forthcoming one. The Citizenship Act was amended in the spring of 1947 to provide the franchise to Chinese and South Asian Canadians, but Japanese Canadians and Aboriginal peoples remained disenfranchised.
26 Obata explains his decision to enlist as follows: "we could not accept any kind of discrimination, even in the matter of service in the armed forces for to do so would be to accept a second-class citizens status." Obata, as quoted in Miki, *Redress*, 222.
27 See Miki, *Redress*; Bangarth, *Voices Raised in Protest*; Fowke, afterword to *They Made Democracy Work*. On immigration issues, see Japanese Canadian Citizens' Association (LAC). Along with the Chinese Canadians Association, the JCCA petitioned the minister of citizenship and immigration and argued that because of the discrimination on immigration issues, Japanese Canadians were "second-class citizens."
28 McAllister, *Terrain of Memory*. On the bill of rights, see Roy, *Triumph of Citizenship*, 209; MacLennan, *Toward the Charter*, 99. MacLennan observes that "the most vocal advocate was George Tanaka, National Executive Secretary of the Japanese Canadian Citizens Association of Toronto. Tanaka was much sought after by other civil libertarians to lend his group's support to the lobbying effort to secure a bill of rights. In a speaking tour of the country in 1948, the association leader argued the case for a Canadian bill of rights." According to MacLennan, "Tanaka linked his support for a bill of rights to his organization's overarching goal to end racial discrimination."
29 Miki, *Redress*, 303.
30 Marshall, *Citizenship and Social Class*, 10–11. For a more recent discussion of the social aspects of citizenship, see Bloemeraad, *Becoming a Citizen*.

31 Oikawa, *Cartographies of Violence*, 319; Bothwell, "Something of Value?," 34. Bothwell explains how identity and citizenship are conflated when citizenship is used to distinguish nation from empire: "Canada's practice of citizenship was merely an extension of colonial practice dating back to the seventeenth century. It was the fruit of recognition that the requirements, and therefore the self-definition, of colonial political communities differed radically from that of the empire as a whole. The values of colonial citizenship, the benefits that membership in the colonial community conferred were different from those of the mother country, even if, in a vast empire, they might still be accommodated. The process of self-definition, of conceiving a separate nationality and a separate citizenship, well illustrates the difficulty of maintaining two standards in a geographically disparate political entity such as the British Empire. But, as generations of politicians, colonial and imperial, might testify, it may also illustrate its inevitability."

32 Scholars use the term *burden of citizenship* most regularly in reference to the Indigenous experience in Australia. The idea is that because the norms of citizenship are essentially assimilationist, citizenship can become a burden on those to whom it is granted. See Wells and Christie, "Namatjira and the Burden of Citizenship," 121; Isin and Nyers, eds., *Routledge Handbook of Global Citizenship Studies*.

33 Oikawa, *Cartographies of Violence*, 9.

34 Kimura Memoir, 31. All references to Kimura's memoir will reference the page numbers of the manuscript as it appears in this book.

35 Ibid., 90.

36 Ibid., 91.

37 Ibid., 54.

38 The federal government ran a Status Adjustment Program from 1960 to 1974 in which Chinese migrants who had entered the country illegally could come forward, confess, and have their status normalized. Twelve thousand people did so, and this process, which also revealed the presence of organized smuggling rings, served to confirm in the minds of many that there was something immoral about the "Asian character." The program remains under-researched, but some key details are available in Roy, *Triumph of Citizenship*, 278; Kelley and Trebilcock, *The Making of the Mosaic*, 364.

39 Oikawa, *Cartographies of Violence*, 68–9 (emphasis in original). The proven loyalty of Japanese Canadians is a recurrent theme in the literature on internment and redress. See Miki, *Redress*, 67.

40 Kimura Memoir, 95–6.

41 Ibid., 43–4.

42 Ibid., 52.

43 Bates, *Year of Finding Memory*, 6. It appears that the discovery of her father's head tax certificate in the same pile had a more powerful effect. Bates writes, "For as long as I had known my father, he had been an old man. But here he was, a youth, staring at

me across time itself. At that moment it seemed as if we both had our lives ahead of us. If only I could find a way into the past and warn him."

44 Omatsu, *Bittersweet Passage*, 35.

45 Ibid.

46 Marlene Mortensen, email exchange with author, 28 August 2015.

47 Frances Nakagawa, interview by author, 28 June 2015.

48 Dennis Madokoro, email exchange with Laura Madokoro, 23 March 2015.

49 Access to Information Request, Citizenship and Immigration Canada.

50 Anno Abraham Makishi fonds, LAC MG30 C115. It is not clear what happened to Makishi during the war. There are no references to his wartime experience in official histories of the Japanese-Canadian community, and there are no records relating to the war years in his archival fonds. Nakayama, *Issei*, 165.

51 After 1947, Canadian-born women had to apply for a citizenship certificate if they married a non-Canadian because they lost citizenship status as a result. This was not the case for my grandmother because my grandfather was also Canadian-born.

52 Marlene Mortensen, email exchange with author, 28 August 2015.

53 Victor Ujimoto, email exchange with author, 9 April 2015. The archival record suggests that applications for Canadian-born persons did occur but, as Ujimoto and Roy suggest, this was most often by persons who were in Japan for a variety of reasons before, during, and after the war. Some served in the Japanese military; others were children when they arrived in the country before the war. See "Certificate of Proof of Canadian Citizenship – Japanese," LAC, RG25, VOL. 4971, 58-BLX-40.

54 Adachi, *The Enemy That Never Was*, 308.

55 Roy et al., *Mutual Hostages*, 178.

56 Ibid., 180.

57 Ibid., 185.

58 Miki and Kobayashi, *Justice in Our Time*, 50. The discussions in cabinet suggest that there was some concern about the deportation of natural-born Canadians. Louis St Laurent, the minister of justice, indicated that existing provisions in the Immigration Act and the Naturalization Act "affected aliens and naturalized British subjects but not persons born in Canada." Under the War Measures Act, "Canadian-born Japanese were subject to deportation, to revocation of their British and Canadian status and to examination by the Loyalty Commission and as such, the government would be going beyond existing legislation in very important particulars." The Loyalty Commission, with a membership of three, had the power to consider individuals referred by the minister of labour and recommend deportation if they were found to be disloyal. St Laurent indicated, "on the other hand, if the proposed Orders were confined to Japanese nationals and naturalized Japanese, there would be no departure from the principles of the present law." Cabinet decided that for the present, "a) the scope of the enquiries of the proposed Loyalty Commission should extend only to persons

of Japanese nationality and naturalized Canadians of Japanese race; b) that repatriation of Canadian-born Japanese should be confined to those who wished to be sent to Japan; and, c) that Orders in Council to provide for deportation and to establish the Loyalty Commission be approved in accordance with the above decisions." When this decision was contested, the government appealed to the Privy Council and noted that "pending the outcome of the appeal, the government repatriate only those persons of Japanese race who still desired to be returned to Japan" and that in the meantime, "the government continue to seek the dispersal of Japanese to all parts of Canada." "Repatriation of Persons of Japanese Race."

59 Sunahara, *Politics of Racism*, 165. Sunahara observes that cabinet had considered this issue earlier but delayed making a decision until the possible backlash in British Columbia could be accounted for.

60 Niwayama, "Caught In-between," 11. The actual numbers break down as follows: 34 per cent were Japanese nationals, 15 per cent were naturalized Canadians, and 51 per cent were Canadian-born. Eighteen per cent were sixteen years of age or over, and 33 per cent were dependent children under sixteen years of age. On the experience of the deportees, see Kage, *Uprooted Again*.

61 The initial discussions in cabinet about revoking citizenship and deporting Japanese Canadians involved not only repatriation but also measures to "deal finally with the segregation of persons in Canada of Japanese race." "Repatriation and Re-settlement of Persons of Japanese Race," Cabinet Conclusions, 2 February 1945, LAC, RG2, Vol. 2636, Item 5555.

62 The sparseness of the file stands in marked contrast to "high-profile" cases such as that of the actress Mary Pickford. Pickford, a Canadian-born woman, lost her Canadian citizenship when she married the American Douglas Fairbanks. She sought Canadian citizenship in 1977, shortly before she passed away. Her case file contains a list of honours, a curriculum vitae, and copies of her birth certificate and passport as well as a slew of correspondence between officials excited about the possibility of welcoming her back as a "fellow Canadian." "Mary Pickford Application for Citizenship," LAC, RG6, Vol. 659. The government did not consistently publish statistics relating to the acquisition of citizenship certificates by Canadians, but from 1952 to 1959 (years for which there are published reports) more than 400,000 people obtained citizenship certificates. Presumably, the majority of these applications occurred as part of the application for citizenship. See *Canadian Citizenship Statistics*.

63 When Minister Walter Harris presented legislation to revise the Citizenship Act in 1952, he indicated that the most significant change was to Section 19, which gave the government greater powers to strip a naturalized citizen of citizenship on the basis of disloyalty. The amendments were the product of Cold War fears about communist infiltration and a desire, on the part of the federal government, to remove communist agitators from the country. There was some debate in the House of Commons

over whether the government was overreaching its power, but the bill ultimately passed without controversy. Scholars have largely overlooked the 1952 Citizenship Act. Kelley and Trebilcock, for instance, ignore it completely in their comprehensive analysis of the history of immigration laws in Canada. See Kelley and Trebilcock, *The Making of the Mosaic*; see "House of Commons Debates, 1952–3."

64 An alien was defined as "a person who is not a Canadian citizen, Commonwealth citizen, British subject or citizen of the Republic of Ireland."

65 "Mackenzie King is Canada's First Citizen."

# Afterword

*Pamela Sugiman*

> As people actually encountered Nikkei people who had moved and spread all over Canada, they soon realized that past discrimination was unjust. They gradually came to know the true value of Nikkei people. The accumulated anti-Nikkei sentiment evaporated, and people became open and warm.[1]

In 1959, the Sugimans, all seven of us – me, my mother and father, my recently widowed aunt, and her three young daughters – moved into a respectable, white (largely Anglo-Saxon and eastern European), middle-class neighbourhood in the west end of the city of Toronto. My parents and aunt pooled their hard-earned savings in an effort, like many working-class people, to create a better life for their children, to provide the next generation with the opportunities that they themselves never had, and to escape from the hardship and cruelty of the past. I was one year old when I moved into this house, one that is still inhabited by my very robust mother, now in her early nineties, now the sole resident. I still visit my mother in this house whenever I can, and my daughter, cousins, and their offspring congregate there to celebrate holidays, birthdays, and other festivities. As always, I cherish my childhood years and my family home, but my memories of growing up on this quiet cul-de-sac are bittersweet.

Recollections of my early years as a *Sansei* daughter, a third-generation Japanese Canadian, are admittedly filtered by the lens through which I currently view the world as a middle-aged academic with considerable years of research and general life experience in tow. Yet my cousins and I still reminisce about our childhood days and the painful realities of being "Asian" and working-class in what was then an extremely homogeneous town.

How visible, odd, and unsettling we must have been to the residents of this staid street. After all, our two-household extended family was packed into a moderately small, single-family dwelling; my mother, father, and I lived on the first floor of the house, while my aunt and cousins occupied the second. Our black hair, slanted eyes, and short stature made us all the more conspicuous. On Sunday mornings, we would pile into, and later file out of, my father's black and orange Diamond taxi cab for our visits to the Bathurst Street Toronto Buddhist Church (the only place in my 1950s and '60s existence where I encountered Japanese Canadians to whom I was not related). Like many others in our community, we were painfully aware of our Japanese "looks." It didn't matter that we were all Canadian-born and fluent in English; our appearance rendered us foreign, and there seemed to be no way of escaping this definition.

School posed some unique challenges. By the time I reached high school, my cousin and I were among a handful of visibly racialized kids in our classes. In our count, three other Asians and one black student made up what some would call the school's "visible minority" population. One day on my way home from school, attacked by snowballs hurled along with jeers of "Chink," "Nip," and "Jap," I was surprised and touched when the popular school athlete John Davy, who lived in the big house on the corner, calmly came to my defence, instructing the boys to "stop it" and leave me alone. In memory, ever since that winter day, I have had the young John Davy on a pedestal. Although it is most likely an act he does not remember, it remains an important one in my repertoire.

Summer road trips, of course, guaranteed encounters with unfriendly strangers who eagerly taunted us with chants of "Go back to where you came from," shouted from the safety of passing cars. Over the years, we learned to anticipate, dread, and at times imagine such remarks behind aggressive stares, even when no words were passed. No matter where we were born or what we had achieved, we were, as Roy Miki has astutely described, "framed by race."

With only slight exaggeration do I claim that my childhood was made traumatic by our family's legendary next-door neighbours. In the eyes of a child, the Murrays epitomized whiteness and middle-class propriety. They conveyed all that we were supposed to be, all that was appropriate, that which my parents and grandparents were not, indeed never could be. We kids were warned never to set foot on the Murrays' well-manicured lawn, not to let our ball roll on to their property, and always to keep our voices hushed in their midst. We tried very hard not to incite any complaints. Periodically, my thoughtful, generous, and, in retrospect, brave mother, with my father's gentle consent, would invite Mr Murray to a weekend dinner when the "Mrs" was out of town visiting her sister. On these occasions, a menu of Hakujin food was a must: meat, potatoes, vegetables, and store-bought dinner rolls. It never occurred to us that perhaps Mr Murray would like to try some Japanese-Canadian food. Instead, we shed our chopsticks for stainless steel cutlery, gohan (sticky Japanese rice) for baked potatoes, and orange pekoe bags replaced the ocha (Japanese green tea).

Back in those days, days to remember, the Sugiman clan did our best to hide or at least to sanitize our Japanese-ness. In the postwar, public world, federal government "repatriation" policies and municipal by-laws made racial assimilation more or less compulsory. While dispossessed of their property and goods, in the privacy, if not isolation, of home, most *Issei* (the first generation) maintained their Japanese identity along with some aspects of tradition and culture (notably, the Japanese language). Many *Nisei* (the second generation), by comparison, had an ambivalent relationship with their "Japanese" origins, largely because of the material and psychic costs of this racial assignment. For my generation, the *Sansei*, assimilation was complete.

We *Sansei* carefully navigated the social institutions of employment and education. For Japanese Canadians, upward class mobility went hand in hand with the assimilation project. While certainly not immune to assimilationist pressures, family was the one arena in which our incomplete history as Japanese Canadians was passed on. Home is where my Japanese-speaking *Bachan* and *Gi-chan* came to visit. It is where we placed our modest shrine before which we put our hands together, reciting "*Namu ami dabutsu, Namu Ami dabutsu, Namu Ami dabutsu*" while we burned incense in a tribute to our deceased ancestors. Deep and profound, these fractured rituals shaped our identities in spite of the racial hegemony that marked Canadian society. These childhood memories of home and family were joyful and powerful yet, at the same time, complicated and destructive.

As I read Kishizu Kimura's memoir, I thought about Mr Murray, John Davy, and the many passing racist strangers whom I encountered throughout my life. The commentaries that make up the rest of this volume, in turn inspired by Mr Kimura's passages, have provided me with both the language and analytical frame for understanding these memories – both Mr Kimura's and my own. Laura Madokoro's insightful discussion of the experiences of Hakujin Canadians as normative contextualizes early yearnings to pass as white, cooperate with Hakujin, and at times to obey, comply with, and even seek their approval.[2] After all, as Tim Stanley reminds us, personal and interpersonal relationships are formed "across the divides of 'race' and culture," though such connections are made within structures of racist dominance, power and subordination, superiority and deference.[3] Just as Kimura dined with the architects and engineers of the dispossession of his own community, he spent many years after the war carefully explaining his actions. Kimura was not naive to the racism that plagued the pre-war years and wartime period. While not always overtly articulated, much of his memoir speaks to the ways in which he exercised individual agency in the face of such racism and how he ultimately chose to represent himself and interpret his decisions in a post-war social and political context.

On this note, Vic Satzewich's inquiry about Kimura's motivation is highly relevant. Satzewich reflects on whether we should view the memoir as a "consciously chosen strategy at the time the events were unfolding" or "a way in which he used his memory and his memoir to justify and explain his actions many years later"[4] Like Stanley, I interpret the memoir not as "passively reflecting an external reality but rather as actively creating knowledge" of the past and the present.[5]

Notable is that Mr Kimura chooses to present what he views as the "facts" of his involvement in the dispossession, as well as those of the wider history of internment, as objective history. Indeed, the memoir's narrative form (which Kimura laboured over) neatly compartmentalizes (as distinct sections of the piece) the facts of the events from personal "reflections" on these events. In this sense, the narrative further reveals a temporal difference between "history" and the man's reflections on this history. The former is presented as fixed in time (with the time period being the years leading up to and during the Second World War), while the latter are presented as fluid, offered with hindsight. It is important to note, I believe, that the memoir as a whole, with all of its component parts, was constructed subjectively and in the decades following the war.

Reading Mr Kimura's memoir as "consciously chosen" prompts other questions. It is a privilege to learn about this man's journal entries. But equally informative is what Kimura does not mention. In any narrative, silences and omissions are meaningful. Who is missing or has little presence in his account? It is likely that Kimura did not see it appropriate to bring his wife and children into his memoir, for he mentions them only briefly. Did they appear in his original entries? That they are directly referenced in the narrative tells us much about intimacy and disclosure and the ways in which relations of gender and race intermingled. Why in places does Kimura rely on the passive voice? Why, less frequently, does he slip into the first person? And why does he at times refer to himself in the third person? At one point in his memoir, Mr Kimura also switches to dialogue, away from the narrative itself. Likewise, "We went to the Buddhist Temple because we'd heard that someone had broken in through a window. It seemed to be simple mischief, and there were about five pots of ashes of the dead with their contents scattered. It was not unusual for Nikkei people to honour the dead collectively, so we told the guard to put the ashes into the large pot."[6] He writes about this with a certain matter-of-factness.

Jordan Stanger-Ross's introduction highlights the banality of racism and the evil of banal racism. Indeed, as Stanley observes, the memoir catalogues "the minutiae of the creation of dominance, showing that it is a system being created piecemeal and in an ad hoc way." In his words, "one small step follows another until racialized Japanese people no longer own any boats and they all have been removed from the coast. The manuscript does not describe the brutality of racist exclusion, yet it does articulate the banality of racist exclusion at every turn."[7] In some ways, racism and injustice hiding behind bureaucratic rule is the most vicious because it is hard to touch and most deceitful and pernicious.

Kimura was complicit in the dispossession of Japanese Canadians. My visceral reaction to his decisions and actions is one of dismay mixed with anger mediated by the passage of time. These are, of course, personal emotions, intimately experienced, meaningful, and entirely rational. Yet I am also able to situate Mr Kimura, and in his memoir he constructs a narrative of reconciliation (and perhaps even of forgiveness). But it is not reconciliation of the Japanese-Canadian community or with non–Japanese Canadians. This is Mr Kimura's personal reconciliation project.

Kimura himself supports the often promoted myth that Canadians of Japanese descent were rounded up and interned for their own "protection" in the midst of wartime hysteria. The dispersal itself was a necessity for the security of the Japanese-Canadian population in the face of racist hysteria of the day. With reference to the anti-Japanese and anti-Chinese riots in 1907, Kimura explains the circumstances of Prime Minister Mackenzie King's wartime decision to remove people of Japanese origin from the west coast: "He must have been afraid now, under wartime circumstances, someone might actually harm Nikkei people, and if such awful things were to happen, the Japanese military might take revenge on Canadian soldiers. I think that the prime minister, after deep deliberation, concluded to send all Nikkei people to a safe place as soon as possible."[8]

He also gives weight to the narrow model minority view of Japanese Canadians and, in the same breath, promotes the popular view that the internment was for the Japanese-Canadian community, a "blessing in disguise": "Common sense among the general public no longer condones anti-Nikkei practices, and I believe there is no room for anti-Nikkei propaganda. It was definitely the behaviour of the Nikkei fishermen who created such an atmosphere, by following the law, making sacrifices, and cooperating with government policy during the war."[9] These are views shared by some Hakujin (though not all) and some Japanese Canadians (though not all). They can be powerful and convincing, and they serve many purposes. For Kimura: "I think these are meaningful points because they could make the Canadian general public recognize *the Nikkei Canadians carried out their responsibility as Canadian citizens* in extremely difficult circumstances."[10]

My own life, my parents' lives, have been in large part a social performance of social citizenship in the face of the failure of legal citizenship, as Madokoro perceptively discusses. Unlike Mr Kimura, we have been deeply critical of the wartime injustices, the racism that continued as my family resettled and rebuilt their lives and home in Toronto in the 1950s and beyond. The property losses were part of a larger legacy of loss. Government policy-makers and political leaders ensured that Japanese-Canadian success rested on racial and ethnic assimilation.

Masako Fukawa sensitively observes, "Although they took place more than seventy years ago, and despite the fact that more than a quarter-century has passed since redress, there still lingers a great sense of sadness and incredulity that these events took place in Canada, a democratic country."[11] This speaks to the Japanese Canadians' performance of citizenship as reifying the "inclusive and celebratory aspects of citizenship" but also as part of an effort "to claim the identity of citizen, while marginalizing how they had been disappointed by the legal status of citizenship."[12]

NOTES

1 Kimura Memoir, 100.

2 Madokoro, Commentary 4, 176.

3 Stanley, Commentary 2, 130.

4 Satzewich, Commentary 3, 149.

5 Stanley, Commentary 2, 123.

6 Kimura Memoir, 70.

7 Stanley, Commentary 2, 135.

8 Kimura Memoir, 97.

9 Ibid., 54.

10 Ibid., 52.

11 Fukawa, Commentary 1, 107–8.

12 Madokoro, Commentary 4, 170.

# Appendix
# Key Individuals and Legal Enactments

*Will Archibald, Monique Ulysses, and Jordan Stanger-Ross*

## Key Individuals

ANGUS, HENRY FORBES – Henry Forbes Angus (born 19 April 1891 in Victoria, BC; died 17 September 1991) was a professor of economics, political science, and sociology at the University of British Columbia, publishing extensively on immigration, international trade, and discrimination against Asian Canadians. He was a member of the Rowell–Sirois Royal Commission on Dominion–Provincial Relations from 1937 to 1940, was part of the Standing Committee on Orientals, and served from 1940 to 1945 as an executive assistant in the Department of External Affairs. In his role in External Affairs, he stood alongside H.L. Keenleyside as one of the key figures in the bureaucracy advocating for just treatment of Japanese Canadians.[1]

AOKI, SADAYOSHI – Sadayoshi Aoki was a Tokyo-trained educator and school principal who ran Japanese language schools first in Cumberland, BC, and later out of the family's home in Vancouver. With the forced removal of Japanese Canadians from the coast in 1942, Sadayoshi Aoki relocated to a sugar beet farm in Iron Springs, Alberta, in an effort to keep his family together. His children had storied lives and careers of their own – his eldest, Ted Aoki, was a highly influential educator and university professor, and his younger son, Harry Aoki, was a renowned musician.[2]

BEECH, WILLIAM JAMES ROBERT – William James Robert Beech (born June 1895 in Slindon, Sussex; died 9 April 1975) was an officer with the Canadian Navy, serving during both world wars, and was, by late 1940, commanding officer over all naval forces on the Canadian Pacific coast. Immediately after the attack on Pearl Harbor, Beech ordered the Navy to round up all Japanese Canadian–owned fishing vessels, thus setting in motion the events that led to the creation of the Japanese Fishing Vessel Disposal Committee. Suspicious of Japanese-Canadian loyalties, Beech advocated for the forcible removal of Japanese Canadians from the coast through late 1941 and early 1942.[3]

CARROTHERS, WILLIAM ALEXANDER – William Alexander Carrothers (born 27 March 1889 in Brookeborough, Ireland; died 29 August 1951 in Victoria, BC) was a professor of economics and public administrator, publishing primarily on immigration and currency. From the late 1920s, Carrothers advocated for the restriction of immigrants from "less assimilable" areas such as Japan and China and suggested that such settlers were afforded too many rights. In the late 1930s, he published racially charged research on "Oriental Standards of Living" and, as an adviser to the Province of British Columbia, submitted a brief including anti-Asian-Canadian positions to the Rowell–Sirois Royal Commission on Dominion–Provincial Relations.[4]

CLARKE, FRED – Fred Clarke was a boat captain and marine surveyor for the San Francisco Board of Underwriters, Vancouver, who was employed by the Japanese Fishing Vessel Disposal Committee to appraise Japanese Canadian–owned fishing vessels. Clarke was familiar with many of the fishing boats from before their confiscation because of his firm's responsibility for a large amount of the marine insurance. The Department of Fisheries briefly considered Clarke for a role on the committee itself but decided instead to appoint Justice Sidney Smith.[5]

COLLINS, GEORGE – George Collins was an engineer and bureaucrat, serving as the assistant deputy minister of public works in Manitoba. After the 5 February 1943 dissolution of the BC Security Commission, Collins was appointed commissioner of Japanese placement and was responsible for the newly created Japanese Division of the Department of Labour. In his role as commissioner, Collins oversaw internment camp operations and plans to send more Japanese Canadians eastwards.[6]

DURKEE, H.S. – H.S. Durkee served as an administrator for both the Japanese Fishing Vessel Disposal Committee and the Advisory Committee on Japanese

Properties in Greater Vancouver. Having assisted A.E. McMaster with the finalization of JFVDC files, records, and accounts, Durkee was hired on 12 May 1943 to replace McMaster as the executive assistant for the Greater Vancouver Advisory Committee.[7]

DURNIN, WILLIAM – William Durnin (born 23 August 1906 in Dungannon, Ontario; died 13 December 1973 in Vancouver, BC) was an officer of the RCMP. He was promoted to corporal in June 1941 and served at that rank until his promotion to sergeant in 1951. He was promoted to staff sergeant in 1955 and retired in 1960 after twenty-nine years of service.[8]

FINN, DONOVAN BARTLEY – Donovan Bartley Finn (born 1900; died 1982) was a Cambridge-educated scientist and bureaucrat. During World War II, he held the position of deputy minister of fisheries from February 1940 to 1947. Following the war, he served as director of fisheries for the Food and Agriculture Organization of the United Nations from 1946 to 1964 and headed a royal commission on marketing Atlantic salted and cured fish from 1964 to 1965.[9]

FISH, GEORGE WILLIAM – George William Fish (born 14 August 1889 in London, England; died 28 April 1964 in Victoria, BC) was an officer of the RCMP and a private serving with the Princess Patricia's Canadian Light Infantry in World War I. He spent from 1934 to 1938 in Vancouver as an inspector in the Criminal Investigation Branch of the RCMP during which time he was a member of the Board of Review for Illegal Immigrants. Leaving the coast and assuming command of the Edmonton Sub-Division in December 1938, he retired at the rank of superintendent in January 1946 in Regina, Saskatchewan.[10]

FUJIWARA, GINJIRO – Ginjiro Fujiwara (born 1884) was an *Issei* who first came to Canada in 1907. Fujiwara was a fisherman originally from Oshima Island in Yamaguchi-ken.[11]

FUKUYAMA, HIDEO – Hideo Fukuyama (born 17 October 1912 in Saga Prefecture, Japan; died 15 June 1947) was an *Issei* who came to Canada at the age of twelve; his father, Magoichi Fukuyama, worked at Premier Goldmine in Premier, BC. By 1941, he was the chief of the Canadian Salt Herring Exporters, the co-operative that Kimura had set up. Displaced to Christina Lake during the mass uprooting of Japanese Canadians from the coast, he died there suddenly in 1947.[12]

GINN, ROY WILFRED – Roy Wilfred Ginn (born 1 December 1892 in Dominion City, Manitoba; died 11 October 1952 in Vancouver, BC) was a Vancouver-area marine lawyer. He was an active yachtsman, serving as rear commodore from 1928 to 1931 and vice commodore from 1933 to 1934 of the Royal Vancouver Yacht Club. In 1933, he purchased 100 acres of land on Penelakut Island, a former Lamalchi First Nations village site that had been confiscated in 1863; the land was held by his widow, Audrey Mavis Ginn, until her own death in 2006.[13]

GOULD, JOHN – John Gould was a Vancouver-area marine surveyor who began his career in 1914 following a seven-year apprenticeship in Liverpool, England, and work for the San Francisco Board of Underwriters. On 7 February 1942, under recommendation from Commander Barney Leitch Johnson, the Custodian of Enemy Property asked him to serve as a surveyor for seized Japanese Canadian–owned fishing vessels. Contrary to Kimura's note, he appears to have worked for the Custodian until 1 August 1942.[14]

HILL, CECIL HENRY – Cecil Henry Hill (born 1886; died 12 May 1953 in Vancouver, BC) was an RCMP officer and a commissioned officer in World War I. During World War II, he was an assistant commissioner on loan to the Department of National Defence where he took an active role in overseeing the uprooting and internment of Japanese Canadians until his retirement in April 1944. In April 1942, Hill suggested to a superior that "unless drastic action were taken" against mounting dissent from *Nisei*, the situation would "get completely out of hand"; in the month following Hill's letter, a number of prominent *Nisei* leaders were given notice of forced removal from the coast.[15]

HOUSSER, GEORGE ELLIOT – George Elliot Housser (born 19 August 1884 in Winnipeg, Manitoba; died 23 August 1977 in Vancouver, BC) was a Vancouver-area lawyer, called to the BC Bar in 1911 and a partner in Bull, Housser, Tupper, Ray, Guy and Merritt. During World War II, Housser was vice-president and director of Canadian Atlas Diesel Engine, the company that provided the appraisal services of Arleigh Pilkey to the JVFDC.[16]

HUME, FREDERICK J. – Frederick J. Hume (born 2 May 1892 in New Westminster, BC; died 17 February 1967) was a career politician, serving as an alderman and mayor of New Westminster from 1934 to 1942 and as the mayor of Vancouver from 1951 to 1958. Invited to chair the Standing Committee on Orientals in British Columbia in 1941, Hume used his position to pressure for the removal of Japanese Canadians from the coast. He is a member of the Hockey Hall of Fame for his tenure as owner of the Vancouver Canucks and his promotion of amateur sport.[17]

IDE, RITSU – Ritsu Ide was an *Issei* and a prominent member of the Vancouver Japanese-Canadian community at the time of the uprooting. In 1922, Ritsu Ide had travelled to Ottawa with Nobutaro Yasuno on behalf of the Amalgamated Association of Fishermen and the Steveston Benevolent Fisherman's Association to protest restrictions on the number of fishing licences for "persons of the Japanese race." As *Iji-kai* (School Maintenance Association) vice-president, Ide was among those who protected and maintained the Vancouver Japanese Language School from its forced closure in 1941 until Japanese Canadians were forcibly uprooted from the coast.[18]

JOHNSON, BARNEY LEITCH – Barney Leitch Johnson (born 1878; died 1968) was a commercial and naval boat captain and, during World War I, was the first Canadian to command a submarine. He was appointed as an advisor to the Department of National Defence in 1938, a position he held while he acted on the Japanese Fishing Vessel Disposal Committee. As the member of the committee most closely associated with the industry, Johnson was responsible for hiring many of the surveyors who appraised the boats.[19]

JONES, CHARLES – Charles Jones (born 19 January 1881 in Whitby, England; died 1 September 1948) was a Vancouver city bureaucrat, alderman, and mayor. Elected alderman in 1940, Jones served as the city council's representative on the Greater Vancouver Advisory Committee tasked with disposing of Japanese Canadian–owned property. He became acting mayor of Vancouver in 1947 upon the death of the incumbent and was elected mayor in 1948 but died soon after taking office.[20]

KEENLEYSIDE, HUGH LLEWELLYN – Hugh Llewellyn Keenleyside (born 7 July 1898 in Toronto, Ontario; died 27 September 1992 in Victoria, BC) was an academic, diplomat, and civil servant. Having joined the Department of External Affairs in 1928, Keenleyside helped to open Canada's first legation in Japan from 1929 to 1936; serving as a special assistant to the prime minister during World War II, he was one of the few people within the Canadian government who strongly protested the treatment of Japanese Canadians and their property. In his later career in public service, he was ambassador to Mexico from 1944 to 1948, commissioner of the Northwest Territories from 1947 to 1950, and director-general of the UN Technical Assistance Administration from 1950 to 1958.[21]

MACINTOSH, MACGREGOR FULLARTON – Macgregor Fullarton Macintosh (born 25 August 1896 in Glasgow, Scotland) was a Conservative politician who was elected as the MLA for The Islands in 1937. Extremely outspoken on the presence of Japanese Canadians in British Columbia, Macintosh publicly favoured the deportation of all Canadians of Japanese descent. Campaigning for the seat of Cowichan-Newcastle in the 1945 provincial election, Macintosh again advocated for the deportation of Japanese Canadians; however, he lost the election and never returned to elected office.[22]

MACKENZIE, DUNCAN EDWIN – Duncan Edwin MacKenzie (born 1869 in Kincarardine, Ontario; died 1944) was a prominent resident of New Westminster who served as the New Westminster market clerk from 1904 to 1920 and manager and secretary of the Royal Agricultural and Industrial Society from 1911 to 1942. As a member of the Custodian's Advisory Committee on Rural Properties until his death in 1944, MacKenzie briefly advocated for Japanese Canadian–owned farms in the Fraser Valley to be sold on the open market instead of sold as a package to Soldier Settlement. However, he quickly changed his mind – at the 1 June 1943 meeting of the Rural Advisory Committee, MacKenzie moved that the committee recommend the sale of 769 Japanese Canadian–owned properties to the Veterans' Lands Act Administration for a fraction of market value.[23]

MCLARTY, NORMAN ALEXANDER – Norman Alexander McLarty (born 18 February 1889 in St Thomas, Ontario; died 6 September 1945) was a Liberal politician, MP for Essex West, and wartime cabinet minister. McLarty held the position of minister of labour from September 1939 until December 1941 and the secretary of state portfolio from December 1941 until April 1945. As secretary of state, McLarty was the titular "Custodian of Enemy Property," although many of the responsibilities of that office were held by bureaucrats E.H. Coleman and G.W. McPherson.[24]

MCLELLAN, JAMES JOSEPH – James Joseph McLellan was a Fraser Valley–area farmer and soldier in World War I. He worked from 1936 to 1941 as a full-time employee of the Fraser Valley Farm Loan Board and was invited to join the Rural Properties Advisory Committee in 1943. He served on the Advisory Committee for only a few days before resigning in order to work for the Veterans' Lands Act Administration, the governmental organization that would later purchase most Japanese Canadian–owned farmland.[25]

MCMASTER, ALFRED ERWIN – Alfred Erwin McMaster (born 1886 in Perth, Ontario; died 1965 in Vancouver, BC) was an administrator and manager who served as executive assistant for both the Japanese Fishing Vessel Disposal Committee in 1942 and the Advisory Committee on Japanese Properties in Greater Vancouver in 1943. Before World War II, he worked at the Powell River Company, a pulp and paper manufacturer, from 1921 to 1936, serving as the vice-president and general manager of the company by the time he left. Departing his position as executive assistant to the urban property committee, McMaster was appointed associate wood fuel controller for the Department of Munitions and Supply by Order-in-Council PC 1943-5490 and, after the war, served as the manager of the Port of Vancouver from 1948 to 1955.[26]

MCMASTER, ROBERT – Robert McMaster was an associate partner of the Vancouver law firm Norris & McLennan. McMaster was one of a group of lawyers that consistently worked with and for the Japanese-Canadian community. This is especially evident through his work with Norris & McLennan, which was heavily involved in Japanese-Canadian challenges of legalized discrimination.[27]

MCPHERSON, GLENN WILLOUGHBY – Glenn Willoughby McPherson (born 29 April 1910 in Portage La Prairie, Manitoba; died 1998 in Vancouver, BC) was a lawyer, bureaucrat, administrator, and security operative who played an integral role in instigating the forced sale of Japanese-Canadian property. Although originally hired as legal counsel, McPherson was promoted to deputy custodian of enemy property and directed Custodian policy regarding the property of some 22,000 Japanese Canadians uprooted from the coast and interned or displaced across Canada. He was one of the people most responsible for the shift in government policy toward forced sales and was responsible for drafting Order-in-Council PC 1943-469, which authorized full-scale dispossession. Secretly an agent for William Stephenson's British Security Coordination, McPherson actively spied upon Japanese Canadians while working in his official role as deputy custodian.[28]

MARTIN, J. ALEXANDER – J. Alexander Martin was an administrator who worked for the Japanese Fishing Vessel Disposal Committee. He worked under the supervision of A.E. McMaster and was assigned to creating inventories of vessels and appraisals. Martin also handled JFVDC business with the Custodian of Enemy Property, who were tasked with handling vessels that they had determined were owned by people residing in Japan and other "enemy" territory.[29]

MATSUYAMA, T. – T. Matsuyama was an *Issei* who was the founder of T. Matsuyama Company (Matsuyama Shokai), an outfit focused on fishing vessels and the fishing industry. A very successful businessman, he invested $200,000 in the establishment of Nanaimo Shipyards Limited on Newcastle Island in 1918. The forced sale of Japanese-Canadian fishing vessels left Matsuyama destitute; he chose to leave for Japan on a Red Cross exchange boat during the war, although he returned to Vancouver in 1953.[30]

MEAD, FREDERICK JOHN – Frederick John Mead (born 29 April 1889 in Sible Hedingham, England; died 9 September 1961 in Vancouver, BC) was an RCMP officer and a lieutenant in World War I. Assistant Commissioner Mead was one of the three men in charge of the British Columbia Security Commission, tasked with overseeing the uprooting and early internment. Mead was broadly supportive of Japanese Canadians, arguing that they presented no security threat.[31]

MENZIES, WILLIAM HALBERT – William Halbert (Hal) Menzies (born 1885 in Ailsa Craig, Ontario; died 31 December 1965) was a real estate agent in Haney, BC. With his business partner, Donald B. Martyn, Menzies built and opened Haney's first real estate office in 1910. Menzies was appointed to the Rural Advisory Committee in March 1943 and was the member of that committee that seconded the motion to sell Japanese Canadian–owned farms in the Fraser Valley to Soldier Settlement for a fraction of market value.[32]

MICHAUD, JOSEPH-ENOIL – Joseph-Enoil Michaud (born 26 September 1888 in Saint-Antonin, Quebec; died 23 May 1967) was a Liberal member of Parliament from 1933 until 1945, serving as minister of fisheries under successive Mackenzie King governments from October 1935 until October 1942 and minister of transport from October 1942 until April 1945. During his tenure as minister of fisheries, Michaud promulgated race-based restrictions on the number of fishing licences granted to Japanese-Canadian fishermen, despite privately expressing hesitations about the policy. Michaud oversaw the Japanese Fishing Vessel Disposal Committee and recommended the policy outlined in Order-in-Council PC 1942-251 banning the granting of fishing licences to "persons of Japanese racial origin" for the duration of the war.[33]

MIWA, KUNISABURO – Kunisaburo Miwa was an *Issei* fisherman who spent much of his career fishing in the Skeena River area. President of the Fishermen's Association, No. 2 District, in 1936, he was a prominent member of the Japanese-Canadian community in northern BC.[34]

MOTHERWELL, JAMES A. – James A. Motherwell was a bureaucrat who served as chief inspector of fisheries for British Columbia from 1921 to 1946. During his tenure as chief inspector, Motherwell oversaw the federal policy to eliminate Japanese Canadians from the BC fishing industry altogether through race-based restrictions on fishing licences. When Japanese Canadian–owned fishing vessels were seized by the Navy in December 1941, Motherwell was integral in assembling the Japanese Fishing Vessel Disposal Committee.[35]

NAKAI, KOHEI – Kohei Nakai (born 1891 in Ujiyamada City, Japan) was an *Issei* who first came to Canada in 1906. Living in the Powell Street area in 1926, by the 1930s he was a crew member on a ship that sailed regularly from Ucluelet and Tofino to Seattle.[36]

NISHIMURA, JUJIRO – Jujiro Nishimura was a Japanese Canadian who served as a trustee for the Japanese Language School in Marpole along with Daishiro Teramura and Kiyomitsu Yamazaki. Before the uprooting of Japanese Canadians in World War II, he ran a grocery store on Hudson Street in the Marpole neighborhood of Vancouver. Following the uprooting, he and his family were interned at McGillivray Falls.[37]

NOGUCHI, MITSUJIRO – Mitsujiro Noguchi (born 3 June 1893 in Imamoto, Japan; died 26 October 1971) was an *Issei* who came to Canada in 1920 from Seattle, where he had worked as a peanut importer and exporter. Noguchi was very active in the Vancouver Japanese-Canadian community and assisted the RCMP with the registration of Japanese Canadians from March to August 1941. In January 1942, as the JFVDC was being formed, several large fishing companies alleged that Noguchi was encouraging Japanese-Canadian fishing vessel–owners to hold onto their boats and push for more favourable terms of sale.[38]

PEARSON, GEORGE SHARRATT – George Sharratt Pearson (born 27 April 1880 in Brierly Hill, England; died 24 August 1966 in Nanaimo, BC) was a grocer and provincial politician who spent from 1928 to 1952 as the Liberal and coalition MLA for various Nanaimo-area ridings. Serving as minister of mines and labour under Premier Pattullo's government and minister of health and welfare under John Hart's coalition government, Pearson was one of many prominent politicians in BC who advocated for restrictions on Asian-Canadian labour and immigration. During World War II, Pearson took an active role in insisting that Japanese Canadians be uprooted from the coast and interned and speculated openly that the loyalties of Japanese Canadians would rapidly shift if the Japanese army landed in BC.[39]

PHILLIPSON, OLIVER WILLIAM – Oliver William Phillipson was a mechanical superintendent and fisherman who had been involved with the BC fishing industry for nearly thirty years by the outbreak of World War II. He was hired to survey boats by Commander Barney Johnson on account of his familiarity with fishing operations. By 1948, Phillipson was superintendent at three different fish-packing plants, overseeing the management, maintenance, and production of each.[40]

PILKEY, ARLEIGH – Arleigh Pilkey (born 3 July 1897) was a service engineer and mechanic specializing in the marine industry. At the time of his hiring by the Japanese Fishing Vessel Disposal Committee, he was a service manager at Atlas Imperial Diesel Engine Company, a job he continued to hold until at least the end of the war. In 1948, Pilkey took up competitive sports car racing after a thirty-year absence, and by 1962 he was the oldest active competition driver in North America.[41]

REEVE, DOUGLAS W. – Douglas W. Reeve was a Vancouver-area realtor working for the firm of Johnston, Reeve and Watson. He served as chairman of the Insurance Financial and Real Estate Bureau of the Board of Trade of Vancouver in 1935 and was the chairman of the Zoning By-Law Board of Appeal for the Vancouver Town Planning Commission by 1947.[42]

REID, THOMAS – Thomas Reid (born 18 April 1886 in Cambuslang, Scotland; died 12 October 1968) was a Liberal Party politician who served as the MP for New Westminster from 1930 to 1949. Renowned for his long-standing anti-Asian-Canadian racism, Reid took on a prominent role in advocating for the internment and deportation of Japanese Canadians in World War II. Rewarded for his nineteen years of service as a Liberal MP, he was appointed to the Senate in 1949 and served there until 1967.[43]

ROBINSON, SAMUEL – Samuel Robinson (born 1870; died 1958) was a mariner, sea captain, and Knight Commander of the British Empire. An employee of the Canadian Pacific Line in 1923, he was caught in the 1923 earthquake that devastated Japan. After securing his ship, *Empress of Australia*, Robinson and his crew assisted in rescuing thousands of refugees.[44]

SAKAMOTO, UNOSUKE – Unosuke Sakamoto (born 14 June 1903; died 28 January 1985) was an *Issei* fisherman. Before World War II, Sakamoto lived in Vancouver, Steveston, and Japan. He fished for forty-five years in the Fraser River for Co-op, Scotch Cannery, and Canfisco. Interned in Minto Mine, he worked in a sawmill as a logger before returning to coast in 1949.[45]

SANSOM, GEORGE BAILEY – George Bailey Sansom (born 28 November 1883 in London, England; died 8 March 1965 in Tucson, Arizona) was a British diplomat and academic. Sansom held various positions with the British legation in Japan, including secretary to the ambassador, commercial secretary, and commercial counsellor, all while working on translations and writing extensively on Japan. During World War II, he acted as adviser to the Ministry of Economic Warfare before being evacuated to the United States and serving there as adviser to the ambassador in Washington.[46]

SATO, TSUTAE – Tsutae Sato (born 1891 in Tanamura machi, Fukushima-ken, Japan; died 23 May 1983 in Vancouver, BC) was the fifth principal of the Vancouver Japanese Language School, serving from 1917 until 1942 and then again from 1952 to 1966. There were about 150 students registered at the Vancouver school when Sato and his wife took over in 1917, and enrollment increased to more than 1,000 by the time the school temporarily closed in 1942 because of the internment. In 1952, after a decade in exile from the coast, the Satos returned to Vancouver and resumed their role as the principals of the Vancouver Japanese Language School until their retirement.

SHEARS, FRANK GOULD – Frank Gould Shears (born 3 March 1885 in London, England) was a bureaucrat who took on a prominent administrative role in the dispossession of Japanese Canadians in World War II. Shears was hired by the secretary of state in 1940 and served as the director of the Vancouver Office of the Custodian of Enemy Property from 1942 until the closure of the office in 1952. As director, he oversaw the forced sale of Japanese-Canadian assets and the payment of claims arising from Justice Henry Bird's royal commission. As one of the longest-serving employees of the Custodian, Shears experienced this history from a unique perspective, privy to the decision-making of his political and bureaucratic masters but also constantly receiving letters and appeals from the Japanese Canadians he helped to dispossess.[47]

SHINDE, MATSUNOSUKE – Matsunosuke Shinde (died 18 March 1962 in Vancouver, BC) was a Japanese Canadian who served as a representative for Japanese-Canadian fishermen from northern BC when vessels were seized by the Navy in December 1941. Together with his older brother Yoshimatsu, Matsunosuke Shinde founded the Sunrise Sawmill Company in 1918 with Fujiichi Matsunaga and Sentaro Namidome. Uprooted to Greenwood in 1942, Shinde lived there until his death in Vancouver General Hospital in 1962 at the age of eighty-three.[48]

SMITH, SIDNEY ALEXANDER – Sidney Alexander Smith (born 1888 in Banffshire, Scotland; died September 1960) was a justice of the Supreme Court of British Columbia from 1940 to 1944 and of the British Columbia Court of Appeal from 1944 until his death in 1960. After serving as a Royal Navy mariner in World War I and a lawyer in the interwar period, Smith was appointed to the Court of Appeal in 1940 after a failed electoral run for the

Liberals in the Vancouver South riding. An expert in marine law, Smith was appointed chair of the Japanese Fishing Vessel Disposal Committee in January 1942 and later served as the chairman of the Advisory Committee on Japanese Properties in Greater Vancouver from 1943 to 1945.[49]

SPARLING, ALBERT WALTER – Albert Walter Sparling (born 12 July 1891 in Pilot Mound, Manitoba; died 20 October 1965 in Kelowna, BC) was a farmer and distinguished major in World War I. During World War II, Sparling worked for the Department of National Defence and was the sole opponent of Asian-Canadian enlistment within the Standing Committee on Orientals. In late 1941 and early 1942, Sparling pressed for the uprooting and internment of Japanese Canadians.[50]

SPRING, W.F. – W.F. Spring was a marine captain, surveyor, and public administrator hired to appraise boats for the Japanese Fishing Vessel Disposal Committee. A safety engineer for the Shipping Federation of British Columbia, Spring left Vancouver shortly after his work for the JVFDC in 1942 to accept a position in Halifax as port loading superintendent. Spring was promoted to controller of the Port of Halifax in March 1944, where he successfully resolved a number of longshoreman labour disputes.[51]

TAYLOR, FREDERICK WELLINGTON – Frederick Wellington Taylor (born 23 June 1884; died 9 June 1979) was an ice hockey player, civil servant, immigration official, and member of the Hockey Hall of Fame. One the earliest hockey professionals, Taylor was first enticed into playing for the Ottawa Senators by an offer of a job with the Department of the Interior, a career path that would continue far past his retirement as an athlete. Taylor played a front-line role as an immigration officer in the infamous *Komagata Maru* incident in 1914 and later worked as commissioner of immigration for British Columbia and the Yukon.[52]

WHITESIDE, DAVID – David Whiteside (died 1947) was a provincial politician and judge who chaired the Advisory Committee on Rural Properties from March 1943 until its dissolution upon his death in early 1947. He was the Liberal MLA for New Westminster for two terms from 1916 to 1924, his chances of running again compromised by a very public party revolt over the loosening of liquor laws. In his tenure as MLA, Whiteside opposed the presence of

Asian- Canadian farmers in the Fraser Valley and condemned a proposed lifting of the head tax imposed on immigrants from China in response to a labour shortage as "very short-sighted."[53]

WHITMORE, A.J. – A.J. Whitmore was a bureaucrat who spent his career with the Department of Fisheries. In 1938, he was part of a federal Interdepartmental Committee on Orientals and appears to have tabled a proposal to that committee from the Department of Fisheries for a four-year program to rid the industry of Japanese-Canadian fishermen. With the retirement of James A. Motherwell in 1946, A.J. Whitmore was appointed chief supervisor of western fisheries, a position in which he reportedly earned the title of "architect of modern salmon management."[54]

WRIGHT, KENNETH W. – Kenneth W. Wright was a lawyer and bureaucrat who served as legal counsel for the Custodian of Enemy Property during World War II. Appointed on 1 June 1942, Wright worked for the Custodian for more than fifteen years before his retirement in 1958. Wright performed a significant role within the Custodian's office in the execution and administration of the dispossession.[55]

YAMAGA, YASUTARO – Yasutaro Yamaga (born 30 March 1886 in Toyohama, Japan; died 1971) was a prominent *Issei* farmer and community leader in Haney, BC. Yamaga used his proficiency in the English language to interpret for and organize Japanese-Canadian farmers in the Fraser Valley, attempting to smooth out relations with white settlers in the face of pervasive racism. He served on the Advisory Committee on Rural Properties from 18 March 1943 to 26 May 1943 when he resigned in protest against the unfair terms of the impending sale of 769 Japanese Canadian–owned farms to Soldier Settlement.[56]

## Key Legal Enactments

Order-in-Council PC 1941-9761 – This order passed on 16 December 1941. On the recommendation of the minister of justice, it mandated: that "[n]o person of the Japanese race shall use or operate any vessel within waters adjacent to the West coast of Canada without the authority in writing of the

Commissioner of the Royal Canadian Mounted Police"; that if a person of Japanese descent "uses or operates a vessel without the authority aforesaid, such vessel may be seized and detained"; and that "[e]very one who contravenes the provisions of this Order shall be guilty of an offence and shall be liable … to a fine … or to imprisonment." Under the authority of this order-in-council, Japanese-Canadian fishers were required to bring their vessels to impoundment areas.[57]

Order-in-Council PC 1942-288 – This order passed on 13 January 1942. Under the authority of the 1927 revised War Measures Act, it created the three-person Fishing Vessel Disposal Committee, comprising Commander B.L. Johnson, Kishizo Kimura, and Hon. Justice Sidney A. Smith serving as chair.[58]

Order-in-Council PC 1942-987 – This order passed on 9 February 1942. It authorized the Fishing Vessel Disposal Committee to charge "one per centum on all monies involved in transactions" regarding the forced dispossession of fishing vessels owned by people of Japanese descent in British Columbia. The Fishing Vessel Disposal Committee decided upon this "disposal charge" because of the "substantially greater than originally estimated" expenses involved in the forced dispossession of fishing vessels. This one per centum charge was then remitted to the Receiver General of Canada, to be included in the Consolidated Revenue Account.[59]

Order-in-Council PC 1942-1486 – This order passed on Tuesday, 24 February 1942. It authorized the minister of justice to "require any or all persons to leave such protected area [100 miles along the coast of British Columbia]"; "prohibit any or all persons from entering, leaving or returning to such protected area except as permitted pursuant to such order"; to restrict the movements of residents in the "protected area"; and to "authorize the detention … of any or all persons ordinarily resident or actually present in such protected area." The protected area itself was created on 16 January 1942 by Order-in-Council PC 1942-365.[60]

Order-in-Council PC 1942-1665 – This order passed on 4 March 1942, establishing the British Columbia Security Commission and mandating the uprooting of all people "of the Japanese race" from coastal British Columbia.[61]

Order-in-Council PC 1942-2483 – This order passed on 27 March 1942. It amended PC 1942-1665, clarifying terms and further clarifying the Custodian's role with respect to property. In a modification of the original clause relating to property, PC 1942-2483 imposed an explicit fiduciary obligation on the part of the government. The vesting of the property of Japanese Canadians in the Custodian was undertaken, according to this order, "for the purpose of protecting the interest of the owner … and the Custodian shall have full power to administer such property for the benefit of all such interested persons, and *shall release such property upon being satisfied that the interests aforesaid will not be prejudiced thereby*."[62]

Order-in-Council PC 1942-6247 – This order passed on 20 July 1942, mandating that all vessels and equipment seized under the authority of Order-in-Council PC 1941-9761 that was not disposed of by 1 August 1942 would be held under the control of the Custodian of Enemy Property. The Custodian of Enemy Property was furthermore vested with the power to "freely negotiate for charters, leases or sales of such vessels and equipment as they own to persons other than those of Japanese origin."[63]

Order-in-Council PC 1943-469 – This order passed on Tuesday, 19 January 1943. Under PC 1943-469, Order-in-Council PC 1942-5523 and its amending Order-in-Council PC 1942-6885 were revoked, and paragraphs 3 and 4 of Order-in-Council PC 1942-6247 were rescinded and amended. These amendments authorized the Custodian of Enemy Property to "liquidate, sell or otherwise dispose of any such vessel or equipment on such terms and conditions as he deems advisable," with full powers being transferred to the Custodian from the Fishing Vessel Disposal Committee.[64]

Regulations Respecting Trade with the Enemy (1939) – These regulations dealt, generally, with two legal issues: (1) what constituted trade with the enemy; and (2) what happened with property, both real and personal, when it was found to belong to enemy subjects. Overall, any commercial or business interactions with an enemy subject, an agent of an enemy subject, or an agent of an enemy state was considered trade with the enemy. The regulations were quite all-encompassing in this regard – likely in an effort to ensure that no business dealings would occur between Canada and an enemy state. Property, in this case, also encompassed all legal conceptions of property. It was not just physical property at stake in these regulations but also debts, credit accounts, promissory notes, etc. With respect to property deemed to be "enemy property," the Custodian was given broad powers: the order was treated as a vesting order, which means that the Custodian had the power to sell, liquidate, dispose of, manage, etc. all of the property that fell within the purview of these regulations. On 4 March 1942, Order-in-Council PC 1942-1665 applied these regulations to "all property situated in any protected area of British Columbia belonging to any person of the Japanese race."[65]

Veterans' Land Act – This statute, initially assented to on 1 August 1942, played an important role throughout the Second World War and in the postwar period as property held by Japanese Canadians ended up under the purview of the director of the Veterans' Land Act. The director of the Veterans' Lands Act was also the director of Soldier Settlement, responsible for the appraisal of agricultural lands owned by people of Japanese descent, which it then acquired from the Custodian of Enemy Property and redistributed to Second World War veterans.[66]

War Measures Act – This Act granted authority to confer certain powers on the Governor in Council in the case of war, invasion, or insurrection. These powers included censorship and broad control of publications; arrest, detention, exclusion, or deportation; control of all ports and waters; control of all forms of transportation; extended powers in relation to trade; and the "[a]ppropriation, control, forfeiture and disposition of property and of the use thereof." The War Measures Act is of critical importance because it granted legal legitimacy to the forced uprooting, dispossession, and internment of people of Japanese descent during the Second World War.[67]

NOTES

1 Hillmer, "Henry Forbes Angus"; Yesaki, *Sutebusuton*, 102–3; Roy, *Oriental Question*; Roy, *Triumph of Citizenship*.

2 Sunahara, *Politics of Racism*, 74.

3 Bosher, *Imperial Vancouver Island*, 132–3; Rawling, "Only If Necessary," 106; Granatstein and Johnson, "Evacuation of the Japanese Canadians, 115.

4 *Canadian Who's Who 1949–1951*, 161; Spafford, *No Ordinary Academics*, 60; H.F.A., "William Alexander Carrothers, 99–100.

5 J.A. Motherwell, memo, 12 January 1942, LAC, RG23, Vol 2292, File: General Correspondence – Disposal of Japanese Fishing Vessels, Folder 2.

6 Robinson, *Tragedy of Democracy*, 189; Oikawa, *Cartographies of Violence*, 130; Ramsden, "Memorable Manitobans.

7 "Minutes," 12 May 1943, City of Vancouver Archives, AM199, Box 513-E-2, File 3; "Organizational Chart, n.d., LAC, RG23, Vol. 2292, File: Japanese Fishing Vessel Disposal Committee. Folder.

8 "Obituaries," *RCMP Quarterly* 39(2) (April 1974): 83.

9 *Canadian Who's Who 1949–1951*, 332; "Government Departments and Their Representatives.

10 "Obituaries," *RCMP Quarterly* 30(2) (October 1964): 83; "Record of Service.

11 Linda Kawamoto Reid, "Research into the Japanese Canadian Liaison Committee Members," 22 July 2015.

12 Ibid.; "Personal Notes across Canada," 28 June 1947.

13 Ginn, "New England Company on Kuper Island," 10–11; *Yachting*, 234.

14 "General Evidence 24 September–30 September, 1948," LAC, RG33-69, Vol. 76.

15 "Obituaries," *RCMP Quarterly* 19(1) (July 1953): 108; Kitagawa, *This Is My Own*, 41.

16 "Descendants of George Housser and Nan Kennedy"; *Canadian Who's Who 1961–1963*, 521.

17 Robinson, *Tragedy of Democracy*, 75; Roy, *Oriental Question*, 217; "Legends of Hockey: Fred Hume"; "Mayors of New Westminster"; MacKinnon, "Mayors of Vancouver."

18 Otsuka, "Remaking an Institution and Community, 16–23; Adachi, *The Enemy That Never Was*, 144.

19 *Barney Leitch Johnson fonds*; "The 100th Anniversary of Canadian Submarines"; "General Evidence 24 September–30 September, 1948"; "General Evidence 4 December–10 December, 1948," LAC, RG33-69, Vol. 76.

20 *Charles Jones Collection*; MacKinnon, "Mayors of Vancouver."

21 "Hugh Llewellyn Keenleyside."

22 Normandin and Normandin, *Guide parlementaire canadien*, 122; Roy, *Oriental Question*, 189; Sunahara, *Politics of Racism*, 11; Roy, *Triumph of Citizenship*, 326.

23 *Duncan Edwin MacKenzie fonds*; Ivan Barnet to Gordon Murchison, 19 March 1943, LAC, RG38-E, Vol. 403, File V-8-10, Part 3; "The Fifth Meeting of the Advisory Committee on Rural Properties," *Canadiana Heritage*, Office of the Custodian of Enemy Property: Vancouver Office, microfilm reel C-9469 RG 117, image 1900, http://heritage.canadiana.ca/view/oocihm.lac_reel_c9469/1900?r=0&s=1.

24 Sunahara, *Politics of Racism*, 91–3; "McLarty, The Hon. Norman Alexander.

25 "General Evidence 13 December 1948–31 January 1949," LAC, RG33-69, Vol. 77.

26 Canada Privy Council, *Canadian War Orders and Regulations, 1943*, 48; *Marine Digest*, 34; Kluckner, *Vanishing British Columbia*, 51.

27 *Canadian Co-operative Digest*; Miki, *Redress*.

28 G.W. McPherson to F.G. Shears, 12 January 1943, Thomas Fisher Rare Book Library, F.G. Shears fonds, Series 1, Box 2, Folder 2: Private and Confidential, 1942–1946; "McPherson Transcript," n.d., University of British Columbia Rare Books and Special Collections, Glenn McPherson fonds, Box 7, File 7-09: Draft Manuscripts.

29 A.E. McMaster to J.A. Martin, 16 March 1942, LAC, RG23, Vol. 2292, File: Japanese Fishing Vessel Disposal Committee, Folder 5: Organizational Chart.

30 Merilees, *Newcastle Island*, 86.

31 *Canadian Who's Who [1949–51 or 1961–63?]*, 708; Sunahara, *Politics of Racism*; "Obituaries," RCMP *Quarterly* 27(2) (October 1961): 147.

32 "General Evidence 24 September–30 September, 1948"; Waite, *Maple Ridge and Pitt Meadows*; Braches, "Whonnock History Notes; "William Halbert Menzies"; "Fifth Meeting of the Advisory Committee on Rural Properties."

33 J.E. Michaud to Ian Mackenzie, 17 January 1940 and 6 February 1942, LAC, MG27-III-B5, Vol. 19, File 29-7: Japanese Fishing Vessels; "Michaud, The Hon. Joseph Enoil."

34 *Labour Organizations in Canada*, 1936, 140; Fukawa and Fukawa, *Spirit of the Nikkei Fleet*, 127; "Wooden Boats of the North Coast – S."

35 Newell, *Development of the Pacific Salmon-Canning Industry*, 235; Harper, *Emigration from Scotland*, 89; Miki, *Redress*, 29.

36 Reid, "Research into the Japanese Canadian Liaison Committee Members."

37 "Nishimura, Jujiro (Card Index)," n.d., Canadiana Heritage, microfilm reel C-9302, http://heritage.canadiana.ca/view/oocihm.lac_reel_c9302/1021?r=0&s=1; Fukawa, "Ebisu Park," 17–21.

38 A.E. McMaster to J.A. Michaud, 30 January 1942, LAC, MG27-III-B5, Vol. 19, File 29-7: Japanese Fishing Vessels; Miki, *Redress*, 41; Reid, "Research into the Japanese Canadian Liaison Committee Members"; "Return: A Commemorative Yearbook."

39 Hobson, "Pearson Bridge Not Named after the Former PM, 46; Roy, *Triumph of Citizenship*.

40 "General Evidence 4 December–10 December, 1948."

41 Shank, *Pilkey Family Genealogy*, 199; Hyde, "Arleigh Pilkey, 24–6; *Pacific Fisherman*, 99; *Pacific Motor Boat*, 9; *Western Fisheries*, 95.

42 *Buildings and Building Management*, 51; *Canadian Railway and Transport Cases*, 271–2; Vancouver Town Planning Commission, *Appearance of the City*, 5.

43 Miki, *Redress*, 35; Sunahara, *Politics of Racism*, 7; City of Surrey Archives; "Reid, The Hon. Thomas."

44 Hammer, *Yokohama Burning*.

45 Reid, "Research into the Japanese Canadian Liaison Committee Members."

46 Nish, "Sansom, Sir George Bailey."

47 F.G. Shears fonds, n.d.; F.G. Shears to K.W. Wright, 27 February 1947, Thomas Fisher Rare Book Library, F.G. Shears fonds, Series 1, Box 1, Folder 1: K.W. Wright, 1945–1950; McPherson to Shears.

48 "Personal Notes across Canada," 31 March 1962; Fukawa and Fukawa, *Spirit of the Nikkei Fleet*, 127; Reeve, "Japanese-Canadians of Silva Bay," 3–8.

49 Moore, *British Columbia Court of Appeal*, 87–8.

50 Barrett, "Jap-Baiter," 64.

51 Stevenson, *Canada's Greatest Wartime Muddle*, 123–33; "Code Cooperation for Marine Safety," *Pacific Marine Review*, 5.

52 "Taylor, Frederick Wellington."

53 Elections British Columbia, *Electoral History of British Columbia*; Campbell, "Liquor and Liberals, 42; Roy, *Oriental Question*, 23.

54 Sunahara, "Chapter I, in *Politics of Racism*; Fitzgerald, "Rise and Demise of J.H. Todd and Sons," 29–30; *Western Fisheries*, 53.

55 K.W. Wright to F.G. Shears, 31 May 1957, Thomas Fisher Rare Book Library, F.G. Shears fonds, Series 1, Box 1, Folder 11: K.W. Wright, 1957–1959.

56 Yasutaro Yamaga, "My Footsteps in Canada," 1958, Japanese Canadian Research Collection, University of British Columbia Rare Books and Special Collections, Box 20, File 20-4: Yasutaro Yamaga – Reminiscences; Yavorsky and UBC Rare Books and Special Collections, "Yamaga Yasutaro"; "Fifth Meeting of the Advisory Committee on Rural Properties."

57 Order-in-Council PC 1941-9761, LAC, RG2-A-1-a, Vol. 1741, File 2468G.

58 Order-in-Council PC 1942-288, LAC, RG2-A-1-a, Vol. 1744, File 2484G.

59 Order-in-Council PC 1942-987, LAC, RG2-A-1-a, Vol. 1747, File 2502G.

60 Order-in-Council PC 1942-1486, LAC, RG2, A-1-a, Vol. 1749; Order-in-Council PC 1942-365, LAC, RG2, A-1-a, Vol. 1744, File 2487G.

61 Order-in-Council PC 1942-1665, LAC, RG2-A-1-a, Vol. 1750, File 2516G.

62 Order-in-Council PC 1942-2483, LAC, RG2-A-1-a, Vol. 1752, File 2531G.

63 Order-in-Council PC 1942-6247, LAC, RG2-A-1-a, Vol. 1767, File 2606G.

64 Order-in-Council PC 1943-469, LAC, RG2-A-1-a, Vol. 1789, File 2710G.

65 Canada Privy Council, "Regulations Respecting Trading with the Enemy" (1939).

66 Veterans' Land Act; "Appendix to the Journals of the House of Commons to Accompany the Fourth Report of the Standing Committee on Public Account, presented to the House on Tuesday, 17th June, 1947," LAC, RG14, Vol. 653, Appendix 8.

67 War Measures Act.

# Bibliography

## Archives and Libraries Consulted

Canadiana Heritage
CBC Digital Archives
City of Surrey Archives
  Senator Thomas Reid fonds
City of Vancouver Archives (CVA)
Barney Leitch Johnson fonds
Charles Jones Collection
Library and Archives Canada (LAC)
  Anno Abraham Makishi fonds
  Ian Mackenzie fonds
New Westminster Archives
  Duncan Edwin MacKenzie fonds
Nikkei National Museum and Cultural Centre (NNMCC)
  Kishizo Kimura fonds
Thomas Fisher Rare Book Library
  F.G. Shears fonds
University of British Columbia Rare Books and Special Collections
  Glenn McPherson fonds

## Books and Articles

"The 100th Anniversary of Canadian Submarines." *Royal Canadian Navy*, 7 July 2014. http://www.navy-marine.forces.gc.ca/en/navy-life/sub-centennial/sub-centennial.page.

Abrams, Philip. "Notes on the Difficulty of Studying the State [1977]." *Journal of Historical Sociology* 1(1) (March 1988): 58–89.

Access to Information Request. Citizenship and Immigration Canada. A-2015-16762/HB. 18 September 2015.

"Act to Amend and Consolidate the Laws Affecting Crown Lands in British Columbia, An." Section 29. In *Statutes of the Province of British Columbia Based on the Session Held in the Twenty-Seventh Year of the Reign of her Majesty Queen Victoria*. Victoria: Richard Wolfenden, 1874.

"Act to Make Better Provision for the Qualification and Registration of Voters, An." In *Statutes of the Province of British Columbia, 1875*. Victoria: Richard Wolfenden, Government Printer, 1875.

Adachi, Ken. *The Enemy That Never Was: A History of Japanese Canadians*. Toronto: McClelland and Stewart, 1976.

Adams, Eric, Jordan Stanger-Ross, and the Landscapes of Injustice Research Collective. "Promises of Law: The Unlawful Dispossession of Japanese Canadians." *Osgoode Hall Law Journal* 54(3) (2017).

Adams, Howard. *Tortured People: The Politics of Colonialism*. Penticton: Theytus Books, 1999.

Ahmed, Sarah. *On Being Included: Racism and Diversity in Institutional Life*. Durham, NC: Duke University Press, 2012.

Alfred, Taiaiake. *Peace, Power and Righteousness*. Toronto: Oxford University Press, 1999.

Allen, Theodore W. *The Invention of the White Race*. Vol. 1 and 2. London: Verso, 1994.

Allred, Jeff. "From Eye to We: Richard Wright's *12 Million Black Voices* (1941), Documentary and Pedagogy." In *American Modernism and Depression Documentary*. New York and Oxford: Oxford University Press, 2012.

Anderson, Kay. *Vancouver's Chinatown: Racial Discourse in Canada, 1875–1980*. Montreal: McGill-Queen's University Press, 1991.

Arendt, Hannah. *Eichmann in Jerusalem*. 1964; repr., New York: Penguin Books, 2006.

– "Race-Thinking before Racism." *The Review of Politics* 6(1) (1994): 36–73.

Atkinson, David. "Out of One Borderland, Many: The 1907 Anti-Asia Riots and the Spatial Discourse of Race and Migration in the Canada–U.S. Pacific Borderlands." In Benjamin Bryce and Alexander Freund, eds, *Entangling Migration History: Borderlands and Transnationalism in the United States and Canada*, 120–40. Gainesville: Florida University Press, 2015.

Avery, Donald. *Reluctant Host: Canada's Response to Immigrant Workers, 1896–1994*. Toronto: McClelland and Stewart, 1995.

Ayukawa, Michiko Midge. *Hiroshima Immigrants in Canada, 1891–1941*. Vancouver: University of British Columbia Press, 2008.

Backhouse, Constance. *Colour-Coded: A Legal History of Racism in Canada, 1900–1950*. Toronto: University of Toronto Press, 1999.

Bangarth, Stephanie. *Voices Raised in Protest: Defending Citizens of Japanese Ancestry in North America, 1942–49*. Vancouver: University of British Columbia Press, 2008.

Barlow, Tani. "Politics and Protocols of *Funü*: (Un)Making National Women." In Christina K. Gilmartin, Gail Hershatter, Lisa Rofel, and Tyrene White, eds, *Engendering China: Women, Culture and the State*, 339–59. Cambridge, MA: Harvard University Press, 1994.

– "Theorizing Women: *Funü, Guojia, Jiating* (Chinese Women, Chinese State, Chinese Family)." *Genders* 10 (spring 1991): 132–60.

Barman Jean. "Beyond Chinatown: Chinese Men and Indigenous Women in Early British Columbia." *BC Studies* 177 (2013): 39–64.

Barrett, Matthew K. "The Jap-Baiter." *Patriots, Crooks and Safety-Firster.* 11 September 2015. http://matthewkbarrett.com/2015/09/11/the-jap-baiter.

Barzun, Jacques. *Race: A Study in Modern Superstition*. New York: Harcourt, Brace, 1937.

Bates, Judy Fong. *The Year of Finding Memory: A Memoir*. Toronto: Vintage Canada, 2011.

Beasley, Edward. *The Victorian Reinvention of Race: New Racisms and the Problem of Grouping in the Human Sciences*. New York: Routledge, 2010.

Belshaw, John Douglas. *Becoming British Columbia: A Population History*. Vancouver: University of British Columbia Press, 2009.

Berton, Pierre. "They're Only Japs." *Maclean's*, 1 February 1948.

Billig, Michael. *Banal Nationalism*. London: Sage, 1995.

Bird, Henry Irvine. "Royal Commission to Investigate Property Claims of Canadian Citizens of Japanese Origin Evacuated from Coast Areas of British Columbia in 1942." *Privy Council Office Archived Commissions*, 1950. http://epe.lac-bac.gc.ca/100/200/301/pco-bcp/commissions-ef/bird 1950-eng/bird1950-eng.pdf.

Bloemeraad, Irene. *Becoming a Citizen: Incorporating Immigrants and Refugees in the United States and Canada*. Berkeley: University of California Press, 2006.

Bolaria, B. Singh, and Peter S. Li. *Racial Oppression in Canada*. Toronto: Garamond, 1988.

Boldt, Menno. *Surviving as Indians: The Challenge of Self-Government*. Toronto: University of Toronto Press, 1993.

Bonnett, Alastair. *Anti-Racism*. London: Routledge, 2000.

Bosher, J.F. *Imperial Vancouver Island: Who Was Who, 1850–1950*. Xlibris Corporation, 2010.

Bothwell, Robert. "Something of Value? Subjects and Citizens in Canadian History." In William Kaplan, ed., *Belonging: The Meaning and Future of Canadian Citizenship*. Montreal and Kingston: McGill-Queen's University Press, 1993.

Braches, Fred. "Whonnock History Notes: Menzies Island." http://whonnock-history.blogspot.ca/2008/01/menzies-island-revisited.html (accessed 4 March 2016).

Brett, E.A. *Colonialism and Underdevelopment in East Africa*. New York: NOK Publishers, 1973.

*Buildings and Building Management*. Porter-Langtry Company, 1935.

Cameron, Craig M. "Race and Identity: The Culture of Combat in the Pacific War." *The International History Review* 27(3) (September 2005): 550–66.

Campbell, Robert A. "Liquor and Liberals: Patronage and Government Control in British Columbia, 1920–1928." *BC Studies* 77 (1988).

Canada. House of Commons. *Official Report of the Debates of the House of Commons of the Dominion of Canada*. Ottawa: Maclean, Roger & Co., 1885.

Canada Privy Council. *Canadian War Orders and Regulations, 1943*.

– "Regulations respecting Trading with the Enemy (1939): (PC 2512 and 2586)." Ottawa: Printer to the King, 1939.

*Canadian Citizenship Statistics*. Ottawa: Dominion Bureau of Statistics, 1952–59.

*Canadian Co-operative Digest*. 1966.

*Canadian Railway and Transport Cases*. Canada Law Book Company, 1952.

*Canadian Who's Who 1949–1951: Volume V*. Orillia, ON: University of Toronto Press, 1951.

*Canadian Who's Who 1961–1963: Volume IX*. Orillia, ON: University of Toronto Press, 1963.

Carlson, Keith Thor, ed. *A Stó:lo-Coast Salish Historical Atlas*. Vancouver: Douglas and McIntyre; Seattle: University of Washington Press; Chilliwack, BC: Stó:lo Heritage Trust, 2001.

Carter, Sarah. *Lost Harvests: Prairie Indian Reserve Farmers and Government Policy*. Montreal and Kingston: McGill-Queen's University Press, 1990.

Chang, Kornel S. "Brokering Empire: The Making of a Chinese Transnational Managerial Elite." In *Pacific Connections: The Making of the U.S.–Canadian Borderlands.* Berkeley: University of California Press, 2012.

"Citizenship Act." *Justice Laws Website.* http://laws-lois.justice.gc.ca/eng/acts/c-29/page-2.html#h-3 (accessed 10 June 2015).

Clarkson, Adrienne. "Belonging: The Paradox of Citizenship." 2014. "CBC Massey Lectures." www.cbc.ca/radio/ideas/masseys (accessed 7 June 2015).

– *Room for All of Us: Surprising Stories of Loss and Transformation*. Toronto: Penguin Books, 2011.

Cohn, Bernard S. *Colonialism and Its Forms of Knowledge: The British in India*. Princeton, NJ: Princeton University Press, 1996.

Crowder, Michael. "Indirect Rule: French and British Style." *Africa: Journal of the International African Institute* 34(3) (1964): 197–205.

– *West Africa under Colonial Rule*. London: Hutchinson, 1984.

Cumbo, Enrico Carlson. "'Uneasy Neighbours': Internment and Hamilton's Italians." In Franca Iacovetta, Roberto Perin, and Angelo Principe, eds, *Enemies Within: Italian and Other Internees in Canada and Abroad*, 99–119. Toronto: University of Toronto Press, 2000.

Daniels, Roger. "Words Do Matter: A Note on Inappropriate Terminology and the Incarceration of the Japanese Americans." In Gail M. Nomura and Louis Fiset, eds, *Nikkei in the Pacific Northwest: Japanese Americans and Japanese Canadians in the Twentieth Century*, 190–214. Seattle: Center for the Study of the Pacific Northwest in association with University of Washington Press, 2005.

Danziger, Edmund J., Jr. *Great Lakes Indian Accommodation and Resistance during the Early Reservation Years, 1850–1900*. Ann Arbor: University of Michigan Press, 2009.

Darroch, Gordon, and Lee Soltow. *Property and Inequality in Victorian Ontario*. Toronto: University of Toronto Press, 1994.

Dashuk, James. *Clearing the Plains: Disease, Politics of Starvation, and the Loss of Aboriginal Life*. Regina: University of Regina Press, 2014.

Davis, P., and J. Lafrance. *History of Naturalization and Citizenship Certificates*. Ottawa: Secretary of State, Citizenship Registration, 1985.

Denzin, Norman. *Interpretive Ethnography: Ethnographic Practices for the 21st Century*. London: Sage, 1997.

"Descendants of George Housser and Nan Kennedy." http://www.housser.net/geh_nkh_/d1.htm (accessed 7 March 2016).

Dickason, Olive. *Canada's First Nations: A History of the Founding Peoples from Earliest Times*. Toronto: McClelland and Stewart, 1992.

"Dominion Policy in Favour of Influx." *Vancouver Daily Province*, 25 July 1907.

Dore, Ron. "The Family." In *City Life in Japan: A Study of a Tokyo Ward*. London: Routledge & Keagan Paul, 1958.

Dower, John W. *War without Mercy: Race and Power in the Pacific War*. New York: Pantheon Books, 1986.

Drake-Terry, Joanne. *The Same as Yesterday: The Lillooet Chronicle the Theft of Their Lands and Resources*. Lillooet, BC: Lillooet Tribal Council, 1989.

Dunae, Patrick, Jason Gilliland, Donald Lafreniere, and John Lutz. "Making the Inscrutable, Scrutable: Race and Space in Victoria's Chinatown, 1891." *BC Studies* 169 (spring 2011): 7–49.

Elections British Columbia. *Electoral History of British Columbia 1871–1986*. n.d.

Fanon, Franz. *Black Skin, White Masks*. 1967; repr., New York: Grove Press, 1991.

Fisher, Robin. *Contact and Conflict: Indian–European Relations in British Columbia, 1774–1890*. Vancouver: University of British Columbia Press, 1977.

Fitzgerald, Mickey. "The Rise and Demise of J.H. Todd and Sons, British Columbia's Enduring Independent Salmon Canners." MA thesis, University of Victoria, 2015. http://dspace.library.uvic.ca:8080/handle/1828/6672.

Foucault, Michel. *"Society Must Be Defended": Lectures at the College de France, 1975–76*. New York: Picador, 2003.

Fowke, Edith. Afterword to *They Made Democracy Work: The Story of the Co-operative Committee on Japanese Canadians*. Toronto: The Japanese Canadian Citizens' Association, 1951.

Fraser Basin Council. *Bridge between Nations: A History of the First Nations in the Fraser River Basin*. Vancouver: Fraser Basin Council, 2013. http://www.fraserbasin.bc.ca/_Library/Ab_NonAb_Relations/bridge_between_nations.pdf.

Frideres, James S., and René R. Gadacz. *Indians of North America*. Don Mills, ON: Pearson, 2012.

Fukawa, Masako. "Ebisu Park." *Nikkei Images* 15(2) (summer 2010).

Fukawa, Masako, and Stanley Fukawa. *Spirit of the Nikkei Fleet: BC's Japanese Canadian Fishermen*. Madeira Park, BC: Harbour Publishing, 2009.

Geiger, Andrea. *Subverting Exclusion: Transpacific Encounters with Race, Caste, and Borders, 1885–1928*. New Haven, CT: Yale University Press, 2011.

Geiger-Adams, Andrea. "Writing Racial Barriers into Law: Upholding BC's Denial of the Vote to Its Japanese Canadian Citizens, *Homma v. Cunningham*, 1902." In Louis Fiset and Gail M. Nomura, eds, *Nikkei in the Pacific Northwest: Japanese Americans and Japanese Canadians in the Twentieth Century*. Seattle: University of Washington Press, 2005.

Gill, Paul, and Manpreet Gill. "Zennosuke Inouye: A Canadian Veteran, the Struggle for His Land." *Surrey History*. www.surreyhistory.ca/inouye.html.

Gilmour, Julie F. *Trouble on Main Street: Mackenzie King, Reason, Race, and the 1907 Vancouver Riots*. Toronto: Allan Lane, 2014.

Ginn, Audrey. "New England Company on Kuper Island." *British Columbia Historical News* 24(3) (summer 1991).

Goldberg, David Theo. *The Racial State*. Oxford: Blackwell, 2002.

– *The Threat of Race: Reflections on Racial Neoliberalism*. Malden, MA: Wiley Blackwell, 2009.

Gough, Barry. *Gunboat Frontier: British Maritime Authority and Northwest Coast Indians, 1846–90*. Vancouver: University of British Columbia Press, 1984.

"Government Departments and Their Representatives: A History." Parliament of Canada. http://www.lop.parl.gc.ca/ParlInfo/Compilations/Federal Government/HistoryOfDepartments.aspx?Department=22736494-a6ff-401b-8cda-7e9db3d3913a&Language=E (accessed 4 March 2016).

Granatstein, J.L. *Canada's War: The Politics of the Mackenzie King Government, 1939–1945*. Toronto: Oxford University Press, 1975.

Granatstein, J.L., and Gregory A. Johnson. "Evacuation of the Japanese Canadians, 1942: A Realist Critique of the Received Version." In Norman Hillmer, Bohdan Kordan, and Lubomyr Luciuk, eds, *On Guard for Thee: War, Ethnicity, and the Canadian State, 1939–1945*, 101–29. Ottawa: Canadian Committee for the History of the Second World War, 1988.

Grant, Nichole E., and Timothy J. Stanley. "Reading the Wallpaper: Disrupting Performances of Whiteness in the Blog 'Stuff White People Like.'" In Awad Ibrahim and Shirley Steinberg, eds, *The Critical Youth Studies Reader*, 172–83. New York: Peter Lang, 2014.

Groff, David. "The Dynamics of Collaboration and the Rule of Law in French West Africa: The Case of Kwame Kangah of Assikasso (Cote d'Ivoire)." In Kristin Mann and Richard Roberts, eds, *Law in Colonial Africa*. London: James Currey, 1991.

Grossberg, Lawrence, ed. "On Postmodernism and Articulation: An Interview with Stuart Hall." *Journal of Communication Inquiry* 10(2) (1986): 131–50.

Haig-Brown, Celia, and David Nock, eds. *With Good Intentions: Euro-Canadian and Aboriginal Relations in Colonial Canada*. Vancouver: University of British Columbia Press, 2006.

Hall, Stuart. "Race, Articulation and Societies Structured in Dominance." In UNESCO, ed., *Sociological Theories: Race and Colonialism*, 305–45. Lanham, MD: Bernan Associates, 1980.

– *Representation and the Media*. Produced and directed by Sut Jhally. Northampton, MA: Media Education Foundation, 2002.

– "The Work of Representation." In Stuart Hall, Jessica Evans, and Sean Nixon, eds, *Representation: Cultural Representations and Signifying Practices*, 13–75. London: Sage in association with the Open University, 1997.

Hammer, Joshua. *Yokohama Burning: The Deadly 1923 Earthquake and Fire That Helped Forge the Path to World War II*. Toronto: Simon and Schuster, 2006.

Hannaford, Ivan. *Race: The History of an Idea in the West*. Washington: Woodrow Wilson Center Press with the John Hopkins University Press, 1996.

Harper, Marjory. *Emigration from Scotland between the Wars: Opportunity or Exile?* Manchester: Manchester University Press, 1998.

Harris, Cole. *Making Native Space: Colonialism, Resistance, and Reserves in British Columbia*. Vancouver: University of British Columbia Press, 2003.

– *The Resettlement of British Columbia: Essays on Colonialism and Geographical Change*. Vancouver: University of British Columbia Press, 1997.

Harvey, Christopher. "The Fish Canneries Reference." 2004. http://www.mackenziefujisawa.com/News_Articles/Oct-7-2004_FishCanneries Reference.pdf.

– "Litigating Racial Discrimination from Prince Rupert to Ottawa to London." *The Advocate* 73(3) (May 2015): 347–54.

Hawkins, Naoko. "Becoming a Model Minority: The Depiction of Japanese

Canadians in the *Globe and Mail*, 1946–2000." *Canadian Ethnic Studies* 41(1–2) (summer–fall 2009): 137–54.

Henry, Frances, and Carol Tator. *The Colour of Democracy: Racism in Canadian Society*. Toronto: Harcourt, 2010.

H.F.A. "William Alexander Carrothers, 1889–1951." *The Canadian Journal of Economics and Political Science/Revue canadienne d'économique et de science politique* 18(1) (1952).

Hillmer, Norman. "Henry Forbes Angus." *The Canadian Encyclopedia*. http://www.thecanadianencyclopedia.ca/en/article/henry-forbes-angus (accessed 3 March 2016).

Hobson, Dave. "Pearson Bridge Not Named after the Former PM, but Nanaimo Politician." *Nanaimo Daily News*, 18 March 2014.

"House of Commons Debates, 19th Parliament, 3rd Session." *Canadian Parliamentary Historical Resources*. http://parl.canadiana.ca.ezproxy.library.uvic.ca/view/oop.debates_HOC1903.

"House of Commons Debates, 19th Parliament, 4th Session." *Canadian Parliamentary Historical Resources*. http://parl.canadiana.ca.ezproxy.library.uvic.ca/view/oop.debates_HOC1904.

"House of Commons Debates, 1944, 19th Parliament, 5th Session, Vol. 6." 4 August 1944. *Canadian Parliamentary Historical Resources*. http://parl.canadiana.ca.ezproxy.library.uvic.ca/view/oop.debates_HOC1905_06.

"House of Commons Debates, 1952–3, 21st Parliament, 7th Session, Vol. 4." *Canadian Parliamentary Historical Resources*. http://parl.canadiana.ca/view/oop.debates_HOC2107_04/1?r=0&s=1.

"Hugh Llewellyn Keenleyside." *The Canadian Encyclopedia*. http://www.thecanadianencyclopedia.ca/en/article/hugh-llewellyn-keenleyside (accessed 7 March 2016).

Hyde, Fred. "Arleigh Pilkey: Old Man, Young Ideas." *Canada Track and Traffic* (July 1962).

Iacovetta, Franca, Roberto Perin, and Angelo Principe, eds. *Enemies Within: Italian and Other Internees in Canada and Abroad*. Toronto: University of Toronto Press, 2000.

Ignatiev, Noel. *How the Irish Became White*. New York: Routledge, 1995.

Isin, Engin F., and Peter Nyers, eds. *Routledge Handbook of Global Citizenship Studies*. London and New York: Routledge, 2014.

Johnson, Hugh. *The Voyage of the* Komagata Maru: *The Sikh Challenge to*

*Canada's Colour Bar*. Vancouver: University of British Columbia Press, 1989.

Jorgenson, Mica. "'Into That Country to Work': Aboriginal Economic Activities during Barkerville's Gold Rush." *BC Studies* 185 (2015): 109–36.

Kage, Tatsuo. *Uprooted Again: Japanese Canadians Move to Japan after World War II*. Translated by Kathleen Chisato Merken. Victoria: Ti-Jean Press, 2012.

Kaplan, Marion A. *Between Dignity and Despair: Jewish Life in Nazi Germany*. New York: Oxford University Press, 1998.

Keevak, Michael. *Becoming Yellow: A Short History of Racial Thinking*. Princeton, NJ: Princeton University Press, 2011.

Kelley, Ninette, and Michael Trebilcock. *The Making of the Mosaic: A History of Canadian Immigration Policy*. Toronto: University of Toronto Press, 1998.

Kelley, Robin D.G. "'We Are Not What We Seem': Rethinking Black Working-Class Opposition in the Jim Crow South." *Journal of American History* 80(1) (1 June 1993), doi:10.2307/2079698.

Kimura, Edmund, and Doris Kimura. Interview by Jordan Stanger-Ross. 4 March 2014. Vancouver.

Kitagawa, Muriel. *This Is My Own: Letters to Wes and Other Writings on Japanese Canadians, 1941–1948*. Edited by Roy Miki. Vancouver: Talonbooks, 1985.

Kluckner, Michael. *Vanishing British Columbia*. Vancouver: University of British Columbia Press, 2011.

Knight, Rolf. *Indians at Work: An Informal History of Native Labour in British Columbia*. Vancouver: New Star Books, 1996.

Knight, Rolf, and Maya Koizumi. *A Man for Our Times: The Life History of a Japanese Canadian Fisherman*. Vancouver: New Star Books, 1976.

Kobayashi, Audrey. "Emigration from Kaideima, Japan, 1885–1950: An Analysis of Community and Landscape Change." PhD thesis, University of California, Los Angeles, 1983.

*Labour Organizations in Canada*. 1936.

Lai, David Chuenyan. *Chinatowns: Towns within Cities in Canada*. Vancouver: University of British Columbia Press, 1988.

Lambertson, Ross. "'The Dresden Story': Racism, Human Rights, and the Jewish Labour Committee of Canada." *Labour/Le travail* 47 (2001): 29–44.

"Legends of Hockey: Fred Hume." *Hockey Hall of Fame.* http://www.legendsofhockey.net/LegendsOfHockey/jsp/LegendsMember.jsp?mem=b196203&type=Builder&page=bio&list=ByName (accessed 4 March 2016).

*Legion Magazine.* "J.L. Granatstein vs. Pamela Sugiman, Face to Face: Should the Canadian Government Have Authorized the Forcible Evacuation Inland of Japanese Canadians during the Second World War." 8 July 2015. https://legionmagazine.com/en/2015/07/face-to-face-should-the-canadian-government-have-authorized-the-forcible-evacuation-inland-of-japanese-canadians-during-the-second-world-war.

Li, Peter. *The Chinese in Canada.* Toronto: Oxford University Press, 1988.

Loo, Tina. "Africville and the Dynamics of State Power in Postwar Canada." *Acadiensis* 39(2) (6 June 2010).

Lutz, John. *Makúk: A New History of Aboriginal White Relations.* Vancouver: University of British Columbia Press, 2008.

McAllister, Kirsten. *Terrain of Memory: A Japanese Canadian Memorial Project.* Vancouver: University of British Columbia Press, 2010.

Mackenzie, John M., ed. *Imperialism and Popular Culture.* Manchester: Manchester University Press, 1986.

"Mackenzie King Is Canada's First Citizen." CBC Digital Archives. http://www.cbc.ca/archives/entry/mackenzie-king-is-canadas-first-citizen (accessed 1 May 2015).

MacKinnon, Donna Jean. "Mayors of Vancouver." *The History of Metropolitan Vancouver.* http://www.vancouverhistory.ca/whoswho_mayors.htm (accessed 4 March 2016).

"McLarty, The Hon. Norman Alexander." *Parliament of Canada: Parlinfo.* http://www.lop.parl.gc.ca/ParlInfo/Files/Parliamentarian.aspx?Item=22bf2cb3-ba5e-4d15-aa66-3b7cb8b7a216&Language=E&Section=ALL (accessed 3 March 2016).

McLean, Lorna. "Education, Identity, and Citizenship in Early Modern Canada." *Journal of Canadian Studies/Revue d'études canadiennes* 41(1) (2007): 5–30.

MacLennan, Christopher. "Toward the Charter: Canadians and the Demand for a National Bill of Rights." PhD thesis, University of Western Ontario, London, 1996.

Mar, Lisa Rose. *Brokering Belonging: Chinese in Canada's Exclusion Era, 1885–1945.* New York: Oxford University Press, 2010.

*Marine Digest*. Marine Digest, 1965.

Marlatt, Daphne. *Steveston Recollected: A Japanese-Canadian History*. Victoria: Provincial Archives of British Columbia, 1975.

*Marpole Richmond Review*. 14 January 1942.

Marsh, Robert. *The Great Transformation: Social Change in Taipei, Taiwan since the 1960s*. Armonk, NY: East Gate Books, 1996.

Marshall, T.H. *Citizenship and Social Class and Other Essays*. Cambridge: Cambridge University Press, 1950.

Mawani, Renisa. *Colonial Proximities: Crossracial Encounters and Juridical Truths in British Columbia, 1871–1921*. Vancouver and Toronto: University of British Columbia Press, 2009.

"Mayors of New Westminster." *New Westminster Heritage*. http://www.nwheritage.org/heritagesite/history/content/mayors.htm (accessed 4 March 2016).

Meggs, Geoff. *Salmon: The Decline of the British Columbia Fishery*. Vancouver: Douglas and McIntyre, 1991.

Merilees, Bill. *Newcastle Island: A Place of Discovery*. Nanoose Bay, BC: Heritage House Publishing, 1997.

"Michaud, The Hon. Joseph Enoil." *Parliament of Canada: Parlinfo*. http://www.lop.parl.gc.ca/ParlInfo/Files/Parliamentarian.aspx?Item=3732C068-0F11-4BF0-8E5A-E3C170A5934A&Language=E&Section=ALL (accessed 4 March 2016).

Miki, Roy. *Redress: Inside the Japanese Canadian Call for Justice*. Vancouver: Raincoast Books, 2004.

Miki, Roy, and Cassandra Kobayashi. *Justice in Our Time: The Japanese Canadian Redress Settlement*. Vancouver: Talonbooks, 1991.

Miles, Robert. *Racism*. London: Routledge, 1989.

– *Racism & Migrant Labour*. London: Routledge, 1982.

Miller, James. *Shingwuak's Vision*. Toronto: University of Toronto Press, 1996.

Montgomery, Ken. "Banal Race Thinking: Ties of Blood, Canadian History Textbooks and Ethnic Nationalism." *Paedagogica Historica: International Journal of the History of Education* 41(3) (2005): 313–36.

Moore, Christopher. *The British Columbia Court of Appeal: The First Hundred Years*. Vancouver: University of British Columbia Press, 2010.

Morawska, Ewa. "From Myth to Reality: America in the Eyes of Eastern European Peasant Migrant Laborers." In Dirk Hoerder and Horst Rossler, eds, *Distant Magnets: Expectations and Realities in the Immigrant Experience, 1840–1930*, 241–63. New York: Holmes & Meier, 1993.

Morita, A. Katsuyoshi. *Powell Street Monogatari*. Translated by Eric A. Sokugawa. Burnaby, BC: Live Canada Publishing, 1989.

Mortensen, Marlene. Email exchange with Laura Madokoro. 28 August 2015.

Muszynska, Alicija. *Cheap Wage Labour: Race and Gender in the Fisheries of British Columbia*. Montreal: McGill-Queen's University Press, 1996.

Nakagawa, Frances. Interview by Laura Madokoro. 28 June 2015.

Nakashima, Kimiaki. "Economic Aspects of Japanese Evacuation from the Canadian Pacific Coast: A Contribution to the Study of Economic Consequences of the Relocation of Social Groups and Displaced Persons; A Thesis." Master's thesis, McGill University, 1946.

Nakayama, Gordon. *Issei: Stories of Japanese Canadian Pioneers*. Toronto: NC Press, 1984.

National Association of Japanese Canadians and Price Waterhouse. *Economic Losses of Japanese Canadians after 1941: A Study*. Winnipeg: National Association of Japanese Canadians, 1986.

National JACL Power of Words II Committee. "Power of Words Handbook: A Guide to Language about Japanese Americans in World War II, Understanding Euphemisms and Preferred Terminology." 2013. https://jacl.org/wordpress/wp-content/uploads/2015/08/Power-of-Words-Rev.-Term.-Handbook.pdf.

"Naturalization Act, 1914." *Canadian Museum of Immigration at Pier 21*. http://www.pier21.ca/research/immigration-history/naturalization-act-1914 (accessed 31 August 2015).

Newell, Diane. *Development of the Pacific Salmon-Canning Industry: A Grown Man's Game*. Montreal: McGill-Queen's University Press, 1989.

– *Tangled Webs of History: Indians and the Law in Canada's Pacific Coast Fisheries* . Toronto: University of Toronto Press, 1993.

Nicosia, Francis R. *Zionism and Anti-Semitism in Nazi Germany*. Cambridge and New York: Cambridge University Press, 2008.

Nish, Ian. "Sansom, Sir George Bailey (1883–1965)." In Lawrence Goldman, ed., *Oxford Dictionary of National Biography*. Oxford: Oxford University Press, 2004.

Niwayama, Yuukichi. "Caught In-between: The Life History of Japanese

Canadian Woman Deportees." *Journal of American and Canadian Studies* 28 (2010).

Normandin, Pierre G., and A. Léopold Normandin. *Guide parlementaire canadien.* P.G. Normandin, 1938.

"Obit – Audrey Mavis Ginn," *Ladysmith Chronicle*, 15 June 2006. http://www.ladysmithchronicle.com/mobile/obits/?id=1267332.

"Obituaries." RCMP *Quarterly* 19(1) (July 1953).

"Obituaries." RCMP *Quarterly* 27(2) (October 1961).

"Obituaries." RCMP *Quarterly* 30(2) (October 1964).

"Obituaries." RCMP *Quarterly* 39(2) (April 1974).

Oikawa, Mona. *Cartographies of Violence: Japanese Canadian Women, Memory, and the Subjects of the Internment.* Toronto: University of Toronto Press, 2012.

Omatsu, Maryka. *Bittersweet Passage: Redress and the Japanese Canadian Experience.* Toronto: Between the Lines, 1992.

"Ordinance to Amend and Consolidate the Laws Affecting Crown Lands in British Columbia (Land Ordinance, 1870), An." In *Ordinances Passed by the Legislative Council of British Columbia, during the Session from 15th February to 23rd April, 1870.* Victoria: Government Printing Office, 1870. *Early Canadiana Online.* http://eco.canadiana.ca.ezproxy.library.uvic.ca/view/oocihm.9_03445_7/63?r=0&s=1.

"Ordinance to Further Define the Law Regulating the Acquisition of Land in British Columbia (Pre-emption Ordinance, 1866), An." In *Ordinances Passed by the Legislative Council of British Columbia, during the Session from January to April, 1866.* New Westminster, BC: Government Printing Office 1866. *Early Canadiana Online.* http://eco.canadiana.ca.ezproxy.library.uvic.ca/view/oocihm.9_03445_3/27?r=0&s=1.

Otsuka, Chihiro. "Remaking an Institution and Community: The Vancouver Japanese Language School after the War." Master's thesis, University of British Columbia, 1995.

*Pacific Fisherman.* M. Freeman Publications, 1945.

*Pacific Marine Review* 30(1) (January 1933).

*Pacific Motor Boat.* M. Freeman Publications, 1941.

Pascoe, Peggy. "Gender Systems in Conflict: The Marriages of Mission-Educated Chinese American Women, 1874–1939." *Journal of Social History* 22(4) (September 1989): 631–52.

Perry, Adele. *Colonial Relations: The Douglas-Connolly Family and the Nineteenth-Century Imperial World*. Cambridge: Cambridge University Press, 2015.

– *On the Edge of Empire: Gender, Race, and the Making of British Columbia, 1849–1871*. Toronto: University of Toronto Press, 2001.

"Personal Notes across Canada." *The New Canadian*, 28 June 1947.

"Personal Notes across Canada." *The New Canadian*, 31 March 1962.

Pettipas, Katherine. *Severing the Ties That Bind: Government Repression of Indigenous Ceremonies on the Prairies*. Winnipeg: University of Manitoba Press, 1994.

Pfaelzer, Jean. *Driven Out: The Forgotten War against Chinese Americans*. New York: Random House, 2007.

Pickles, Katie. *Female Imperialism and National Identity: Imperial Order Daughters of the Empire*. Manchester: Manchester University Press, 2002.

Porter, John. *The Vertical Mosaic*. 1965; repr., Toronto: University of Toronto Press, 2015.

Price, John. "Canada, White Supremacy, and the Twinning of Empires." *International Journal* 68(4) (December 2013).

– *Orienting Canada: Race, Empire and the Transpacific*. Vancouver: University of British Columbia Press, 2011.

Ramsden, Sarah. "Memorable Manitobans: George Collins." *The Manitoba Historical Society*. http://www.mhs.mb.ca/docs/people/collins_g.shtml (accessed 3 March 2016).

Rawling, Bill. "Only If Necessary: Canada's War against Japan, 1941–45." In Greg Donaghy and Patricia E. Roy, eds, *Contradictory Impulses: Canada and Japan in the Twentieth Century*. Vancouver: University of British Columbia Press, 2009.

Razack, Sherene. *Race, Space and the Law: Unmapping a White Settler Society*. Toronto: Between the Lines, 2002.

"Record of Service." *Birth of a Regiment: Princess Patricia's Canadian Light Infantry, 1914–1919*. http://birthofaregiment.com/soldier-details.php?id=1463 (accessed 7 March 2016).

Reeve, Phyllis. "The Japanese-Canadians of Silva Bay." *SHALE* 25 (March 2011).

"Reid, The Hon. Thomas." *Parliament of Canada: Parlinfo*. http://www.lop.parl.gc.ca/ParlInfo/Files/Parliamentarian.aspx?Item=EAD8EC08-

81D6-44DD-B076-E1054FA170C7&Language=E&Section=ALL (accessed 4 March 2016).

"Return: A Commemorative Yearbook." *Issuu*. https://issuu.com/ubyssey/docs/2_returns_yearbook_ubc (accessed 4 March 2016).

Roberts-Moore, Judith. "Office of the Custodian of Enemy Property: An Overview of the Office and its Records, 1920–1952." *Archivaria* 22 (summer 1986): 95–106.

Robinson, Greg. *A Tragedy of Democracy: Japanese Confinement in North America*. New York: Columbia University Press, 2009.

Ronen, Avihu, Hadas Agmon, and Asaf Danziger. "Collaborator or Would-Be Rescuer? The Barenblat Trial and the Image of a Judenrat Member in 1960s Israel." *Yad Vashem Studies* 39(1) (April 2011).

Roy, Patricia. *The Oriental Question: Consolidating a White Man's Province, 1914–41*. Vancouver: University of British Columbia Press, 2003.

– *The Triumph of Citizenship: The Japanese and Chinese in Canada, 1941–67*. Vancouver: University of British Columbia Press, 2007.

– *A White Man's Province: British Columbia Politicians and Chinese and Japanese Immigrants, 1858–1914*. Vancouver: University of British Columbia Press, 1989.

Roy, Patricia, J.L. Granatstein, Masako Iino, and Hiroko Takamura. *Mutual Hostages: Canadians and Japanese during the Second World War*. Toronto: University of Toronto Press, 1990.

Said, Edward W. *Orientalism*. New York: Vintage Books, 1979.

Satzewich, Vic. *Racism and the Incorporation of Foreign Labour: Farm Labour Migration to Canada since 1945*. London: Routledge, 1991.

Satzewich, Vic, and Nik Liodakis. *"Race" and Ethnicity in Canada: A Critical Introduction*. Toronto: Oxford University Press, 2013.

Satzewich, Vic, and Linda Mahood. "Indian Affairs and Band Governance: Deposing Indian Chiefs in Western Canada, 1896–1911." *Canadian Ethnic Studies* 26(1) (1994): 1–40.

Satzewich, Vic, and Terry Wotherspoon. *First Nations: Race, Class and Gender Relations*. Regina: University of Regina Press, 2000.

Scott, James. *Domination and the Arts of Resistance: Hidden Transcripts*. New Haven, CT: Yale University Press, 1990.

Shank, Luella Mae. *A Pilkey Family Genealogy, 1774–1998*. L.M. Shank, 1998.

Shibata, Yuko, Shoji Matsumoto, Rintaro Hayashi, and Shotaro Ilda. *The*

*Forgotten History of the Japanese Canadians: Volume I: Japanese Canadians in the Early Fishing Industry in BC*. Vancouver: New Sun Books, 1977.

Simms, Glenda. "Racism as a Barrier to Canadian Citizenship." In William Kaplan, *Belonging: The Meaning and Future of Canadian Citizenship*. Montreal and Kingston: McGill-Queen's University Press, 1993.

Slack, Jennifer Daryl. "The Theory and Method of Articulation in Cultural Studies." In David Morley and Kuan-Hsing Chen, eds, *Stuart Hall: Critical Dialogues in Cultural Studies*, 113–30. London: Routledge, 1995.

Snyder, Timothy. *Black Earth: The Holocaust as History and Warning*. New York: Tim Duggan Books, 2015.

Spafford, Shirley. *No Ordinary Academics: Economics and Political Science at the University of Saskatchewan, 1910–1960*. Toronto: University of Toronto Press, 2000.

Stanger-Ross, Jordan. Interview by Pamela McCall. *Pamela McCall Show*, CFAX 1070 (Victoria). 28 August 2014. 38:35–57:00. https://soundcloud.com/pamela-mccall-cfax/august-28-11am.

– "Telling a Difficult Past: Kishizo Kimura's Memoir of Entanglement in Racist Policy." *BC Studies* 181 (spring 2014): 39–62.

Stanger-Ross, Jordan, Eric Adams, and Laura Madokoro. "Lessons from the Japanese Canadian Internments: Policies Built on Fear Won't Make Us Safer." Op-ed. *Globe and Mail*, 16 January 2016. http://www.theglobeandmail.com/opinion/policy-built-on-fear-wont-make-us-safer/article28250602.

Stanger-Ross, Jordan, Nicholas Blomley, and the Landscapes of Injustice Research Collective. "'My Land Is Worth a Million Dollars': How Japanese Canadians Contested Their Dispossession in the 1940s." *Law and History Review* 35(3) (2017).

Stanger-Ross, Jordan, and the Landscapes of Injustice Research Collective. "Suspect Properties: The Vancouver Origins of the Forced Sale of Japanese-Canadian-Owned Property, WWII." *Journal of Planning History* (2016). doi:10.1177/1538513215627837.

Stanley, Timothy J. "'The Aryan Character of the Future of British North America': John A. Macdonald, Chinese Exclusion and the Invention of Canadian White Supremacy." In Patrice Dutil and Roger Hall, eds, *John A. Macdonald at 200: New Reflections and Legacies*, 115–40. Toronto: Dundurn, 2014.

– "'Carrying into the Schools What Already Exists in Every Other Institution of Society': Colonialism and the Discourse on Chinese School Segregation in British Columbia during the Early Twentieth Century." *International Journal of Educational Policy, Research and Practice* 1(4) (2000): 453–69.
– *Contesting White Supremacy: School Segregation, Anti-Racism, and the Making of Chinese Canadians.* Vancouver: University of British Columbia Press, 2011.
– "The Strong Poetry of Won Alexander Cumyow: Solidarity across Time and Space." In Nicholas Ng-A-Fook, Award Ibrahim, and Guiliano Reis, eds, *Provoking Curriculum Studies: Strong Poetry and Arts of the Possible in Education.* New York: Routledge, 2016.
– "Why I Killed Canadian History: Conditions for an Anti-Racist History in Canada." *Histoire sociale/Social History* 33(65) (2000): 79–103.
Stevenson, Michael D. *Canada's Greatest Wartime Muddle: National Selective Service and the Mobilization of Human Resources during World War II.* Montreal and Kingston: McGill-Queen's University Press, 2001.
Stoler, Ann Laura. *Race and the Education of Desire: Foucault's History of Sexuality and the Colonial Order of Things.* Durham, NC: Duke University Press, 1995.
Sugiman, Pamela. "'These Feelings That Fill My Heart': Japanese Canadian Women's Memories of Internment." *Oral History* 34(2) (autumn 2006).
Sumida, Rigenda. "The Japanese in British Columbia." Master's thesis, University of British Columbia, 1935.
Sunahara, Ann Gomer. *The Politics of Racism: The Uprooting of Japanese Canadians during the Second World War.* Toronto: James Lorimer, 1981.
Switzer, Anne-Lee. *Gateway to Promise: Canada's First Japanese Community.* Victoria: Ti-Jean Press, 2012.
Takai, Yukari. "Navigating Transpacific Passages: Steamship Companies, State Regulators, and Transshipment of Japanese in the Early-Twentieth-Century Pacific Northwest." *Journal of American Ethnic History* 30(1) (spring 2011): 7–34.
Takaki, Ronald T. *Double Victory: A Multicultural History of America in World War II.* Boston: Little, Brown, 2000.
Takata, Toyo. *Nikkei Legacy.* Toronto: NC Press, 1983.
Tateishi, Doug. "The Inevitable Antiracist Educator: Reflections of Sansei

Student and Teacher." *Critical Literacy: Theories and Practices* 14(1) (2014): 50–63.

Taylor, Diana. "Scenes of Cognition: Performance and Conquest." *Theatre Journal* 56(3) (2004).

"Taylor, Frederick Wellington." Komagata Maru*: Continuing the Journey*. http://komagatamarujourney.ca/node/4383 (accessed 7 March 2016).

Tennant, Paul. *Aboriginal Peoples and Politics: The Indian Land Question in British Columbia, 1849–1989*. Vancouver: University of British Columbia Press, 1990.

Truth and Reconciliation Commission of Canada. *Canada's Residential Schools: The Final Report of the Truth and Reconciliation Commission of Canada*. 5 vols. Montreal and Kingston: Published for the Truth and Reconciliation Commission by McGill-Queen's University Press, 2015.

Truth and Reconciliation Commission of Canada. *Honouring the Truth, Reconciling for the Future: Summary of the Final Report of the Truth and Reconciliation Commission of Canada*. Truth and Reconciliation Commission of Canada 2015. http://www.trc.ca/websites/trcinstitution/File/2015/Honouring_the_Truth_Reconciling_for_the_Future_July_23_2015.pdf.

Ujimoto, Victor. Email exchange with Laura Madokoro. 9 April 2015.

Vancouver Town Planning Commission. *The Appearance of the City*.

*Veterans' Land Act*. SC 1942, c 33.

Voyageur, Cora. *Firekeepers of the Twenty-First Century*. Montreal and Kingston: McGill-Queen's University Press, 2008.

Wa, Gisday, and Delgan Uukw. *The Spirit in the Land: Statements of the Gitksan and Wet'suwet'en Hereditary Chiefs in the Supreme Court of British Columbia, 1987–1990*. Gabriola, BC: Reflections, 1992.

Waite, Donald Ender. *Maple Ridge and Pitt Meadows: A History in Photographs*. Waite Bird Photos, 2008.

Walls, Martha Elizabeth. *No Need of a Chief for This Band: The Maritime Mi'kmaq and Federal Electoral Legislation, 1899–1951*. Vancouver: University of British Columbia Press, 2010.

Ward, W. Peter. "British Columbia and the Japanese Evacuation." *Canadian Historical Review* 57(3) (1976): 289–308.

– *White Canada Forever: Popular Attitudes and Public Policy toward Orientals in British Columbia*. Montreal: McGill-Queen's University Press, 1978.

Ware, Vron. *Beyond the Pale: White Women, Racism, and History*. London: Verso, 1992.

*War Measures Act*. RSC 1927, c 206.

Weinberg, Gerhard L. "Halting the Japanese Advance, Halting the German Advance; Keeping Them Apart and Shifting the Balance: December 1941 to November 1942." In *A World at Arms: A Global History of World War II*, 310–65. Cambridge and New York: Cambridge University Press, 1994.

Wells, Julie T., and Michael F. Christie. "Namatjira and the Burden of Citizenship." *Australian Historical Studies* 31(114) (2000).

*Western Fisheries*. Interpress Publications, 1957.

Whitaker, Reg, and Greg Kealey, "A War on Ethnicity? The RCMP and Internment." In Franca Iacovetta, Roberto Perin, and Angelo Principe, eds, *Enemies Within: Italian and Other Internees in Canada and Abroad*. Toronto: University of Toronto Press, 2000.

Wickwire, Wendy. "Teit, James Alexander (until 1884 he spelled his surname Tait)." In *Dictionary of Canadian Biography Online*, vol. 15. University of Toronto/Université Laval, 2005. http://www.biographi.ca/en/bio/teit_james_alexander_1884_15E.html.

"William Halbert Menzies." *Geni_Family_Tree*. http://www.geni.com/people/William-Menzies/6000000003956678696 (accessed 4 March 2016).

Wilson, Kathleen. "Introduction: Three Theses on Performance and History." *Eighteenth-Century Studies* 48(4) (2015).

Winant, Howard, and Michael Omi. *Racial Formation in the United States: From the 1960s to the 1980s*. New York: Routledge and Kegan Paul, 1986.

"Wooden Boats of the North Coast – S." http://www.halfmoon.ca/boats/boatsS.html (last updated 9 September 9 2012; accessed 7 March 2016).

Wright, Richard. *Twelve Million Black Voices: A Folk History of the Negro in the United States of America*. London: L. Drummond, 1947.

*Yachting*. CBS Magazines, n.d.

Yamaga, Yasutaro. *History of Haney Nokai (Farmer's Association)*. North York, ON: 4 Print Division of Musson Copy Centres Inc., 2006.

Yavorsky, Greg, and University of British Columbia Rare Books and Special Collections. "Yamaga Yasutaro – An Inventory of His Papers." July 1977.

Yee, Paul. "Sam Kee: A Chinese Business in Early Vancouver." *BC Studies* 69–70 (spring–summer 1986): 79–96.

Yesaki, Mitsuo. *Sutebusuton: A Japanese Village on the British Columbia Coast*. Vancouver: Peninsula Publishing Company, 2003.

Yonekura, Harry. Interview by Masako Fukawa. 2002. Toronto.

Young, Robert J.C. *Postcolonialism: An Historical Introduction*. Oxford: Blackwell, 2011.

Yu, Henry. *Thinking Orientals: Migration, Contact, and Exoticism in Modern America*. New York: Oxford University Press, 2001.

Zimmerman, David. *Top Secret Exchange: The Tizard Mission and the Scientific War*. Montreal and Kingston: McGill-Queen's University Press, 1996.

# Contributors

WILL ARCHIBALD is an MA candidate in the Department of History at the University of Victoria. Their thesis, "Unsettling Aliens," interrogates the intersections among settler colonialism, Indigenous dispossession, and the historical racialization of Asian Canadians in British Columbia. Their work is rooted in the interdisciplinary insights of settler colonial studies and critical ethnic studies.

MASAKO FUKAWA is a former school administrator and teacher specializing in the story of Japanese Canadians. With her husband, Stanley Fukawa, she is co-author of the award-winning *Spirit of the Nikkei Fleet* (Harbour Publishing, 2010). She is also the editor and author of collected materials, teacher resources, and websites on related topics. Fukawa lives in Burnaby, BC.

LAURA MADOKORO is assistant professor in the Department of History and Classical Studies at McGill University. She is the author of *Elusive Refuge: Chinese Migrants in the Cold War* (Harvard University Press, 2016) and numerous scholarly articles on race, humanitarianism, and migration.

JANE MASUTANI has been a columnist for the Vancouver Island newspaper *The Island Word* for many years. She has been a long-time proofreader and collaborator in English translations with her husband, Matsuki.

MATSUKI MASUTANI is a professionally trained and certified translator who has been working in the field since 1989. His translated work includes *Reconciliation, Repentance, and Redress* (Anglican Church of Canada), *Legacy of the Asahi Baseball Team* (Nikkei National Museum), and *Mothertalk* (Soshisha Publishing, Tokyo) as well as translations for radio and film.

VIC SATZEWICH is professor of sociology at McMaster University. His most recent book, *Points of Entry: How Canada's Visa Officers Decide Who Gets In* (University of British Columbia Press, 2016), won the 2016 John Porter Tradition of Excellence Book Award of the Canadian Sociological Association.

JORDAN STANGER-ROSS is associate professor of history at the University of Victoria and project director of Landscapes of Injustice. He is the author of *Staying Italian: Urban Change and Ethnic Life in Postwar Toronto and Philadelphia* (University of Chicago Press, 2009). His writing on the dispossession of the property of Japanese Canadians has appeared in *BC Studies*, *The Journal of Planning History*, and *Law and History Review*.

TIMOTHY J. STANLEY is professor of education foundations and antiracism education in the Faculty of Education at the University of Ottawa. He specializes in the history and theory of racism in Canada, Chinese-Canadian history, and antiracism education. He is the author of the award-winning book *Contesting White Supremacy: School Segregation, Anti-Racism, and the Making of Chinese Canadians* (University of British Columbia Press, 2011) as well as numerous articles and chapters on related topics. He is the former interim dean of the Faculty of Graduate and Postdoctoral Studies.

PAM SUGIMAN is professor of sociology and dean of arts at Ryerson University and the chair of the Oral History Cluster of Landscapes of Injustice. She is the former president of the Canadian Sociological Association and a former director of the National Executive Board of the National Association of Japanese Canadians.

MONIQUE ULYSSES is a doctoral student in the Department of History at Yale University. She specializes in histories of twentieth-century popular culture in Mexico and the United States as related to divergent understandings and representations of racialized gender identities. Her work is guided by and devoted to anti-racist, intersectional, and decolonial feminisms.

# Index